To my parents for the good times in the old times,
and to Anne for my new times.

Altered States

Postmodernism, Politics, Culture

edited by Mark Perryman

LAWRENCE & WISHART
LONDON
In Association with Signs of the Times

Lawrence & Wishart Limited
144a Old South Lambeth Road
London SW8 1XX

First published in Great Britain 1994

© Lawrence & Wishart Limited

Each essay © the author, 1994

Cover design: Jan Brown Designs
Cover photo: Abel Lagos
Photoset in North Wales by
Derek Doyle & Associates, Mold, Clwyd.
Printed and bound in Great Britain by
Biddles Ltd, Guildford.

Contents

Section Two: Crossing the Border –
The Postmodernism of Global Times

Section Three: Faces to the Future –
Towards a Twenty-First Century Left

Acknowledgements

The ideas and impetus that led to this book sprang from a seminar series, also entitled 'Altered States' organised by the London-based discussion group, *Signs of the Times*, in the winter of 1992. *Signs of the Times* (for fuller details of publications and events see page 279) grew out of a highly successful *Marxism Today* group that met in Haringey through the late 1980s and early 1990s. We would like to make special mention of Kay and Joe Ball, and Arthur Mendelsohn who helped to organise the Haringey *Marxism Today* group throughout this period. *Signs of the Times* seeks to continue to develop, debate and discuss the ideas first originated by the magazine *Marxism Today* under the rubric New Times. A most special debt is owed to the inspired editing of *Marxism Today* by Martin Jacques which allowed a thousand fruitful flowers to bloom, ideas that relentlessly engaged with reality rather than the thunderous rhetoric that is so often passed off as politics in journals of ideas and current affairs.

This book would not have been possible without the broader project of 'remaking the political' that *Signs of the Times* has situated itself within. Helping to carry that project forward, we would like to thank in particular the following who help to organise the group's activities, Geoff Andrews, Sarah Cassidy, Diana Coben, Anne Coddington, Kevin Davey, Jeremy Gilbert, Richard Glover and Stefan Howald. Special thanks are also due to Anne Coddington for advice on the introduction to this book, and to Kevin Davey for commissioning and supervising the chapters by Michael Rustin and Ken Worpole, plus the interview with David Dabydeen. The series of seminars that provide the basis of this book were held at 'Anna's Place', a superb Swedish restaurant on Hackney's Newington Green that provides most pleasant and unusual surroundings for our deliberations. We are extremely grateful to the avuncular proprietor, Anna Hegarty, who continues to allow us to meet there.

We would also like to thank our transcribers, Helen Bailey, Bernard Knight, Ian McCormick and Helen Taylor, for typing up the texts of the original talks.

This book is part and parcel of our ambition to spread the ideas raised in our seminars and discussion. In this regard the newspaper *New Times* has been particularly helpful in providing valuable space for articles and interviews arising from our group's activities.

The editing, production and publication of this book would, of course, not have been possible without the enthusiasm and expertise of the staff at Lawrence & Wishart. The friendly hands provided by Lindsay Thomas, Ruth Borthwick and Sally Davison provided the guidance and advice that made editing the book not only a new, but hopefully successful, enterprise. And as always the designer, Jan Brown, provided an unmissable contribution, providing us with not only a very fine cover but also originated our own group's logo.

And finally, a great roar of a thank you to Darren Anderton and all the boys from White Hart Lane for the almost weekly inspiration their performances provided throughout the editing of this book.

Mark Perryman, October 1993

Notes on Contributors

David Dabydeen is Lecturer in Caribbean Studies at the University of Warwick. His most recent book is the novel, *Disappearance* (1993).

Kevin Davey is one of the convenors of the discussion group, *Signs of the Times*. A Lecturer in Journalism at Hackney Community College, he is a regular contributor to *New Times* and *Tribune*.

Andrew Gamble is Professor of Politics at Sheffield University. One of the prime originators of *Marxism Today*'s analysis of Thatcherism in the 1980s, and author of *The Free Economy and the Strong State: The Politics of Thatcherism* (1988), he is currently writing a study of Friedrich Hayek.

Marc-Henri Glendening is a political researcher. A former Chair of the Federation of Conservative Students, he is now a member of the Libertarian Alliance and is currently involved with the launch of Diversity – The Campaign for Lifestyle Freedom.

Adam Lent is a research student at Sheffield University investigating changes in the Labour Party during the past decade. He is a regular contributor to *New Times*.

Angela McRobbie is Principal Lecturer in Sociology at Thames Valley University. Her book, *Postmodernism and Popular Culture*, is to be published by Routledge in 1994.

David Morley is Reader in Communications at Goldsmiths' College, London. His book, *Television, Audiences and Cultural Studies* was published in 1993.

Mark Perryman founded the *Signs of the Times* discussion group in early 1992. He was formerly Circulation Manager on *Marxism Today* and was closely involved with their highly original approach to organising events and conferences. He is now the Marketing Director for a publisher of sports and leisure magazines and writes regularly for *New Times*.

Greg Philo is the Research Director of the Glasgow University Media Unit. He was a founder member of the Glasgow University Media Group whose latest book, *Getting the Message*, was published in 1993. He is himself the author of *Seeing and Believing* (1990).

Michael Rustin is Professor of Sociology at the University of East London. He is the author of *For a Pluralist Socialism* (1985), and *The Good Society and The Inner World* (1991).

Anne Showstack Sassoon is Professor of Politics and Director of the European Research Centre at Kingston University. The author of *Gramsci's Politics* (1987) and editor of *Women and the State* (1987), her current work is concerned with equality, difference and citizenship.

Wendy Wheeler is Senior Lecturer in English Literature and critical theory at the University of North London. Her current research and writing is concerned with the domestication of the sublime in contemporary English fiction.

Ken Worpole is a writer and social critic. He has worked extensively with Comedia, the research and policy development network, since the early 1980s. His most recent book is *Towns for People* (1992).

Introduction: The Remaking of the Political

It had to happen. After postmodernism, post-Fordism, post-Marxism and post-feminism we are now being offered the 'post-political'.[1] The implication is that we are entering an age where the central focus of new thinking and collective activity is moving away from the political party. Politicians, and party leaders in particular are held not just in disrepute but in popular contempt. Corruption increasingly rears its ugly head, whilst the defence of vested interests remains almost systemic within the party establishments. Young people are universally disenchanted with the party system; the brightest and best who not so long ago would have joined a party as a way to fulfil their ideals are now far more likely to be drawn to the work of charities, the voluntary sector, research foundations and the more enlightened of the transnational corporations. Entire communities are ill-served at best, and excluded at worst, by parties that once would have championed their demands. The political party is creaking with old age and appears incapable of adjusting to the times in which we now live.

One of the best summaries of this situation is to be found in the *Manifesto for New Times*, and is worth quoting at some length:

1. Over the last thirty years our personal lives from consumption to sexuality, have become increasingly political. Politics is less and less confined to a distinct realm

1

of parties, resolutions, manifestoes and elections. The agents of political change have become more diverse and complex.

2. The expansion of politics in society has contributed to changing the role of the state. The idea of the state managing society, playing an extensive role in delivering solutions and services is being superseded. There is a widespread desire for a state which is capable of taking determined strategic action to sort out problems, but this is matched by a desire for a less intrusive, paternalistic state, allowing people to reach their own solutions to problems.

3. Politics and power are becoming increasingly internationalised.

4. Social upheaval has been accompanied by the fragmentation of old political constituencies and allegiances. This has been accompanied by the rise of new sources of collective identity and attachment, which do not readily fit the old straitjackets of right and left.

The central point of this analysis is that, because of its institutional form the political party is incapable of renewal, let alone transformation. The empirical evidence that accompanies this analysis makes distinctly sobering reading. To quote four recent reports. Firstly, a survey of Labour Party members by Patrick Seyd and Paul Whiteley revealed that in 1992 which was a general election year just 56 per cent of members had taken part in a party campaign or attended a party meeting, this figure had fallen from the 82 per cent recorded in 1989. In addition 49 per cent of members admitted to being less politically active in 1992 compared to five years ago. The picture is of a party that is not only experiencing chronic membership decline, but those members who do remain are becoming 'de-energised'.[3] Secondly, in the wake of the humiliating July 1993 by-election defeat at Newbury the depth of the decline in the Conservative Party's grassroots resources came out into the open for the first time. Typically this was best measured for the Tories by the drying-up of financial support from local members. Not only was the party being forced to make redundant many of its treasured full-time agents but local parties were becoming seriously lacking in the manpower and expertise to mount effective election campaigns.[4] Thirdly, following her high-profile resignation from the leadership of the Green Party – an organisation which for some represented the renewal of old party politics – Sara Parkin penned a most interesting account of the factors that had led to the party's decline, 'Too many Green Party members are unable to move beyond whatever single issue they favour. This has led to conflicts that have chased away those committed to the larger project of creating a society that is truly sustainable. In Britain there are now probably more genuine Greens outside the Green Party than in it.'[5] Fourthly, whilst the Liberal-Democrats through spectacular by-election victories, sweeping local government gains and concentrating on such issues as electoral reform, environmentalism and higher taxes to fund education have been able to develop as a most effective third party force in British politics, they are is failing to attract a new generation to their ranks. In a survey of the party membership 73 per cent were found to be over 46 years of age, and just 4 per cent were under 26 years.[6] Four very different contexts, but the common message is one of decline. And whatever the short-term solutions currently on offer, from cut-price membership deals to more effective fund raising, they will all ultimately fail unless a new sense of purpose is found that can give identity and pride to party membership.

Of course no one would seriously suggest that parties, because they form governments, won't remain absolutely central to the future of politics. Indeed, it was for this reason that after 1989 and the ushering in of multi-party democracy to eastern Europe that the civic movements which had created the conditions for such a momentous development, disappeared with rancorous rapidity. But it remains the case that the state has a declining importance in our everyday lives. Entire areas of life have become politicised in a way which hardly even registers at the bottom of party agendas and thus their previously hegemonic role as vehicles for 'concerned citizens' has fallen into disuse. Moreover, in this situation political parties are proving almost wholly incapable of meaningful change. For example, the Labour Party now lacks a vibrant inner-party life, is losing its active membership and thus a presence in the communities it seeks to represent, has little or no appeal for young people, and demographically it is dominated by forty-something white collar public sector workers.

To pretend that the party-form has *ever* provided a particularly large space for the study, development and discussion of new thinking would be to look at the past with rose-tinted spectacles. Yet an electorally successful Labour Party, or at least one that carried a spirit of hope for future success, did spawn a range of official, and unofficial, satellites where thinking could be pursued, and ideas channelled back into the party via the trade unions, local parties, sympathetic MPs and the party press. Today such a culture is all but extinct. This is not to decry the valuable work that has been undertaken by bodies like the Institute for Public Policy Research, the Plant Commission on Electoral Reform and the Commission on Social Justice, but they are locked into an agenda that is largely determined by pre-existing electoral needs. Electoral considerations hold down even the most recalcitrant of thinking caps. It was in reaction to this mind-set that the New Times analysis of the late 1980s[7] floated free from short-termism. Such freedom is important within any political firmament. As Bryan Gould put it in a review of the first of the New Times discussion papers, 'Facing up to the Future':

The Communist Party may, by comparison with the Labour Party's record of achievement and hopes of office, have little by way of a political future to look forward to. Travelling light, however, seems to have freed them to look to the future with an open mindedness and intelligence which *the Labour Party, imprisoned by its past achievements, hostage to its aspirations, has not always found easy to demonstrate.*[8]

When the Party Stops

The post-war years saw a sad succession of attempts by an increasingly independent-minded left to provide this kind of open yet incisive strategic intervention of ideologicised forward thinking. The original 1956 New Left emerged in reaction to Khrushchev's secret speech and the Soviet invasion of Hungary. Its anti-Stalinism provided an effective challenge to the way in which Marxism as both a theory and supposed guide to practice had become the almost exclusive preserve of interpretations provided by the Communist Party.[9] The rich diversity of rebellions, events and ideas that coalesced in 1968 was the next catalyst for opening minds to the potential for new forms of thinking and organising.[10] In the mid-1970s feminism represented a growing movement concerned with inserting the personal into the political, encouraging local self-management initiatives and developing a critique of the inadequacies of a Leninism that had come to dominate much of the post-1968 revolutionary left. Feminism also articulated the need to inaugurate prefigurative forms of organisation that challenged the millenarianism of the left (whether the millennium was represented by a general election or the storming of a Winter Palace). This feminist-led perspective was best represented by the hugely influential book, *Beyond the Fragments*.[11] By the early 1980s this stream was one of the principal instigators behind the foundation of the Socialist Society which in its founding statement set out the following aims: 'It would help create a new forum and common framework for considering fundamental questions of socialist programme and purpose. It would address itself to the implications of new radical currents of thought. It would bring together intellectual workers and worker intellectuals ...'.[12] Much of this intellectual, strategic and political process of renovation came to fruition under the benign and hugely imaginative Labour regime that took control of London's Greater London Council in 1981, only to see the council abolished by the vengeful Thatcher government just five years later in 1986.[13]

However good the founding principles, each and every one of these very different initiatives ended up failing. Though thankfully, that hasn't stopped people trying. Three of the most recent attempts are, the launch of Democratic Left out of the remnants of the British Communist Party; the launch of *Renewal* – a 'Journal of Labour Politics'; and the foundation of the think-tank Demos. The following extracts from these three sources give a flavour of their noble intentions, which still remain unsatisfied in terms of a transformation of the wider realms of politics culture.

'The project is the renovation of our society along environmental, democratic and socially just lines. The challenge is to open up dialogues, that help towards the convergence of visions that could enable a range of distinctive forces to enter into coalitions.' – Democratic Left[14]

'The combination of Conservative hegemony and ineffectual opposition has led to a progressive de-politicisation and passivity in public life ... there is an urgent need for popular, broad-based campaigns.' – *Renewal*[15]

'Politics ... feels like a cultural backwater, like some declining sector of the economy: defensive, unimaginative, and no longer able to attract the brightest and the best. Once politics and parties were at the forefront of change, but today innovation is more likely to come from the laboratory of a global company, an environmental campaign or the energy and commitment of a voluntary organisation.' – Demos[16]

Out of History

The immense problems any attempt to break the political mould faces points to the need to take the long view in politics. This is not to retreat into an apolotical historiography, divorced from the pressing needs of today. But it is to recognise the depth of the difficulties the left currently finds itself in. This is a central motivation behind both this book, and the discussion group, *Signs of the Times*, from which the book has evolved. Alongside this 'long view' there is a growing imperative to address the harsh realities of empirical analysis, particularly with regard to the break-up of old class formations, changes in traditional models of voting behaviour, and the trans-formation of socio-cultural norms. In place of this unfortunately we are all too often ill-served by a ready predilection for superficiality and posturing. It is our hope that this book will serve up little of either, and in his opening chapter Andrew Gamble certainly addresses full-square the present predicament the Labour Party finds itself in: 'The Conservatives' victory [in 1992], although slight in terms of votes, was crushing in terms of the percentage of the vote, and emphasised once more the long-term resilience and dominance of the Conservatives in British politics.'[17]

The difficulty Labour and its attendant left has in coming to terms with the long term dominance of the Conservative Party and its own long march of decline – psephological, sociological and organisational – is surely intimately connected to the single most devastating trait of today's Labour Party: 'a defensive, conservative political formation, trapped in a particular style of politics and still finding it difficult to appeal beyond its traditional electorate.'[18]

From Popular Culture to Unpopular Politics

This innate conservatism meant that even when Labour's communications and campaigns were being directed by the decidedly modernist Peter Mandelson and his acolytes in the Shadow Communications Agency,[19] the images and language they projected spoke of a strictly passive role for electorate and party alike. Indeed it was during the Mandelson era that ventures that had at the outset promised to break the grip of labourist conservatism came to a speedy and spectacular end, namely the party magazine *New Socialist* and the pop-cultural alliance Red Wedge. There remains on the left a gaping chasm between popular culture and unpopular politics. There are very few signs of a politics emerging that in terms of reaching out to people, is both inspiring and able to provide the services of representation that communities look to parties to deliver. It is in this sense that notwithstanding the updating of Labour's electoral appeal there remained a major failure to construct a common sense and language, never mind icons and institutions of identification, that could enable voters and party members to make sense of the Kinnock leadership's fast-moving policy shifts on issues ranging from unilateralism to Europe to taxation and renationalisation. In his chapter Greg Philo sums up the importance that should have been given to generating a popular language and common sense around Labour's new message, he describes this process as creating – 'a sort of template through which people interpret their own experiences and desires.'[20]

The Long Goodbye

Modernisation is a key element in any template of explanation. In this respect Mike Rustin is most forthright and prescient in setting out the need for the left to focus on the 'unfinished business' of New Times. The present-day popular disenchantment with such institutions as the monarchy, the judiciary, the police service and parliament points to a substantial breakdown of a previously deeply entrenched English antipathy to the modern, preferring instead the security of tradition and ritual. Such a breakdown is not in itself necessarily progressive, witness the birth of Murdochian republicanism, but what it does provide is a moment of scrutiny and critique. For those who at this precise moment prefer to retreat into the shell of the certainty of class politics. Rustin offers a bold alternative, 'socialism without class'.[21]

In projecting any future movements of change the question must be asked from where will the sources of radicalism emerge? Those sources that do exist are now largely outside the parties, indeed the prospects for new thinking within the parties appears to be becoming quite dismal if the comments of informed, and clearly disenchanted, insiders such as Bryan Gould are to be believed: 'Labour seems to be infected by ... a difficulty in making up its mind, and a paralysing caution about doing or saying anything that might offend anybody.'[22] Of course this isn't a recent phenomenon, it is a process that has been unravelling since at least the mid-1980s. The issues which have energised great swathes of people since then, both domestically and internationally, are marked out by their near total marginalisation from traditional party-politics. AIDS, Third World famine, the environment being three of the most potent issues of this kind in recent years. At the same time networks of self-organisation – not just sectional and defensive, but full of momentum and expansion – have emerged. These range from ravers and travellers, to local trading and barter schemes, to independent football supporters groups. Green consumerism has offered a very direct and personal way to express a deeply held set of convictions scarcely represented in the political mainstream. Similarly the growth of a 'pink economy' provides lesbians and gay men with a very different way of defending their interests to the traditional route of lobbying for representation within the party establishments. These movements cannot be easily located on a simple left/right axis, instead they stand apart, and often have little or no interest in earning a position on that axis. This is a change that many of today's thirtysomething generation witnessed through their late teens and twenties. The first great mass movement that I took part in was the Anti-Nazi League in the late 1970s, then in the early 1980s I turned out for CND, and in the mid-1980s for the miners. Each of these campaigns was not only spearheaded by the extra-parliamentary left, but also enjoyed a relatively close and fruitful relationship to the parliamentary left, in the form of the Labour Party. The campaigns and movements that now persist enjoy little of this access to the citadels of the mainstream, they are resolute outsiders, and are thus far more prone to exclusion, or at best localisation (in the wider sense of

the word). This includes the last great campaign; the
anti-poll tax revolt which existed largely at a local level,
generating widespread civil disobedience whilst what
organisational support it did enjoy came largely from
libertarians, greens, anarchists, the voluntary sector and
the far left. It was this diversity that gave the campaign its
vitality, but it was the dilution of a link to the mainstream
of politics and the resultant free hand this afforded the far
left that meant in the end the campaign, even at the
moment of victory, in fact represented the last gasp of the
old times. It failed to deliver a culture of co-operation in
place of party or factional battles for control, and was
unable to preserve diversity in the face of those – in this
case particularly the Militant Tendency and the Socialist
Workers Party – who sought control.[23] Patrick Marber, in
his column in the London weekly *Time Out* sums up very
well the disillusion these years of distance from the body
politic has produced – 'My generation, by which I mean
first time voters in 1983, were too young for punk and too
old to dance. Consequently we are neither rebels nor
hedonists, our calling card is irony, we are the glib
generation and we have chosen to cast ourselves into the
political wilderness. That's why we vote Labour and
cultivate our gardens.[24] There is no more poignant
epitaph for the death of politics.

From the Depths of Despair

The depth of these difficulties point to the desperate need
to open up, to adopt inclusive rather than exclusive ways
of talking and organising, and indeed some well-deserved
humility in seeking to listen and learn from the new
radical forces that are attracting a level of support,
commitment and activity that is largely absent in left circles
outside the well-drilled ranks of the latter-day Leninist
sects.

However, in pointing to the potent, and very often
highly original, appeal of these new sources of radical
ideas and action it is important not to become entrapped
in a new version of an old essentialism. The dead-end that

all essentialisms offer has been admirably charted by the work on radical democracy by Ernesto Laclau and Chantal Mouffe.[25] Their theories have been most effectively explained in this collection by Adam Lent.[26] Lent places at the centre of any progressive politics the democratic imperative, necessitating structures and ideas that permit alternative conclusions to be always free to exist, and not simply exist in a vacuum but with the permanent capacity to upset whatever has been allowed to become the intellectual status quo. This strikes at the very heart of the organised Marxist tradition (and particularly its surviving Leninist variant in parties such as the Socialist Workers Party) – that sees revisionism, ie the ability to revise the party orthodoxy – as the ultimate in the betrayal of principle. Similarly it deconstructs the terrible timidity and dismissal of ideas that Labourism has come to represent. Such a theoretical and practical perspective would seek to create a political culture founded on pluralism, constantly sensitive to internal and external threats of absolutism, and cherishing rather than suppressing the free-flow of ideas and open minds that a politics of dialogue rather than *diktat* necessitates.

Unpicking the Patchwork

Such a perspective fits neatly into both critiques of left-economism and social-movement essentialism, whilst paying attention to the positive ideas associated with the notion of a new politics of identity and difference.[27] However to turn these ideas from what can often be simply a celebration of the narcissistic to the potential for renovation and transformation that they most certainly do possess requires what Suzanne Moore has poignantly described as: 'Identity must hold on to the idea that it's always strategic and not some essential truth. Those who are entirely sure about their identities are the people we should fear. We have to hold on to a much looser idea. So we have to anchor this free-floating desire for change in a way that doesn't weigh it down. *Identity politics will fail if it becomes about finding one's self. It has to be about finding other*

people'.[28]   Coming   to   terms,   however   critically,
with the implications of 'identity politics' means engaging
with the wide-ranging, and hugely vexed, debates around
postmodernism. Suzanne Moore, again, points to the
well-deserved suspicion that the merest mention of
postmodernism can provoke: '... I'm suspicious about
postmodernism's   supposed   all-purpose   nature,   its
become like some sort of super glue. If you want a theory
that starts off talking about architecture and ends up
talking about the universe, well as they say at Burger King,
"You want it, you got it." While talking about the end of
any grand narratives post-modernism is itself a grand
narrative.'[29] Nevertheless, as Angela McRobbie illustrates
in her *tour de force* introduction to the second section of this
collection,[30] postmodernism does represent a vital concept
in developing an understanding of social and cultural
change, a concept that is all the more necessary in an age
where   the   left   has   displayed   such   an   inability   to
understand the particularities of the condition we are
living in. With precious few exceptions – mainly at a local
level, the left either unthinkingly accommodates to trends
in popular culture or remains in blissful ignorance of
those trends. Whilst as a site of learning and contestation
culture remains largely outside the ambit of Labourists
and Leninists alike. Such a gross strategic error not only
makes left politics profoundly boring and out of touch, it
also means that vital areas of everyday life are left prey to
interventions from the right. Angela McRobbie pointedly
reminds us that of all the current theorisations of culture it
has been postmodernism that has most ably looked at the
roots of the process of the construction of the subject; that
has refused to take the subject, and its construction, as a
given and that has interrogated the condition of its past,
present and future existence. Angela McRobbie quotes
Jane Flax who gives this estimation of postmodern theory:
'At its best postmodernism invites us to engage in a
continual process of disillusionment with the grand
fantasies that have brought us to the brink of
annihilation.'[31] It is this process that Wendy Wheeler links
to the crisis of parliamentary politics. In her contribution

to the opening section Wheeler untangles the questions of nostalgia and desire from their traditional place in the lexicon of cultural politics and seeks to place them at the heart of a highly original account of the successes of Thatcherism and the failures of oppositional politics.[32] Her reading of the role of nostalgia in giving a sense of meaning to the present is intimately connected with the analogy of the relationship between centre and margin which is so important to postmodernism. This highly problematic relationship demands, for Wheeler, both a space for 'communal identification' and 'more fluid collective identifications'. It is within this apparent contradiction of mixing the local and the global, at every conceivable level, that a state of hybridity may emerge that runs counter to the essentialism that has ended up bedevelling much of what passes itself off as radicalism.

Back to the Future

The nature of the original New Times analysis gave it the potential to run counter to essentialist tendencies. The context and outcome of this contest of wills is the subject of Kevin Davey's review of the continuing significance of the components of New Times.[33] In outlining the importance of New Times as a model of analysis of epochal change Martin Jacques in his original *Marxism Today* editorial had been at pains to stress that what he was presenting was an analysis of an objective situation rather a line of advance which more traditionally-minded editors might have been expected to serve up, thus: 'It is the left which seems backward-looking conservative, bereft of new ideas and out of time. In short, the right has appropriated New Times. Unless the left can come to terms with those New Times it must remain on the sidelines. *But coming to terms with New Times means first understanding what New Times, are, what they mean.*'[34]

It should not be such a surprise then to find a group of forward-thinking Conservatives taking this analysis as their starting point to find ways to perpetuate, and in their own way improve upon, the Tory hegemony of the last fourteen years and more. This is the basis of Marc-Henri Glendening's very different contribution to this collection.[35] For those who see irony as a natural part of postmodern discourse there is something peculiarly rewarding to find a group of Tory dissidents critiquing the inadequacies of conservatism in a manner more than faintly reminiscent of our own critique of the inadequacies of labourism. For the postmodernist, clearly, the mirror never lies.

The City Without Limits

Contemporary intellectual debate has a bewildering tendency to fly away from the realities it must address. It needs securing in order to develop ideas which have substance. The urban space, and particularly the inner-city, is a potent provider of this crucial process. The city represents both shadowy ideals and concrete forms, indeed it is a key space where the narratives of everyday life are acted out, most recently set out in a range of books dealing with postmodern city realities.[36] As Ken Worpole points out in his chapter, it is the city that provides a space where the engagement between cultural theory and lived experience can be examined and practised. He goes on to claim: 'It is probably the city that now serves as the key organising principle for social hope at the end of the twentieth century'.[37] This is not to decry progressive developments in rural areas and small towns. After all in Britain it is in the decidedly non-metropolitan South-West that dealignment and realignment have opened up the most fruitful opportunities yet for co-operation and dialogue between the parties of opposition and have thrown home counties Tories into turmoil. Meanwhile it is in run-down inner-city areas that the Nazi British National Party have acquired a level of support to make a frightening, if hopefully, temporary electoral break-through backed by a horrific rise in the number of racially-motivated attacks. Nevertheless it is the metropolitan unit which is emerging as a new 'city-state' and that could yet provide a basis for the re-organisation of politics to meet the new needs of next century.

The concept of space is closely connected to the discussion around globalisation and localisation.[38] David Morley's chapter[39] focuses on the impact of this discussion on the global media of film, television and radio. He makes a strong case for not underestimating the strength of the influences at work when we digest cultural products, and in particular he asks us to pay special attention to the continuing pervasive influence of Americanisation. Indeed as all our contributors argue, the question of power expressed through culture must be a key part of any radical estimation of local and global balances of forces. Cultural power works through the oft-quoted analogous conditions of boundary, borderline and the 'other' which sets limits to any notion of universalism. The interview with writer and poet, David Dabydeen, which closes the second section of this collection[40] deals with these questions in a notably vivid fashion. Dabydeen makes an impassioned call not just for the recognition of the inexorably political nature of the construction of global identities and social relations, but also for an understanding of the ways in which that recognition must transform what we have formerly perceived as 'the political'. This transformation forces a re-evaluation of where we come from, and who we are. Such a process demands an unravelling of the complexity of social and cultural identity which will necessarily reveal painful grievances which cannot be suppressed in the name of the false totem of unity. However the revelation and pain will take us nowhere if it ends up trapping us in guilty victimhood rather than uncovering the potential to put an end to the sources of the grievances.

Only Connect

For all these very necessary ventures the body politic in general, and the left in particular, is poorly equipped, characterised as it is by a spirit of intellectual exhaustion. The radical project of communism, that came to a sorry end with the fall of the Berlin Wall, has bequeathed few fragments of any note. Memories of a long-past Prague spring, of experiments in a self-managed socialist economy and of a resurgent Eurocommunism are almost all that are left, and they remain for the present most certainly only memories. Similarly west European socialism and social-democracy has found the energies that propelled it into office across Europe in the late 1980s somewhat wanting, to say the least, as the pace of change has relentlessly accelerated. As a result socialism has found itself not simply out of office, but out of time. Western capitalism throws up crisis after crisis, but socialism quite simply is no longer viable as the answer to those crises and the questions it raises – of justice, equality, peace and collective solutions to shared problems remain unanswered. The Third World liberation movements that once offered a picture of far-away militant inspiration are no longer the force they once were. It is undoubtedly true that the implications of a looming global environmental catastrophe are still very much with us, but the Green parties are racked with division and the confusion of role that the seemingly contradictory demands of social movement and parliamentary party have imposed upon them. For the right, the 'end of history' not surprisingly provoked a period of smug self-satisfaction. This in turn has been speedily wiped away in the face of the fearsome rise of forces to its right, whether nationalist, fascist or religious-fundamentalist. The right's hegemony that some thought would reign untroubled after the end of communism is facing a whole new range of challenges on its right flank, whilst domestically the mid-term disenchantment with John Major's grey regime has been fuelled by the enduring rise of the Liberal Democrats in the Tory heartlands of the South and South-West. That disenchantment with the government is partly a result of the emergence of issues which have impaled division on the heart of the Conservative Party in much the same way that the 1980s inner-party strife struck the Labour Party with the same malaise. From the corruption of party donations, to Maastricht, to the level of public sector expenditure, via open disquiet with the character of the Prime Minister's leadership qualities the British right is divided in a whole number of new ways which could yet spell electoral defeat.

The problems of the current Conservative Party are a welcome break from the anxieties that living through an age of uncertainty necessarily provoke, intellectually, politically and culturally. The current age is characterised by the multiplicity of moments of flux that we see and feel around us. There are no longer any obvious and reassuring lines of linear political development that one can follow until their forward march reaches one's chosen rainbow's end. As Anne Showstack Sassoon outlines in the closing chapter of this collection,[41] shifts in intellectual attitudes are needed in order to underpin a grander expansion of our ways of seeing, hearing and understanding the political. And this expansion of our political imagination must bring with it a new-found emphasis on empathy if our intellectual work is to rid itself of its isolationism. To 'remake the political' requires a culture where meaningful and thoughtful dialogues take place well beyond the narrow and depleted ranks of the party faithful. Dialogues which are as at ease with 'sonic hedgehogs' and the chart-topping antics of 'Take That' as the lofty ideas and ideals of political economy.[42] The practice must be rigorously inclusive, existing in an open, rather than a closed space. The messages projected should be unashamedly of today, rather than trapped in a compromised yesterday of dubious parentage. The remaking of the political starts with the subtle, but ends with the significant. It is a transformation that belongs in the crowded rooms of tomorrow.

Mark Perryman

Notes

[1] See Martin Jacques, 'The End of Politics' in the *Sunday Times*, 18.7.93.
[2] The Communist Party of Great Britain, *Manifesto for New Times*, Lawrence & Wishart, London 1990, pp 48-50.
[3] 'Party Activity Slows', report in the *Guardian*, 7 August 1993. See also Patrick Seyd and Paul Whiteley, *Labour's Grass Roots*, Clarendon Press, Oxford 1992.

4 'Cash Crisis hits Tories as PM falters', report in the *Sunday Telegraph*, 8 August 1993.

5 'Grassroots Warm to Labour', report in the *Guardian*, 20 September 1993.

6 Sara Parkin, 'How fresh-look Greens could be good for you', in the *Guardian*, 3.6.93.

7 Stuart Hall and Martin Jacques (eds), *New Times – The Changing Face of Politics in the 1990s*, Lawrence & Wishart, London 1989.

8 Bryan Gould, 'A map of the battlefield for the Left', in the *Guardian*, 25 June 1988.

9 See, Oxford University Socialist Discussion Group (eds), *Out of Apathy*, Verso, London 1989.

10 See David Caute, *Sixty-Eight*, Hamish Hamilton, London 1988 and Ronald Fraser, *1968*, Chatto and Windus, London 1988.

11 Sheila Rowbotham, Lynne Segal and Hilary Wainwright, *Beyond The Fragments*, Merlin Press, London 1979.

12 The Socialist Society, Founding Statement January 1992.

13 See Ken Livingstone, *If Voting Changed Anything They'd Abolish It*, Collins, London 1987.

14 Democratic Left, 'Renovation – A Discussion Document', January 1993.

15 Editorial in *Renewal*, issue one, January 1993.

16 Demos, Founding Statement, March 1993.

17 Andrew Gamble, in this collection, p 27.

18 Andrew Gamble, *op cit*, p 38.

19 See Colin Hughes and Patrick Wintour, *Labour Rebuilt*, Fourth Estate, London 1990.

20 Greg Philo, in this collection, p 47.

21 Mike Rustin, in this collection, pp 88–89.

22 Bryan Gould, 'Why Britain deserves better than today's Labour Party', in the *Daily Mail*, 24 August 1993.

23 See Beatrix Campbell, 'Dangerous Liaisons', in *Marxism Today* April 1990. Also, Danny Burns, *Poll Tax Rebellion*, AK Press, Stirling 1992 for an excellent anarchist account of the anti-poll tax campaign.

24 Patrick Marber, 'Sees Red', in *Time Out*, 8 September 1993.

25 See Ernesto Laclau, *New Reflections on the Revolution of our Time*, Verso, London 1990. Also, Chantal Mouffe (ed), *Dimensions of Radical Democracy*, Verso, London 1992.

26 Adam Lent, in this collection, pp 218–239.

27 See Jonathan Rutherford (ed), *Identity*, Lawrence & Wishart, London 1990.

28 Suzanne Moore, 'Faith, Hope and Identity', in *In These Times*, Signs of the Times Discussion Paper Number 4, September 1993.

29 Suzanne Moore, *op cit*.

30 Angela McRobbie, in this collection, pp 113–132.

31 Jane Flax, quoted in McRobbie, *op cit*, p 126.

32 Wendy Wheeler, in this collection, pp 94–109.

33 Kevin Davey, in this collection, p .195–217.

[34] Martin Jacques, 'New Times', in *Marxism Today*, October 1988.

[35] Marc-Henri Glendening, in this collection, pp 240–260.

[36] See Mark Fisher and Ursula Owen, *Whose Cities?*, Penguin, Harmondsworth 1991; Patrick Wright, *Journey through the Ruins*, Radius, London 1991; Elizabeth Wilson, *The Sphinx in the City*, Virago, London 1991; Beatrix Campbell, *Goliath*, Methuen, London 1993.

[37] Ken Worpole, in this collection, pp 162.

[38] See Erica Carter, James Donald and Judith Squires (eds), *Space and Place*, Lawrence & Wishart, London 1993.

[39] David Morley, in this collection, pp 133–156.

[40] Interview with David Dabydeen, in this collection, pp 74–191.

[41] Anne Showstack Sassoon, in this volume, pp. 261–277.

[42] In an interview in September 1993 with Radio One's *Newsbeat* programme Labour leader John Smith admitted that he had never heard of a computer game, 'Sonic the Hedgehog' which had sold millions of copies that year and was totally unaware of the then current number one teen-pop sensations 'Take That'. Such levels of ignorance are not uncommon amongst politicians.

Section One:
On the Home Front —
Parliament, Parties
and Power

Loves Labour Lost

ANDREW GAMBLE

In April 1992 the Conservatives won their fourth consecutive general election victory. The result was a surprise, not least to the Conservatives themselves. Throughout the election campaign the opinion polls had consistently predicted that neither party would gain an overall majority. The final poll of polls constructed from the four leading polls and published on the morning of the election gave Labour a lead of 0.9 per cent. (The actual result was a Conservative lead of 7.5 per cent). The Exit polls of the BBC and ITN suggested that the Conservatives would not win more than 305 seats, twenty-one short of a majority. (They won 336). Had the polls been right there would have been a hung parliament and the Conservatives would have been perceived as having lost the election since they were defending a parliamentary majority from 1987 of one hundred seats. In these circumstances they would have found it extremely difficult to stay in office. Even if Labour had not won enough seats to become the largest single party, the political initiative would have moved decisively in its favour.

A hung Parliament would have meant that Labour would have secured a substantial swing. The events of the campaign would then have appeared in a very different light. Labour's Sheffield rally would have been interpreted as the springboard which launched Labour to victory. Labour's health broadcast would have been presented as brilliantly highlighting the health issue and wrong-footing the Tories. Even Labour's tax plans would have been hailed as a success, by defusing the tax issue and persuading many sceptical voters to trust Labour on the economy.

The actual result delivered a reduced but still sizeable Conservative majority of twenty one. In the deluge of criticism, blame, and recrimination which followed, it is easy to forget how widespread was the conviction during the campaign that Labour was on its way. Typical banner headlines were 'Tory row over strategy grows'; 'Top Tories get jitters as campaign wobbles'; 'Fear grips the City'; 'Hung Parliament looms'; 'Polls point to defeat for Tories'. In the *Observer* the weekend before election day twelve leading psephologists and commentators gave their assessments of the outcome. One predicted an outright Conservative victory, one an outright Labour win. All the others predicted that there would be a hung Parliament; the only point on which they differed was which party would have the largest number of seats.

The basis of these expectations was the opinion polls. An overwhelming majority of the polls published during the election campaign had suggested that the outcome of the election would be a hung parliament. It was the unanimity of the polls which misled so many commentators. A single poll might be wrong, but any bias or error, it was believed, could be corrected by taking the average of the leading polls. It was that average that pointed inexorably to the loss of the Conservative majority. So authoritative have polls become in contemporary electoral politics because of their successful record in accurately predicting the results of elections that no one believed they could be seriously mistaken. Polls have always permitted themselves a margin of error, but the actual error was more than four times the permitted margin. It was the largest error in the history of opinion polling. Almost everyone was fooled. This explains why the result of the election came as such a shock.

But should it have been such a shock? In a longer perspective it does not appear so. The surprise is rather that Labour appeared at the time of the election to be in such a strong position. Labour, it is true, had built up a commanding lead in the opinion polls during 1990 and

had won some important by-elections, particularly at
Mid-Staffordshire and the Vale of Glamorgan. The
unpopularity of specific government policies, such as the
poll tax and the health reforms, and the worsening
economic situation had caused a plunge in the ratings of
both the government and the Prime Minister, Margaret
Thatcher. Many Conservative MPs had begun to perceive
Thatcher as an electoral liability. That was a key factor in
the background to the dramatic events in November 1990
which culminated in her removal as Conservative leader.
The most dominant Conservative leader since Churchill,
who had never lost a national election, and who had
secured three general election victories, was dumped with
only eighteen months of the Parliament still to run and in
the midst of a major security crisis – Iraq's invasion of
Kuwait.

Thatcher's removal stunned her supporters and there
were bitter recriminations in the Conservative Party which
have continued up to the present.[1] Adverse poll ratings
alone would never have removed her. What precipitated
the leadership crisis was the division in the Cabinet over
European policy and the handling of the economy.
Nevertheless the change of leader appeared to work
wonders for the Conservatives. Before Thatcher's removal
Labour held a lead in the opinion polls of ten percentage
points. This was down from the very high levels achieved
in the spring, but still a comfortable margin. As soon as
Thatcher was replaced by John Major the polls performed
a somersault and the Tories were catapulted into a small
lead, which they held through Christmas 1990 and
through the Gulf War in the spring of 1991.[2] The lead
disappeared in the summer, but reappeared in the
autumn.

Many commentators were surprised that Major did not
call an early general election – either just after he became
Leader, or immediately after the Gulf War. It seems likely
that had Michael Heseltine become leader he would have
gone to the country at the earliest possible moment. Major
was not under the same pressure to establish his authority
within the party – he was the preferred successor of the

ousted leader and had taken no part in the regicide. Another factor seems to have been the economy. Major and Lamont were convinced that the recession would not last and that recovery was certain to be evident by the autumn, and at the very latest by the following spring. Against the background of a strongly reviving economy they calculated that they could coast to victory. By waiting until the autumn of 1991 they could make absolutely certain.

What threw out all their calculations was the failure of the economy to come good. The green shoots glimpsed so confidently in the spring obstinately refused to thrive. So important has the relationship become between the economic expectations of voters and their voting intention that Conservative strategists were not prepared to risk an election. It had to be postponed from the autumn until the spring. Yet despite the unveiling of new spending plans, and many ministerial attempts to talk up the recovery, the economy still obstinately failed to oblige. The Tories found themselves having to fight an election against the background of the deepest recession since 1945 and an apparent revival in Labour's electoral fortunes. Many observers thought that the Conservatives had boxed themselves in and that Major had made an error in not going to the country earlier.

But that judgement turned out to be false. The Conservatives were not boxed in. The Sheffield rally and the 'war of Jennifer's ear' (over Labour's party election broadcast on the long waiting lists in the National Health Service) had very little to do with it. The result vindicated the judgement widely held at the end of 1990 that with Thatcher gone the electoral task for Labour was too great. On paper the Labour party needed a swing of 8 per cent to gain an outright majority, and a swing of 4 per cent to deprive the Conservatives of their majority. It needed to win 97 seats more than it won in 1987. These targets were greater than any party had managed to achieve in any election since 1945. The swing Labour actually achieved was 2.1 per cent but it did better in winning seats, capturing an extra 42; this was however still less than half of what it needed. Analysis of the results has shown that the way in which votes were distributed nationally in 1992 favoured Labour by enabling it to win more seats than it deserved on the basis of its share of the vote. To have won outright, therefore, Labour actually needed a smaller swing than the 8 per cent which was estimated before the election. But the swing it needed was still much greater than the one it actually achieved.[3]

Had the recovery come when Norman Lamont expected it, and the Conservatives had called an election in November 1991 and been returned with a majority of around fifty, there would not have been the same sense of shock that was felt only a few months later in April 1992 when the Conservatives came back with a majority of twenty one. The shock quickly turned to relief on the right, and a renewed sense of confidence; on the left it produced a mood of despair and deep disappointment. For a short period in those weeks leading up to the election the centre-left in British politics, which had been shut out of office and marginalised in political debate for thirteen years, suddenly glimpsed the possibility of a hung parliament and a new agenda opening up for constitutional change, new alliances, and the possibility of breaking the stranglehold of the Conservatives on government. It was that which was ripped away in the early hours of 10 April, 1992.

The Conservatives' victory, although slight in terms of votes, was crushing in terms of the percentage of the vote, and emphasised once more the long-term resilience and dominance of the Conservatives in British politics. In the aftermath of the election it was reasonable to ask why the Conservatives should ever lose office again. A political system with a mass electorate has been established in Britain only since 1885. 1992 was the first time any party in this period had won four general elections in a row. The Tories under Lord Liverpool won four consecutive elections in the first two decades of the nineteenth century, but that was in the unreformed House of Commons, elected by only 2 per cent of the population, and when party organisation in the modern sense did not exist.

Landmarks on the Electoral Map

Significant elections allow a redrawing of boundaries and a reshaping of our understanding of the past. After the 1992 election result the period between 1940 and 1979 assumes a more distinct profile. It is the period when Labour achieved its greatest success, a period when it was almost on terms of equality with the Conservatives. Including the period of the war-time coalition government both parties were in government for twenty-two years between 1940 and 1979. This is the only time in the modern era when Britain has had a true two-party system, in the sense of a system in which there were two major parties with a reasonable opportunity of forming a government after each election.

In the 1920s and 1930s there was a dominant party system, in which the Conservatives were the normal party of government and the opposition to them was split. The vote of the Labour Party was increasing in this period but it never went above 40 per cent. Labour was able to form

Table 1

Election Year	Conservative %	Conservative Seats	Labour %	Labour Seats	Lib/All/LDP %	Lib/All/LDP Seats
1945	39.8	213	48.3	393	9.1	12
1950	43.5	299	46.1	315	9.1	9
1951	48.0	321	48.8	295	2.5	6
1955	49.7	345	46.4	277	2.7	6
1959	49.4	365	43.8	258	5.9	6
1964	43.4	304	44.1	317	11.2	9
1966	41.9	253	47.9	363	8.5	12
1970	46.4	330	43.0	288	7.5	6
1974	37.8	297	37.1	301	19.3	14
1974	35.8	277	39.2	319	18.3	13
1979	43.9	339	37.0	269	13.8	11
1983	42.4	397	27.6	209	25.4	23
1987	42.3	376	30.8	229	22.6	22
1992	41.9	336	34.4	271	17.8	20

two governments, in 1924 and 1929, but both were minority governments, and neither lasted long – the first less than a year, the second just over two years. By contrast the Conservatives' share of the vote rarely fell below 40 per cent and in their best years went much higher. In 1924 they won 48.3 per cent of the vote; in 1931 55.2 per cent; in 1935 53.7 per cent. The percentage margin they held over Labour in those three elections was 15.3 per cent, 24.6 per cent, and 15.8 per cent respectively.

Since 1979 a big gap has once again opened up between the two parties. In absolute terms the Conservatives' share of the vote does not match the levels they achieved in the 1920s and 1930s, but in relative terms they once again have a significant lead. In 1979 they had a 6.9 per cent lead; in 1983 14.8; in 1987 11.5 per cent; and in 1992 7.5 per cent. Labour has recovered from its slump in 1983, but its absolute share of the vote is still below its 1979 level. If Labour continues to make progress at the rate it achieved between 1983 and 1992 it will need not one but two elections before it pushes its vote above 40 per cent. Unless the electoral system delivers Labour a freak victory Labour will need not one more heave but at least two more heaves.

These changes are the reasons why the period between 1940 and 1979 now seems to belong to another age. Labour has not won more than 40 per cent of the vote at any general election since 1970, six elections and twenty-three years ago. At all seven elections from 1945 to 1970 Labour had over 40 per cent of the vote and in several was close to 50 per cent. The period also contains the only two occasions when Labour has won a parliamentary majority of more than ten seats – 1945 and 1966. Looking at British political history since the decisive widening of the franchise in 1885 it is obvious that the Conservatives are the dominant force. Between 1945 and 1979 Labour was at least on equal terms with the Conservatives. Since 1979 even this has no longer been the case (see Table 1).

1983: The Watershed Election

While 1979 is often seen as the key watershed election in the Thatcher era, the Conservative victory in 1992 shows that it is 1983 which is even more important. The result in 1979 could have been reversed, and for a time it looked as though it would be. No government in the previous twenty years had been re-elected after serving a full term. The government had changed hands every five years on average – in 1964, 1970, 1974, and 1979. The depths of unpopularity to which the Thatcher government quickly plunged made it likely that this would be its fate also. Three factors changed this; the split in the Labour Party in 1981 which led to the formation of the Social Democratic Party (SDP) and the formation of the Alliance, an electoral pact between the SDP and the Liberals; the Falklands War, which might have been a disaster, but was turned, not least by Thatcher herself, into a triumph; and the recovery of the economy from the deep recession of 1980-81, which brought back prosperity to key parts of the Conservative electorate, particularly in the South-East.

These three factors allowed the Conservatives to hold their vote steady in the 1983 election, while the opposition parties fought for second place. The electoral system rewarded the Conservatives with a huge parliamentary majority of 144. But the real significance of 1983 was not the number of seats which the Conservatives won but their percentage lead over the other parties. Both have diminished since 1983, but both still exist. If the polls had been right the vote in 1992 would have divided between the three main parties 40/40/18. The actual result was 42/34/18. Labour won more seats than it deserved to on a strictly proportional basis, which made the election seem closer than it actually was. The percentage share of the vote shows how far Labour still has to go to recover from 1983. In 1992 the Conservatives polled two million more votes than Labour. Yet the circumstances for a Labour victory could hardly been more propitious. The election was fought during a recession, the severity of which was blamed on the government by the electorate, and after a period in which Conservative rule had been highly unpopular. As a result of mis-timing the electoral and the economic cycle, the government had been forced to call an election at a time not of its own choosing. Even so Labour was defeated; indeed it did not even come close to overtaking the Conservatives in terms of its share of the popular vote.

Today 1983 looks like the election which re-aligned British politics and solidified a political and electoral structure which gave a permanent advantage to the Conservatives, making Conservative victories a more likely outcome of general elections than Labour ones. Labour victories may still occur, in part because the party is benefiting under the present electoral system from the regional concentration of its vote and the small size of the electorate in many of its constituencies. But in other respects the balance of the system has shifted against the party. Labour's base of support is too small relative to the Conservatives' to make it an equal contest. Ivor Crewe points out that the number of Labour identifiers in the electorate declined sharply during the 1980s. Conservative identifiers outnumber Labour identifiers by 45 to 33 per cent. The range of the normal vote for each party is 28–40 for Labour, 37–45 for the Conservatives, and 14–26 for the Liberal Democrats. The overlap between the bottom of the Conservative range and the top of the Labour range means that Labour victories are still possible, but not probable. Conservative victories are much more likely.[4] To this extent the two-party system which existed for forty years has been superseded by a dominant party system.[5]

Some dispute this conclusion. Certainly the rituals of two-party politics continue to flourish. There is still a leader of the Opposition, still balance to be preserved on party political broadcasts, still the impression that the Labour Front Bench is the government-in-waiting. But the British have always been very good at preserving rituals long after the real substance which gave rise to them has disappeared. The British constitution and parliamentary system requires an opposition to assist in the legitimation of the actions of the executive. The opposition parties are happy to perform their allotted role, and are gradually being transformed into a permanent opposition.

The trend towards a dominant party system is reinforced by the new consensus on policy. One of the most significant legacies of the Thatcher era on British politics was the way in which it changed the priorities of policy in several areas and the agenda of policy debate.[6] Signs that Thatcherism was becoming exhausted at the end of the 1980s and that a new radical interventionist agenda was emerging not just in Britain but around the world have been eagerly seized on. But the obituaries may be premature. There remains a considerable untapped potential in the New Right agenda, which may well be picked up again in the future. The themes of choice, opportunity, and competition are too central to modern Conservatism in the way that it has been redefined during the Thatcher era to be easily abandoned.

The influence and relevance of this agenda is one of the reasons that explains Labour's shift on so many issues, from the sale of council houses to privatisation, from industrial relations legislation to taxation, from defence to the European Community. After the polarisation in policies which opened up between the parties during the 1970s and early 1980s, the policy gap has narrowed sharply, until by the 1992 general election the differences were marginal. Although the Conservatives had made some adjustments, abandoning a few of the more radical proposals of their third term, in particular the poll tax, most of the movement was from Labour. The Labour leadership, in order to make the party electable again, abandoned its alternative economic strategy, emphasising instead the party's traditional role as the defender of collectivist, public sector, welfare programmes. The manifesto on which Labour fought the 1992 election had few radical proposals of any kind.

Does this mean that Britain can look forward to everlasting Conservatism? It would not make Britain exceptional. There are relatively few functioning two-party systems in the world, in the sense of political systems in which there is a fairly regular alternation of political parties in government. They require a balance between political forces which occurs sometimes but not often. Far more common are political systems in which one party is dominant and rules relatively uninterruptedly for long periods. Examples include the Swedish Social Democrats from the 1930s until the 1970s, the German Christian Democrats after 1945 and again since 1981, and the Japanese Liberal Democrats throughout the post-war period. In all these democracies those parties which are not part of the ruling alliance have been excluded from participation in government for long periods. As a result the culture and structure of the opposition parties and the government parties comes to be quite different. In several dominant party systems, such as in Japan, corruption has become endemic as a mode of running the system. Another feature of such systems is that the opposition becomes more and more remote from government, the boundary between the state elite and the ruling party begins to blur.[7] In the last hundred years the British system has been relatively free of corruption, in part because of the strong ethos of public service among civil servants and other public sector workers. The restructuring of the state under the Thatcher government, through the privatisation and hiving off of so many functions and services to private bodies or to new, autonomous, public agencies, and the highly partisan exercise of government patronage in the making of public appointments and the awarding of contracts, risks destroying that ethos and creating conditions in which corruption will seep into the political system.

The spectacular collapse of the standing of the Major government in the six months following its general election triumph in April 1992 might suggest that the dangers of a dominant party system in Britain have been exaggerated. The government's reputation for economic competence was weakened by the persistence of the recession into 1993 and by the collapse of the main plank of its economic policy – sterling's membership of the

Exchange Rate Mechanism – in September 1992. This was compounded by highly inept government handling of major issues – such as pit closures, the future of the Leyland Daf plant, and the education reforms. Even more seriously, the unity of the party was threatened by the deep rift over the ratification of the Maastricht Treaty.

If the Conservatives cannot restore unity in their own party and cannot win back their reputation for economic competence before the next election their ability to continue dominating British politics would be threatened. But provided they do not actually split in a way which would bring the government down, the Conservatives have a long time to recover before they need to call another election. John Major lacks the ideological vision and radical drive which his predecessor had. But that may be an asset. The government still intends to carry on the main lines of the education and health reforms of the 1980s and to finish privatising what little remains of the old nationalised industries. But beyond that it has no radical agenda or any clear sense of direction. In one sense this makes opposition harder. There are unlikely to be clearcut issues like the poll tax which can become a focus for organising opposition. The main opportunities for the Opposition will stem from government muddle and incompetence, both of which appear to be in plentiful supply.

Those are powerful weapons in the hands of a competent opposition, but they may not be enough by themselves to deliver victory. At the next election the Conservatives will benefit from the redistribution of constituency boundaries perhaps by as many as fourteen seats.[8] The swing Labour needs to unseat the Conservatives and the number of seats it has to capture requires an exceptional swing of 5 per cent. To have a majority of one seat in the next Parliament, Labour has to capture another 47 seats, and to have a working majority it would have to win over 60. The Conservatives will attempt to realign the economic cycle with the electoral cycle and to hold an election in 1996 in the wake of a tax-cutting budget and an improving economy. Once entrenched, a dominant party system is hard to overturn. In such systems – Japan used to be a good example until 1993 – whatever the scandals, whatever the maladministration, whatever the unpopularity of the ruling party between elections, when it came to the election itself, enough voters still endorsed it, however reluctantly. Commanding opinion poll leads and resounding by-election victories in the mid-term of a Parliament signify little about the prospects of the opposition parties in a general election.

One of Major's key advantages at the 1992 election was that he was able to present his government as a new government which did not have direct responsibility for the actions and policies of the Thatcher government. In terms of personnel there is a solid basis in fact for this claim. It is remarkable that in the Cabinet John Major appointed after the 1992 election the only minister who was in Thatcher's first Cabinet in 1979 was Michael Heseltine. Such a circulation of elites is not particularly common in political systems, where the old guard tends to hang on for as long as possible. The age of the Conservative Cabinet by contrast has continued to fall. There are grumbles about the calibre of some of the new ministers, but there is no dispute that the Conservatives have proven adept at renewing themselves. Their problem is not new faces but new ideas.

The Kinnock Legacy

How is Labour responding to its fourth election defeat? The party is divided between modernisers and traditionalists, those who believe that the party needs a radical rethink not just of its policies and its organisation but also of its ethos and its approach to politics, against those who believe that the fundamentals of Labour politics do not need changing.[9] This debate centres on different estimates of how much further Labour's recovery needs to go and therefore upon what was achieved and not achieved during Neil Kinnock's period as leader.

Kinnock will go down in Labour Party history as a successful moderniser and reformer of this most conservative of parties. Under him the party introduced major organisational and policy reforms. He was a highly successful party manager, who re-established the dominance of the leadership in the determination of the party's policy and image. He achieved this by splitting the left in the Labour Party and re-establishing the links of the Labour leadership with the trade unions. Without Kinnock Labour might well have split again, and become marginalised within the political system. In 1983 the Alliance parties were only two percentage points behind Labour. In 1992 the gap between Labour and the Liberal Democrats was seventeen points. Kinnock's main achievement was to ensure that Labour would remain the main party of opposition, and that the 1981 split did not lead to its replacement by a new, centre party, in the way that Labour had replaced the Liberals after their split in 1916.

A key feature of the changes Kinnock initiated was a far reaching policy review.[10] Changes were recommended on the European Community, on defence, on markets, on industrial relations law, and on council house sales. What the policy review did not touch was Labour's commitment to collective universal welfare services, funded out of progressive taxation. The Croslandite redistributive agenda of the 1950s and 1960s was preserved, but the alternative economic strategy of the 1970s with its emphasis on public ownership and protection was abandoned.

The policy review was criticised for not going far enough. It contained relatively few radical proposals for reforming the public sector or the nature of the Labour Party's trade union links, rethinking the politics of redistribution or devising a new strategy for economic management. But what it achieved was considerable. Labour fought the 1992 election on a manifesto which contained little that any Labour MP who left the party in 1981 to join the SDP could have disagreed with.[11] Under Kinnock Labour moved closer to being a Social Democratic Party, on the European model, than ever before.

During 1989 and 1990 it appeared that Kinnock's

strategy of moving the Labour Party back to the centre and changing its image was paying off. Between 1983 and 1987, the first phase of Kinnock's leadership, Labour never secured above 40 per cent support in the polls. After 1989, however, Labour crossed that threshold and when the poll tax row was at its height, at the beginning of 1990, Labour achieved 50 per cent, even briefly 55 per cent. This was the highest opinion poll rating Labour has achieved at any time in its history. It did not mean that Labour was capable of taking 55 per cent of the votes in a general election, but it was a sign that Labour had made a breakthrough in how it was perceived by the electorate. For a time it did seem that the two-party system was back.

The electoral threat which Labour posed to the Conservatives in 1990 caused considerable alarm in government circles. It convinced many Conservatives that something had to be done about very divisive issues like the poll tax, and raised doubts about Thatcher and her style of leadership. As suggested earlier it is unlikely that electoral unpopularity alone would have provided a pretext on which Thatcher could have been removed. But the resignations in the Cabinet did provide a pretext, and an opportunity for a plausible leadership challenge in 1990. Even so, Thatcher nearly survived. Only 152 Conservative MPs voted for Heseltine on the first ballot, 52 less than voted for Thatcher. But Thatcher was four votes short of the margin she needed to clinch victory on the first ballot, and that failure proved decisive in persuading her to quit.

Thatcher's abrupt departure transformed the political climate. The Conservatives were able to reinvent themselves and remove many of the negative reasons voters had for voting against them. In one sense this was a tribute to Kinnock. His new Labour Party was a key factor in the defeat of radical Thatcherism and the removal of Margaret Thatcher. The level of support for Labour, the anti-poll tax campaign, and Conservative unpopularity on so many issues did ultimately force change in the ruling party.

From another perspective, however, this success also

showed up a deeper failure. Labour had become a more
successful electoral competitor of the Conservatives but on
the Conservatives' own ground. In the 1992 campaign it
was often hard to tell the policy positions of the two parties
apart. Kinnock delivered a Labour party which was
distinct enough from Thatcher's radical Conservatism, but
not from Major's safety first Conservatism. The similarity
between the two parties in policy terms meant the election
centred on issues of trust. Which party did voters trust to
manage the economy and create the conditions for future
prosperity? By a considerable margin the answer went in
favour of the Conservatives.[12]

Kinnock had modernised his party and made it an
electoral competitor again, but he had not found a way of
giving Labour the kind of identity and radical agenda
which would have allowed it to seize the ideological and
political initiative from the Conservatives. For all
Kinnock's efforts Labour still appeared a defensive,
conservative political formation, trapped in a particular
style of politics and still finding it difficult to appeal
beyond its traditional electorate. Kinnock succeeded in
stopping any further decline in Labour's credibility and
clawed back some of the lost votes, but in doing so he
helped to make the old Labourist conception of the party
plausible again. A substantial body of opinion in the party,
stretching from Roy Hattersley and Margaret Beckett to
John Prescott and Tony Benn are resisting in particular
the suggestion that Labour should embrace the cause of
electoral reform. They are not persuaded by the
arguments of the psephologists that the structural balance
of the electorate has moved against Labour, making a
future Labour victory unlikely, if not impossible. They are
unwilling that Labour should give up the chance of
forming a majority government on its own at some point
in the future.

The modernisers point to the task that Labour and the
other opposition parties face if the Conservatives are to be
dislodged. In 1996 Labour is going to need a bigger swing
(at least 5 per cent) than it has achieved in any election
since 1945. It has the handicap of the boundary changes.

It has the problem of how it can distinguish its policy from that of the Conservatives, at the same time increasing its rating for economic competence.

It also faces the continued long-term decline of Labour's core support, a decline which certain government policies since 1979 have been designed to assist. The old connections between trade unions, collective welfare provision, the public sector, and local government is waning. The nexus of interests, attitudes, institutions, and policies that formed the Labour movement appears no longer capable of delivering national electoral majorities. It still dominates certain regions, and it still constitutes Labour's base – its heartland, its tradition, and its history. But it no longer represents an expanding, dynamic, and progressive force.

One hundred years ago it was the Labour movement which was the focus for working class self-reliance, independence, initiative, and self-help. What has happened since that time is that many of these values have become associated with institutions outside the Labour movement. Some of them have been appropriated by the Conservatives. For many working people, particularly in the South of England it is the Conservative Party which represents their aspirations to be socially mobile and to be independent, aspirations which formerly were represented by the Labour movement. For an increasing part of the electorate the Labour movement has come to represent primarily the public sector, many of whose programmes are perceived as helping the disadvantaged and the dependent rather than the solid core of the independent working class. Labour has retained its support much better in the North and in Scotland, where it is still the leading party, but in the South it has lost a large part of its traditional electorate. Some of it came back in 1992 but not nearly enough.

Labour has to decide what kind of party it wants to be. Its traditional working class base, concentrated as it is in the North and Scotland, is not large enough to give it electoral victory. It is also failing to win sufficient support from key sections of the electorate, particularly women.

Labour had two per cent less support than the Conservatives among men but ten percent less support among women. The only age cohort where Labour had a majority was young women aged between 18 and 24. But in all the other age cohorts Labour has much less support than the Conservatives. A key question for Labour therefore is why so many women beyond the age of 24 find it difficult to identify themselves with the party.

Many of the modernisers link that problem directly with the party's continuing identity as primarily a party of and for the trade unions. The trade union connection was at the heart of Labourism in the past because it was an organised interest which provided a sense of purpose and identity. But the trade union link is now at the heart of Labour's problem as it struggles to make itself a more pluralist party, with which a wider range of groups and voters can identify. Too many at present feel excluded, and this restricts Labour's appeal to the electorate. The modernisers argue that Labour's decline stems from its failure to respond to the new aspirations and life-styles of many voters. Labour has become out of touch with important changes in civil society.

Prospects of Realignment

One obvious problem for the modernisers is that Labour never has been a dynamic, radical, modernising, energising force in British politics. It has always dragged its feet, its conception of politics and of opposition has been doggedly conservative. One of the reasons why Labour has been such a congenial partner for the Conservatives in the twentieth century is that Labour, in practice, accepted a subordinate role within a political system and a political culture shaped predominantly by the Conservatives. It is not an accident that the main architect of constitutional changes has been the Conservative Party. Labour, for the most part, has devoted its energies to achieving recognition and protection by the state for the special interests of the British Labour movement. The political settlement that was worked out in the 1940s gave Labour what it sought, and provided several decades of consensus government. The significance of the Thatcher era was that the Conservatives repudiated key elements of that settlement. Thatcher recognised, correctly, that it was no longer necessary to accommodate the interests of the Labour movement in the way in which previous Conservatives had thought prudent.

Under Thatcher the political map was reshaped, and Conservative dominance re-imposed after a period in the 1970s when some of the foundations of Conservative hegemony appeared to be crumbling. One strategic response to this new Conservative ascendancy, much canvassed on the left, has been the various proposals for political realignment. But there are significant obstacles to its realisation. The Liberal Democrats hoped through the 1980s that they could become the core of a new realigned centre-left, but that hope has receded with Labour's revival. In 1992 the Liberal Democrats failed to hold their vote above 20 per cent. They still have substantial support, but are no nearer than they were twenty years ago to making the decisive breakthrough in seats that they need. They are also handicapped because while the activist base of the Liberal Democratic Party wishes to see the party position itself as a left-of-centre party, a substantial part of the electoral support of the Liberal Democrats leans to the Conservatives. Much of that support might go across to the Conservatives rather than support a left-of-centre alliance between the Liberal Democrats and Labour.

Three options for some kind of realignment on the centre-left to break the Conservative hold on power are often discussed. The first is the formation of a completely new party. The name Labour would be abandoned, along with the trade union link. The new party would be non-socialist and would combine Liberal Democrats, Labour, and other groups. The second is the negotiation of an electoral pact between Labour and the Liberal Democrats, to try and win more seats from the Conservatives. The third is the creation of a broad alliance between all radical and left-of-centre parties and groups, aimed at the creation of a radical agenda for modernising Britain.

All face significant obstacles. The third option is perhaps the most interesting, because it would involve an attempt to develop a new style of politics, based on an understanding between many different groups and forces on the left. Labour would be obliged to become a new kind of party – more open, less exclusive, and less insistent on its prerogative to dictate the agenda of left politics.

Any prospects for Labour moving in this direction depend on whether Labour commits itself to constitutional reform, particularly electoral reform. The recommendations from the Plant Commission show how divided the party is between its traditionalist and modernising wings. A pledge to introduce electoral reform would do nothing immediately to break the monopoly of the Conservatives, since the conservatives can only be ousted in an election fought under the existing rules. But it would be a signal of the kind of party Labour means to be in the future, because it would indicate that Labour was prepared to embrace the politics of dialogue, negotiation, pluralism, and compromise, in a bid to unify the centre-left. It would signal a move away from old style Labourist, winner-takes-all politics, which tends to believe that labour can be self-sufficient and can win enough votes to form a Labour government in the future without the need to rethink how a broad alliance for radical change can be reconstructed in this country.[13]

But apart from helping to reconstruct a viable electoral coalition to defeat Conservatism, the crucial advantage of electoral reform is that it might create the political support necessary for a programme of long-term reconstruction. If Labour had formed the government after the 1992 election it would have had to deal with the crisis in the public finances, the pressure on sterling in the ERM, and the continuing recession.[14] It would have been put under such pressure by the financial markets and by the Tory tabloid press that it would quite likely have been an extremely short-lived government. Labour would have performed its role in the political system by demonstrating once again its 'incompetence', and paved the way for the return of the Conservatives. Only if the electoral rules are altered to allow a much more broadly-based consensus to emerge will the radical, long-term reconstruction of the British economy become possible.

A second aspect of the next phase of Labour's modernisation is the development of a radical policy agenda. Norman Tebbit's advice to Labour is that the party should become a second capitalist party. Then the voters/consumers could choose which team of managers they thought better qualified to run the economy. Such advice if heeded would complete Labour's transformation into the SDP. There are forces tugging Labour in that direction, but if Labour did go that way, there would be little point in having a Labour Party at all.

If Labour seeks to renew itself as a radical force in British politics it needs to develop initiatives in a number of areas; the economy, the environment, citizenship, welfare. At the most general level it needs to rethink why the party has become more closely identified with the state (despite being so seldom in office) rather than with civil society. One hundred years ago it was the other way round. The Labour movement was a force outside the state, in important respects antagonistic to it. In seventy years of collectivism the Labour movement tended to become an arm of the state, often indistinguishable from it. A new radical politics requires that it breaks free again.

It may also need to rethink the politics of redistribution. It is hard to imagine a credible party of the centre-left that is not concerned with redistribution. But the result of the 1992 election underlines that it is becoming very difficult to assemble an electoral coalition that will vote for redistribution or support the kind of interventionist economic measures that in the past have accompanied it. The difficulty for any party of reform is acute. The long-term policies that are required to reconstruct the economy require a sacrifice of consumption and short-term austerity. The challenge is to develop a programme that can command the support of both voters and the financial markets and deliver long-term growth and welfare. The establishment of the Commission on Social Justice is a positive sign that Labour is at least prepared to contemplate some fundamental rethinking on its positions on tax, interventionism, and welfare.

Conclusion

Conservative dominance will not be easily overturned. The Conservatives are entrenched and their opponents are divided. The party enjoys many advantages over its competitors – in funding, membership, and press and business support. Its ideas are the ruling ideas. It has set the policy agenda for more than a decade, and it can rely on a large core vote which is concentrated in the South of England, where the bulk of the constituencies now are.

Unless the Conservatives destroy themselves by openly splitting they will have to be ousted by Labour. Despite the failings of the Major government, Labour will do well to continue its advance at the next election. It would be an exceptional result for Labour to win the next election outright. But it is not impossible. Much depends on the ability of the leadership to unite the party around a set of policies and a political style that can give Labour a distinctive, radical profile and broaden its appeal. Labour will not win the kind of landslide it requires unless it breaks decisively with its past and helps to create a momentum for radical change which gives voters positive reasons for switching to Labour. Geography, social structure, and history all seem to be against it. But British politics remains unpredictable. The country is in a mess, and many of the solutions of the 1980s have been discredited. Labour has an opportunity to relaunch itself and become the focus of a new radical politics. Will it take it?

Notes

[1] For an account of Thatcher's fall see P. Norton 'The Conservative Party from Thatcher to Major' in A. King (ed), *Britain at the Polls 1992* Chatham House, New Jersey, 1993, pp 26-69.
[2] The relative impact of particular events such as the removal of

Thatcher and the Gulf War on voting intentions has been analysed by David Sanders 'Why the Conservative Party Won – Again' in A. King (ed), *Britain at the Polls 1992*, Chatham House, New Jersey 1993, pp 171-222. His conclusion is that the impact of such events is normally short-term and transitory, and is less important than the state of the economy and voters' perception of economic well-being.

3 Full details are provided in Butler D. & Kavanagh D., *The British General Election of 1992*, Macmillan, London 1992. See especially chapter 13 and Appendix 2. Labour's relatively high votes in Conservative-held marginals gave rise to the assertion that 1000 more votes in the right constituencies would have made Labour the largest single party. Such a result would have been freakish since Labour's share of the vote would still have been substantially below the Conservative share.

4 See the analysis in Ivor Crewe, 'Voting and the Electorate' in Dunleavy P., Gamble A., Holliday I., & Peele G., *Developments in British Politics 4*, Macmillan, London 1993.

5 The concept of a dominant party system is analysed by Anthony King in 'The Implications of One-Party Government' in A. King (ed), *Britain at the Polls 1992*, Chatham House, New Jersey 1993, pp 223-248.

6 See the classic account by Stuart Hall, *The Hard Road to Renewal*, Verso, London 1988.

7 See the discussion by Anthony King 'The Implications of One-Party Government', *op cit.*

8 For an estimate see Butler & Kavanagh, *The British General Election of 1992 op cit.*, Appendix 2.

9 For an analysis of the debate inside the Labour Party see Patrick Seyd, 'Labour: the Great Transformation', in King A. (ed), *Britain at the Polls 1992 op cit.* pp 70-100.

10 The Policy Review is analysed in P. Alcock et al (eds), *The Social Economy and the Democratic State*, Lawrence and Wishart, London 1989; and Martin Smith and Jo Spear (eds), *The Changing Labour Party*, Routledge, London 1992.

11 An argument made strongly by Ivor Crewe 'The Policy Agenda: A New Policy Consensus?' *Contemporary Record*, 3 (February 1990) pp 2-7.

12 See the summary provided by David Sanders of this important argument 'Why the Conservatives Won – Again' in A. King (ed), *Britain at the Polls 1992 op cit.*

13 Hobsbawm makes a strong plea for such an alliance in *Politics for a Rational Left*, Verso, London 1989.

14 I have explored some of the constraints which Labour's economic policy cannot avoid in 'The Labour Party and Economic Management' in M. Smith & J. Spear (eds), *The Changing Labour Party op cit.*, pp 61-74.

Politics, Media and Public Belief

GREG PHILO

To understand public beliefs about politics we must analyse how political parties have used the media. The crucial issue is how successful they have been in establishing strands of political belief which make sense and 'work' with voters. Of course, the media can distort political ideas and report stories in a way which is partial or simply untrue. But the dominance of the New Right in the 1980s, and Labour's electoral failures, cannot be adequately explained in such terms. The crucial issue is that Labour was much less efficient than the Conservatives in developing coherent political ideas and making them into a form of popular consciousness. Think back over this period, it is not hard to make up a list of popular political phrases which explained Conservative political thinking. The list could include 'there is no alternative', 'a shareowning/homeowning democracy', 'popular capitalism', 'enterprise culture', 'the miracle economy', 'one-sided disarmament'. There were others such as 'the winter of discontent' or 'picket line violence' which in a sense the Conservatives made their own by consistent repetition in political statements and party broadcasts. The phrases came to specify a particular way of understanding trade unions and their harmful effects. These images and the political analysis they carried with them were used all through the 1980s by the Conservative Party in their advertising and political broadcasts. The journalist Michael Cockerell has written extensively on the use of the media by politicians[2]. He commented to us in an interview: 'Ever since 1978/79 Saatchi and Saatchi used all those shots with the doomy music in their party political broadcasts. This time (1992) they used it again and put it into black and white ... on cancer wards closed, patients left to die. They used it in every election since 1979.'

Just before the 1987 election, Mrs Thatcher, appeared for a major interview on the BBC programme *Panorama*. She actually took in with her the newspapers' headlines from the 'winter of discontent' of 1979 and waved them in front of the interviewer's face, to make her point. It is not hard to see how the New Right phrases and images were imprinted onto political memories.

But if we try to make a list of political phrases which are associated with the Labour opposition, it becomes clear very quickly that it cannot be done. There are certainly general areas where the Labour party 'scores' better in popular judgement than the Conservatives, such as on health or welfare benefits. But this is because of Labour's traditional policies towards these issues. There are no 'Labour phrases' from popular political debate which are comparable in the sense that they explain immediately what the Conservatives are doing wrong and what Labour would do about it.[3] This is much more than saying that the Conservatives had the best sound-bites. The importance of such phrases is that they can act as key elements of political consciousness. They can form a sort of template through which people interpret their own experiences and desires for example, the wish to own a home or buy a council house. They can also effect how people interpret new information from the media (for example, reports of trade union influence in the Labour Party or reports suggesting rapid economic decline if Labour is elected).

The purpose of this chapter is to explain this absence of 'Labour phrases' and to show the consequence of this – both in electoral failure and in the much broader problem of Labour's inability to develop an alternative public consciousness.

The New Right and Social Democracy

The most important battleground of political ideas in the
1980s was the economy. It is a crucial area since it
underpins most political issues. Voters may express
concern about child benefits, pensions or health. But they
also know that these have to be paid for and that economic
collapse necessarily undercuts social welfare. The Labour
MP Harriet Harman acknowledged this after the last
election when she noted that the Labour Party's 'general
credibility problems over the economy may have led some
women to disregard promises to increase pensions and
child benefit'. (*Guardian* 16 July 1992)

But there is another reason why arguments over the
economy were especially important. They provided the
key point of difference between the social democratic and
consensual ideas of the post-war period and the New Right
thinking of the 1980s. The essence of social democratic
theory was to reduce class conflict and to promote
consensus politics by providing social 'services' such as free
education, health, social security and housing. It also
included a sustained commitment to full employment with
a high degree of state intervention in the economy and the
public ownership or control of national industries. This
would mean, in theory, that resources were reallocated
from the top of the society towards its lower sections. In
the post-war period, both Labour and Conservative
administrations had pursued or endorsed such consensual
politics.

The essence of the New Right approach as developed by
the Conservatives from 1979, was to put this process of
reallocation into reverse. The theory was that state
spending would be reduced on social services and that the
government would no longer intervene in industry to
promote full employment. Specifically, they would no
longer subsidise failing industries – indeed the 'monetary'
conditions would be set (through, for example, high
interest rates) whereby many firms would be hard put to
survive. Employees would therefore have to accept
whatever wages were on offer or suffer the consequences

of their firms going bankrupt. After the 1983 election in Britain, this political programme was developed to encompass the selling of the profitable public industries into private hands. Another key area of New Right policy concerned the trade unions who were expected to oppose these political policies and to resist the lowering of wages. They were weakened by new laws and by using state funds to defeat them in specific conflicts for example, financing the use of oil-fired power stations to win the miners strike of 1984–85. The new process of distributing resources would be completed by substantial tax cuts for the better off, who would in practice also benefit by purchasing shares in the new private industries at very low rates and by using their economic position to benefit from the share and property markets. With such incentives, it was claimed that a new spirit of enterprise and growth would be released into the economy and there could eventually even be a 'trickle down effect' which would benefit the less priviledged.

The New Right approach clearly implied redistribution towards the better off. But at the end of the 1970s, the strength of post-war consensual values was still such that this element of new right philosophy was not at the forefront of Conservative political statements. Instead, the focus initially was on general tax cuts, the promise of economic efficiency, rationalisation, stopping bureaucratic waste and combating the alleged dire effects of trade unions. This analysis of the economy only made sense if it was believed that the essential difficulty was state intervention in industry with the subsidising of artificially high wages. These were seen by the New Right as being produced by unions who imposed 'restrictive practices'. But a major problem facing Britain and other Western economies in this period was the threat of competition from the powerful economies of the Far East. Their strength came from a combination of relatively low wages combined with high technology plus new management and 'lean production' techniques. Britain had not had a particularly high wage economy in the post-war period. Its persistent failure was on investment levels relative to its major industrial competitors. Already by 1976 a Toyota car-worker in Japan was working with the equivalent of £11,000 of equipment, while a British Leyland car worker had only £1,000 worth. Monetarism had little to offer in terms of redressing such a crucial area of imbalance.[4]

But the Conservatives did roll back many of the social policies of the post-war years. Between 1979 and 1989 the value of pensions and unemployment benefit fell as a percentage of average earnings. By 1989, 25 per cent of all children were living at a level which was below half of the average income. In 1979 10 per cent of children had been in this position. By contrast, the top one fifth of the population did better in the same period and their real income increased by 40 per cent over the ten years[5]. In the same period the publicly owned industries such as telecommunications, gas and electricity were put into private ownership. However, the Conservatives were not successful overall in cutting public spending. Indeed it was increased at various points such as before the 1987 election, in order to win support. The National Health Service, which was a major recipient, was too popular to be seriously cut or replaced with a private scheme (although it was subjected to controversial reforms in the name of efficiency).

The most damaging effect of the New Right policies was on the economy as a whole. The monetarist theory which was applied between 1979 and 1981 in the form of high interest rates resulted in the destruction of approximately 20 per cent of Britain's manufacturing capacity. This was particularly felt in areas such as the West Midlands which had specialised in engineering and machine tool production. It was an important factor in the inability of British industry to meet consumer demand when the economy expanded rapidly in the period before and after the 1987 election. At that time the increases in public spending had put more money into the economy, but the crucial factor was a huge increase in personal borrowing. The Conservatives had encouraged this by removing restrictions on credit and bank lending from 1980 onwards. Personal credit (including mortgages) increased from £90 billion at the end of 1980 to £282 billion by the end of

1987. There was also more money to be spent because of the issuing of cheap shares from the once publicly owned industries. These could be sold for an immediate profit. The very predictable result of having all this extra money in the economy was a consumer spending boom which sucked in large amounts of imports. By 1988 there was a major balance of payments crisis. Britain's deficit to the rest of the world for a single year in 1989 was £19.01 billion.

Another effect of the growth of borrowing and credit was to produce the spiralling of house prices – particularly in the South East of Britain. The overall rate of inflation also began to rise and there were fears that the economy was running out of control. From 1989 the Conservatives moved to a policy of high interest rates to slow the economy, to cut demand and squeeze out inflation. The effect was to usher in the second recession in ten years. The growth that had taken place in 1986 and 1987 had been seen by some people as evidence of the 'miracle economy' but the output figures for the period as a whole show that this was something of a mirage. In the thirteen years from 1979 to 1992 manufacturing output rose by just 4.5 per cent in Britain, the lowest figure for any major industrial country.[6]

The Labour Response

This record as it unfolded should have given the Labour opposition grounds to criticise the New Right and monetarism in at least two areas. The first was on the issue of social morality and the second was on the competence with which the economy was being run. The issue of morality relates primarily to the policy of redistributing social resources towards the top of society. This means much more than simply expressing anger about unemployment or the condition of the poor and deprived (which Labour certainly did raise as an issue). What was missing from the Labour response in the 1980s was the promotion of an alternative theory of social distribution. It is the difference between saying that the poor should be helped and saying that the resources of the society should be reorganised to abolish the production of poverty. It means using the wealth of the society to develop new priorities for the economic system. This would require, at the very least, describing to the population of Britain the parameters of the society in which they live – for example stating clearly that 5 per cent of the population own half of the total private wealth. But such arguments raise important ideological issues which the leadership of the Labour party in its search for the 'middle ground' of politics preferred to avoid. This alarm, at the ideology of their own 'side', in part accounts for the absence of Labour phrases. In the 1980s Labour stopped trying to explain the nature of the social and political world to potential voters.

This was very clear in the debate over the privatisation of the public industries. The main Labour opposition seemed transfixed by the prospect that 20 per cent of the population might end up owning shares.[7] Their critique of the programme was substantially that the shares were being sold too cheaply. They were unable to mount a campaign defending the right of most people to own crucial industries or to say simply that if 20 per cent had shares then the other 80 per cent of the population would have their ownership taken away. The absence of a major Labour campaign meant that there was no development by them of a popular consciousness on the significance of ownership. There was no raising of the simple concept that profits from public industries actually belonged to the public and could, in principle, be used for spending on socially useful projects.

In practice the effect of the privatisation programme was to transform very large public monopolies into private monopolies. The potential consequences of this had been spelt out very early in the 1980s (in, for example, the *Diverse Reports* series in 1983 on Channel 4 television). Later, there were howls of anguish from consumers and the popular press about what was seen as the extortionate profits made by new private companies such as British Telecom ('£90 A SECOND!' *Daily Mirror* headline, 21.5.92). But when these complaints occurred, the Labour

Party was not in a position to refer back to a political campaign which explained and predicted the difference between public and private ownership. There were no Labour phrases or alternative explanations already situated in popular discourse to focus this discontent.

The second area of possible criticism also shows some extraordinary gaps in popular understanding. This area relates to the competence of the New Right in running a capitalist economy. All through the 1980s, the Labour opposition did complain about the failures of monetarist policy as they occurred (such as rises in unemployment and the destruction of manufacturing). But to have a long term effect on popular consciousness each failure needs to be explained and linked to the others to form a coherent alternative critique.

There were four elements in the history of the monetarist experiment which were crucial in developing such an alternative. The first was the use of revenues from the oil industry. In the 1970s, when oil was discovered in the North Sea, there had been great popular expectations about the use of the revenue for the regeneration of industry and the rebuilding of the social and economic infrastructure. That this was not done, was perhaps the greatest failure of the 1980s. By 1983, manufacturing capacity had been seriously cut and unemployment had risen to 3 million people (from 1.5 million in 1979). The cost to the exchequer of the unemployment was estimated at around £12 billion for a single year. In this period oil revenues were not far from this amount. Yet this simple explanatory theme – that the oil money was wasted on unemployment – was not promoted as a consistent part of the opposition case and did not enter everyday political consciousness. This equation of wasted oil money and unemployment is not accurate or perfect as economic analysis but as a tool for shaping political understanding of the economy it works very well. The second element, linked to this was the destruction of approximately 20 per cent of manufacturing between 1979 and 1981. This could have been imprinted into collective historical memory with every bit of the force of other events such as the 'winter of discontent'. As it was, the Labour Party was so preoccupied with its own internal dissention and the break away of the Social Democratic Party in 1981 that it was unable to form a coherent and lasting response. But the impact of the economic destruction on political views was tremendous at the time. Unemployment went above 2.5 million people for the first time since the 1930s, and between April and July 1981 there was an extensive series of riots in inner city areas. It was as if the most dire predictions of what would happen if consensus collapsed, had suddenly come true. Support for Margaret Thatcher in opinion polls fell to just 20 per cent of the popular vote. But the economic collapse and the surrounding events such as the riots were then allowed to pass from our political memories. They were not made into a persistent focal point of Labour's political advertising and broadcasting, or constantly recalled in the manner of the 'winter of discontent'.

The third element in this history follows from the weakness of manufacturing and the consequent inability of Britain to compete in international markets. In 1983, for the first time in industrial history, Britain imported more manufactured goods than it was able to export. This unhappy 'record' for New Right policies should also have been fixed in the political equivalent of neon lights. Michael Cockerell commented on this in relation to his own work on the media impact of different political leaders. He noted the use made of the media by Harold Wilson, the Labour prime minister. Wilson had taught at Oxford University and in Cockerell's words, his speeches, while in power, 'were like a tutorial for the British people'. Some still remember the phrase 'the white heat of technology' with which Wilson had promoted Labour in the 1964 election. Cockerell commented on the New Right's 'record' on manufacturing imports that: 'You can imagine someone like Wilson really hammering that into the public consciousness'. (Interview July 1992). But by the early 1980s the Labour Party had lost the ability to establish such patterns of understanding through sustained political rhetoric. Consequently the Conservatives were allowed to argue that the destruction of manufacturing was helping to make the economy more efficient. They pointed to increases in productivity and made the words 'leaner' and 'fitter' a part of the common language of economics. It is, of course, technically correct to say that if the weaker sections of a manufacturing economy are closed down then the average productivity of those that remain will go up. But this is like saying that we could improve the average health of the nation by going into hospitals and killing all the sick people. The crucial issue is what happens when there is a need for the industries which have disappeared rather than being brought back to health. The Conservatives again circumvented this by arguing that some industries such as engineering and shipbuilding were somehow 'old' and 'traditional', while Britain should be looking to the new 'sunrise' industries such as electronics and computing. This overlooked the problem that Britain's competitors in the Far East and elsewhere already had an unassailable lead in the 'sunrise' sector and were continuing to supply the world with 'old' products such as ships as well. There was also the outstanding difficulty that when any economic upturn did occur in Britain, much of the necessary machine tools and high quality engineering products needed to cope with an increase in orders would now need to be imported. But because these elements of economic understanding were missing from routine public knowledge, the Conservatives were able to make the crucial conceptual jump of presenting unemployment as a sign that the economy was getting *better* rather than as a sign of its structural weakness.

The fourth element in this history is the period of economic expansion before and after the 1987 election. The crucial moment in this was when manufacturing output finally returned to the level that it had been in 1979.[8] It was a high point of the 'bubble economy' which had been produced by the increase in personal credit, financial de-regulation, and the pumping of money into the economy through increased state spending, cheap shares and tax cuts. The bubble was punctured after 1988

with high interest rates and the second recession since
1979. In the period from 1979 to 1992, the Japanese
economy actually expanded by 60 per cent. Yet when
British output finally returned to where it had been in
1979, the Conservatives were able to present this as a
triumph, as if the Japanese and other competitors had
been patiently waiting for the British to catch up. The
press headlines tell the story:

'INDUSTRY POWERS TO RECORD OUTPUT' (*Daily
Express*, 17 September 1987)
'FACTORY   OUTPUT   HITS   RECORD   FOR
THATCHER' (*Daily Telegraph*, 17 September 1987)

It is extraordinary that the Labour opposition had
abandoned so much of the territory of economic
argument. Labour did not routinely make international
comparisons with countries such as Japan and crucially
had not established in popular understanding the central
issues of the waste of oil revenue, the destruction of
manufacturing in 1981 and the 1983 'record' of being
unable to compete internationally. The absence of such an
interpretive framework for understanding the economy
had a crucial impact on the Labour Party's ability to win
popular support. This was most obvious in the elections of
1987 and 1992. Research at Glasgow University by
Professor Bill Miller has now shown that in the 1987
campaign over half the population believed that the
Conservatives were 'best on economic matters for
themselves and their family'[9]. They had, in fact, a 25 per
cent lead in this over the Labour Party. Why was the
Labour Party so unable to contest this area?

Labour's Image Problem

There were several reasons in the early 1980s why the
Labour Party's ideological message was diffuse and
confused. After the electoral defeat in 1979, there was an
intense and acrimonious debate between the right and left
wing in the party, and in 1981 a right wing faction split
from it to form the Social Democratic Party. The Labour

Party did not have a well developed communication
strategy in this period and this, combined with the trauma
of the splits and divisions, affected its ability to offer clear
messages. It was apparent at the time that many
professionals within the party actually preferred the
messages of party broadcasts to be bland rather than to
risk upsetting one or other of the factions. By the 1983
election, the Labour Party was still in confusion. The
political opposition to the Conservatives was divided with
the emergence of the Social Democratic Party who were
now in alliance with the Liberals. Conservative support
had meanwhile been solidified by the Falklands War and
Mrs Thatcher was re-elected, but with 600,000 less votes
than in 1979. Labour's electoral defeat produced a new
leadership within the Labour Party and a decisive change
was made in its communications strategy. Labour chose
the 'dream ticket' of Neil Kinnock as leader and Roy
Hattersley as deputy on the assumption that they would
unite the party and be electorally acceptable to the 'middle
ground' of voters. Labour had watched the grooming of
Margaret Thatcher's television image by Gordon Reece,
her media adviser, and the hiring of Saatchi and Saatchi by
him to advertise their message. The Conservatives had
also set up a sophisticated communications machine run
by Cecil Parkinson for the 1983 election, which could
co-ordinate all major Conservative speakers to focus on a
specific issue for a single day. In response, the Labour
Party brought in Peter Mandelson, an ex-television
producer as their Director of Communications. They
believed it was time to promote and control the images
which the public were to associate with the Labour Party.
To achieve this they decided to give a new authority to
communications and advertising professionals, who were
now brought in to form the Shadow Communications
Agency. The minutes of a 1986 Campaign Strategy
meeting record the decision:

> A paper from the Director of Campaigns and Commu-
> nication was before the meeting. In it, he referred to the
> need to secure sound professional support for future

campaign communications activity and the availability of
a range of outside expertise to meet this need. It was
proposed to structure this expertise in the form of a
Shadow Communications Agency. (24 February 1986)

It was a fateful decision since it moved Labour in the
direction of promoting vacuous images, rather than ways
of understanding. The party leadership had misunderstood the strength of the Conservative position.
Beneath the glossy packaging which the New Right had
used, there were two very powerful elements. The first
was a relatively coherent ideology. By this I mean that it
was internally coherent and could seem to make sense,
whatever its disastrous potential effects in practice. The
popular phrases deployed by Mrs Thatcher on 'the wealth
makers' and 'not taxing successful industry and commerce'
and 'rewarding effort' had a strong resonance in the
culture of the Conservative 'natural' supporters in the
middle and lower middle classes.

The second strength was the actual relationship which
the Conservatives enjoyed with the 'wealth owners' i.e.
those who controlled the industrial and financial economy.
If Labour abandoned the ideological territory of the
economy, then the claim of the Conservatives to be the
obvious party to manage this area would be strengthened
– especially since they were the stated preference of the
'business class'.

Nonetheless, Labour pressed on with its new direction
and the red flag became the red rose. One of the major
influences affecting this move had been a BBC *Panorama*
programme made by Michael Cockerell, called *The
Marketing of Margaret*. It was broadcast shortly after the
1983 election and it contrasted the new communications
machine of the Tories with what it portrayed as the
shambles of the Labour campaign. John Underwood, the
Labour Party Director of Communications after Peter
Mandelson, commented on the programme's effect:

> The Cockerell programme did have a profound impact.
> There was a very strong feeling that Labour had to take on
> these communications developments. There is no question

that in the 1987 election they used professional communication techniques for the first time. This was behind the
rise and rise of Peter Mandelson ... The story of 1983 to
1987 was that it was the flight not just from ideology but
from policy. Neil Kinnock and Peter Mandelson spoke
constantly of transforming the *image* of the Labour Party.
(Interview, July 1992)

In this period Labour's new communication strategists
believed that Kinnock and his wife were a youthful and
glamorous couple who could be marketed in something
approaching a presidential style. Hence in the run up to
the 1987 election there were triumphal rallies with stars
such as Glenda Jackson introducing Kinnock as 'Britain's
next prime minister!!' A special Labour broadcast was
commissioned to promote Kinnock, dubbed by some as
'Neil and Glenys – The Movie'. It was made by Hugh
Hudson, (of *Chariots of Fire*) and is described by Cockerell
as 'a vaseline-lensed biography of the Labour leader, with
musical accompaniment'[10]. The projection of the positive
Kinnock image continued right up to the 1992 election
with what one editorial referred to as 'Mr Kinnock's
relentlessly orchestrated round of babies, balloons and
beaming bounds' (*Guardian*, 9 April 1992)

The strategy did not succeed in terms of establishing
Kinnock's credibility with a wider public. But the
promotion of him in this way had other important
consequences. The intention was to give him a bouncy,
upbeat image. He had to be associated with brightness and
success, so pictures of bleak industrial landscapes or
economic destruction were thought to be inappropriate.
Labour thus began to vacate the crucial territory of how
the population understood their own history. They did it
in favour of a philosophy which was appropriate only for
influencing short term consumer purchases. In a letter to
us in 1988, Bryan Gould, the Labour Shadow for Trade
and Industry, outlined the approach and the difficulties of
stressing 'bad news' on the economy: 'Our problem is that
no one thanks the bringers of bad news and it is very hard
to get the communications strategy right without
appearing "whingers" '. In the 1980s this had become a

catchword of the New Right and was used repeatedly by them to criticise the doubters in their own party. It is symptomatic of how much ground the Labour Party had lost that the word should enter their own vocabulary as a potential description of themselves.

In the event, Labour's bouncy images were no match for the actual economic growth which the Conservative Chancellor Nigel Lawson had produced before and after the 1987 election. In June 1988 Peter Shore, the veteran Labour politician, very frankly acknowledged that 'on economic and external policy, there is not the sense of confidence we (once) had ...' (Channel 4 *A Week in Politics* 24 June 1988)

There were other factors in 1987 which may have contributed to Labour's election defeat, such as the confusion over their defence policy and the obvious divisions which still existed in the party over this. But the decision to focus on projecting positive images rather than winning ideological or policy battles was crucial – not least because it continued to form the Labour approach in the following years. The decision makers in the party actually believed that the 1987 campaign had been a success, but that the party had been held back by the 'negative' associations which it still had for some key groups of voters. The main negatives were seen as the unilateralist defence policy and the continued presence of the left wing Militant Tendency. As John Underwood commented in his interview with us: 'The period after 1987 was about removing the negatives – dumping unpopular policies rather than replacing them with anything else ... But the first rule of communications is that you can only tell the truth better'.

His point was that the image techniques and getting the lighting and camera angles right, could not make up for the absence of policy. By the end of the 1980s the Labour Party had actually reduced the areas which could clearly differentiate them from the Conservatives. Underwood again, 'After removing all the negative policies by 1992, in marketing parlance, the party had lost its USP (unique selling proposition).'

John Underwood also pointed to the irony of John Smith's alternative 'budget' which was presented to the media just before the 1992 election. It was based on a clear political philosophy and was redistributive in the sense of moving wealth from the top of society to those most in need. As such, it was one part of the counter to New Right thinking which Labour could have developed through the 1980s. But by this time the political framework to understand it in this way was no longer present in popular political debate. Instead of understanding it in terms of its principle and intention, the budget was discussed in terms of its details, i.e. exactly how many people would be better off. Underwood: 'The Smith budget was redistributive – but there was no over-arching vision of the future into which the budget fitted. Arguments about it came down to its details rather than what it was for. Was John Smith right that eight out of ten would benefit or were the Tories right that people would all pay £1,200 extra tax?' (Interview, July 1992)

It had been a long time since the leaders of the Labour Party had spoken very clearly about who owned the economy and the parameters of wealth. In Britain, the great bulk of private wealth is in fact owned by the top 20 per cent of the population. But in seeking the elusive 'middle ground' the Labour Party had substantially moved away from rhetoric which raised issues such as class or private ownership. Instead, they had focused attention on the plight of those who had suffered most during the 1980s. They had raised the issues of unemployment, the condition of the inner cities and the homeless. But this had led voters to associate Labour with 'minorities' as if the majority of the population were 'well off' compared to the minority who were not. This is one reason why John Smith's budget was misunderstood, because a majority saw itself as being taxed to help the minority. But given the reality of the distribution of wealth in Britain it was possible for Labour to speak of eight out of ten people being better off.[11] But such a claim would only make sense to people if it was explained in the context of how wealth was actually distributed. Labour needed to speak in terms of

the 20 per cent who did well and the 80 per cent who did not
– just as they could have spoken of the 20 per cent who had
profited from the privatisation programmes and the 80 per
cent who were losing their share of the public industries.

The 1992 Election

The election of April 1992 was closely fought and more
difficult for the Conservatives than in 1987. The economy
was now clearly moving into recession with rising
unemployment, falling house prices and an increase in
bankruptcies. From the middle of 1990 to the beginning
of 1992 economic output actually contracted by over 4 per
cent. The Conservatives blamed the world recession and
were able to pass over the structural weakness of British
industry. There was real concern in the electorate for the
poor and the homeless, which Labour was seen to
represent and very deep worries about the future of the
health service. But once again, Labour lost the election
largely because key groups of voters decided that they
could not trust Labour on the economy. Larry Whitty, the
Labour Party general secretary, concluded in his report on
the defeat that: 'Fears of high tax plus the general unease
about our economic competence or general distrust of the
party and its leadership took their toll' (*Report to Labour
NEC*, June 1992)

Another report by David Hill, the party's director of
communications, acknowledged the power of the Conservative strategy in establishing elements of popular
consciousness over a long period of time: 'Our major long
term problem appears to be the fact that we carry too
much baggage from the late 1970s and early 1980s
to persuade people that they can fully trust us. Even
though many of those voting were very young during
these times, *they have been subjected to constant reminders*'
(June 1992,)

The failure in Labour's approach was the absence of
such 'constant reminders' on the crucial economic
moments of the 1980s. I do not mean that there were no
inputs from Labour throughout that period. It is certainly

possible to point to comments and speeches from politicians such as John Smith, Bryan Gould and Gordon Brown on issues such as the balance of payments and the low level of growth and investment. But in the millions of political words which were spoken in this period, the Labour effort on this was essentially at the periphery. There was no major drive to build an alternative popular understanding of what had gone wrong and what was to be done about it. This also highlights a key difference between the British and US elections of this year. In America the Democrats destroyed the Republicans by focusing relentlessly on the economic failures of Reagan and Bush. In the Labour Party Manifesto of 1992, there is no discussion of the Conservative economic record.

From 1987 the Labour Party approach had been to remove what was seen as the negative elements affecting voters and to stress the positive associations that the public made with the party (for example the National Health Service). The assumption was that by keeping all of the positive elements dancing before the consumers' eyes, the product will take on an acceptable 'glow'. But political decisions and beliefs are more complex than consumer purchases. It is possible to change the colour of a soap powder packet without the public seeing this as an expression of bad faith. But the changes in Labour policies which were designed to increase its market appeal (for example on defence) were actually seen by voters as evidence that the Labour leadership was untrustworthy. This was a clear result of opinion research conducted after the election in the marginal constituencies of areas such as Essex.[12]

There is another problem with this approach of stressing the 'positive'. It neglects the underlying frameworks of understanding which people use to interpret new political information. For example, the underlying belief might be that a good health service or education system requires a sound economy. If so, there is no point in stressing simply health and education even if the market research shows that the party does 'well' on these issues. The consequences of using an advertising philosophy for political selling had not been thought through. One senior Labour Party worker from the Shadow Communications Agency remarked ruefully: '... You went hard on the things that you think will win you votes. But you can never do enough on health to make up for the economy' (Interview, July 1992)

Labour and 'Economic Competence'

Labour had focused much of its propaganda effort on the personal qualities of Neil Kinnock and the Conservative leader, Margaret Thatcher. The intention was to praise the first and to damn the second for having a personal style which was autocratic and domineering. An approach based on personalities was one result of the flight from ideology and policy. It was necessary to focus on the superficial qualities of the product, because the deeper social and political arguments had been largely ruled out. The Conservatives, therefore, confused Labour greatly when they dropped Margaret Thatcher as leader in 1990 and brought in the more 'moderate' John Major. The Conservatives still had serious problems, but they enjoyed one decisive advantage over Labour. This was the close relationship which they had with the business class – the owners of financial and industrial capital. It had always been Labour's problem to argue convincingly about what they would do in the face of the unremitting hostility of this group. How could Labour manage, control or change the capitalist economy? In each election that Labour had won since 1945, they had provided an answer to this. Under Attlee in 1945, it had been that they would take over key sections of the economy and run them in the public interest. In 1964, Wilson had some success in portraying the traditional political and economic establishment as being incompetent. It would be Labour that would introduce the 'white heat of technology'. Later, in 1974 Wilson had presented the political leadership of the Conservatives as socially divisive after two miners' strikes, the 'three day week' and 'state of emergency' introduced by Edward Heath. According to Wilson, a

Labour policy of social consensus would get the economy moving again and the country back to work.

But, by the end of the 1980s, the Labour Party had no answer as clear as any of these. They had missed the opportunity of labelling the Conservatives with fearful images of social division (such as the street riots of 1981). On the crucial question of the economy, Labour's approach was to develop links with the business class and to try to show that Labour was competent in economic management. This point was made very clearly by Bryan Gould in a Channel 4 broadcast in 1987 in which he set out his views on the future of the Labour Party: 'We have to show that we can produce wealth as well as arguing that it should be better used and more fairly distributed. What we have to do is to show that Labour knows how to run the economy – and do it more efficiently than the Tories' (Channel 4, 19.00, 25 September 1987)

In the period before the 1992 election, John Smith embarked on an extended programme of developing contacts in the City. From 1990, he visited merchant bankers, brokers, dealers and industrialists in the City of London in what was referred to in the Labour Party as the 'prawn cocktail circuit'. Labour's manifesto for 1992 conveys the general sentiment of this with the headline 'A government which business can do business with'[13].

But there is a fundamental problem for Labour if it becomes closely associated with the interests and preferences of the business class. The problem is, what happens when that class makes it clear that it already has a political party which it prefers and predicts economic chaos at the very mention that Labour might be elected. It was this which gave the Conservatives a decisive advantage and in pressing it home they had key allies in the media.

The Media Link

By the end of the 1980s, financial and City news had become central areas of media reporting, especially on television. This was one consequence of the dominance of the Conservatives and their promotion of the merits of share ownership, entrepreneurs and business dealing in general. Consequently, movements in the City were routinely reported and 'experts' from merchant banks and finance houses were consulted for their apparently neutral opinions on the latest trade or financial news. This gave them an important status as 'impartial' commentators.[14] 'Good news' for them and for television was a healthy stock market and shares rising. In electoral reporting, the preferences of the City were made absolutely clear by referring to such share movements. On ITN, when Labour took the lead in opinion polls the City sounded near to collapse:

> *Newscaster*: Billions of pounds were wiped off the value of shares this morning, as the City, which traditionally prefers a Conservative government, took fright at the clear Labour lead in the opinion polls.
> *Industrial correspondent*: It was headlines like these (refers to headline in *The Times*) showing Labour pulling into the lead which helped to turn City dealing room screens red. At the start of trading this morning billions of pounds were wiped off shares....
> (ITN, 12.30, 1 April 1992)

The BBC told a similar story, reporting that 'In the City, worries about a Labour victory pushed share values down sharply ...' (BBC1, 18.00, 1 April 1992) Such coverage has a long history. Before the 1987 election, the 'good news' for the City was the Conservatives taking the lead: 'The Tory lead in the polls may be wafer thin, but it's good enough for the City where dealers and investers are in confident mood. Share prices are going up and up....' (BBC 2, 22.25, 6 February 1987)

If the city and the business class are seen as crucial movers in economic health, then such coverage must help the Conservatives. This is especially so if there is no counter-ideology providing constant reminders of the damage which the Conservatives and the City have actually done to the economy. In this sense virtually all of the media could be seen as operating against the interests of Labour merely by reporting the movements and intentions of this class in the face of a Labour victory. For example, the *Guardian* in March 1992 reported on its front page about the movement of millions of pounds out of the country: 'Millions of pounds are leaving Britain with every opinion poll that puts the Opposition ahead, winging out via electronic transfer systems to all points of the compass' (*Guardian*, 26 March 1992)

The article pointed out that £870 billion, or half of the total personal wealth (excluding houses) was con- trolled by just 5 per cent of the population and that: 'By freighting a large proportion of this mobile capital abroad, the rich are reducing further the spending power in the economy.'

A large transfer of capital into other currencies would also mean a run on the pound and that an incoming Labour government would be pushed into putting up interest rates. The *Guardian* would not of course draw the same political conclusions from this as the right wing press. But this analysis is not so different from the front page 'warnings' in papers such as the *Daily Mail*:

WARNING
A Labour government will lead to higher mortgage payments. There is no doubt about it. Interest rates will rise within days of Kinnock entering Number Ten. (*Daily Mail*, 7 April 1992)

This was also the sense of the *Sun*'s start message on its election day front page: 'If Kinnock wins today will the last person to leave Britain please turn out the lights' (*Sun*, 9 April 1992)

We can find other versions of such warnings on television news, in this case from a City expert speaking on ITN: 'If Labour were to win, I think people would be worried about public spending, public borrowing and what might happen to the exchange rate' (ITN, 12.30, 1 April 1992)

It is perhaps no surprise that opinion poll research after the election showed serious worries amongst some voters about Labour's economic competence.[15]

One of the questions raised at the time of the 1992 election was whether the media was responsible for Labour's defeat. The answer is that they must be seen as contributing to it since the issue of economic competence was so crucial. Shortly before the election, opinion polls showed Labour on approximately 40 per cent of the popular vote and the Conservatives around 37 per cent. The actual result gave the Conservatives 41.9 per cent and Labour 34.2 per cent. The 8 per cent of voters separating the two parties might well have been influenced by the media, once these people were confronted with the possibility that an 'incompetent' and 'untrustworthy' Labour party would actually be elected. But there is another point which underlies this – that is the responsibility which Labour had for the formation of its own image. It had vacated, throughout the 1980s, key areas of political argument and this was why, in the end, it had no answer for those who moved against them. And these, it must be said, are a very small proportion of the electorate. The crucial issue for Labour is why it went into the election with only 40 per cent of the vote. The Conservatives in thirteen years of government had achieved a series of 'records' which were unparalleled this century on riots, crime, unemployment, the destruction of manufacturing and the trade balance, as well as major controversies over health, education and the poll tax. When the Conservatives had first come to power in 1979 Labour had achieved 37 per cent of the vote. Yet after thirteen extraordinary years the Labour vote was still only 34 per cent. It is clearly not enough for Labour simply to blame the tabloid press for its defeat. We cannot make judgements about the impact of media without analysing the input of Labour itself. Some of the decisions which made the party unelectable came from within it.

After the 1992 Election

The void in public consciousness over the history of Britain's decline raises other important issues. For example, what if Labour had won the 1992 election? The crisis of 'Black Wednesday' in September 1992 and the collapse of the pound would have occurred even earlier and it is not hard to see that Labour would immediately have been blamed for it, given the low level of public trust in their economic competence. As it is, the absence of popular understanding means that many people are casting around for equally improbable explanations and solutions. There has been popular xenophobia about the Germans as if they, rather than British governments, were responsible for the collapse of industry and manufacturing. In October 1992, opinion polls showed 45 per cent of the population wanting the return of Margaret Thatcher as if she was innocent of the economic chaos foisted on the country in the 1980s.

The problem for the Labour Party is that it is still confining itself to discussing the economy in terms of the ERM, managed exchange rates, shadowing currencies and the other technicalities of fiscal policy. But public understanding of such issues appears to be very limited. Past research on television audiences has indicated this and we have recently produced pilot studies to investigate public knowledge of the economy. Some of these were on groups of undergraduate students who were just beginning a first year social science course. A number had actually studied economics and other related areas before entering university. Yet in this sample, over 90 per cent did not know why the pound goes down when there is a balance of payments crisis or anything about an issue such as how or why Britain 'shadowed the Deutschmark'. This has important implications for the understanding of political debates. For example, on the 24 September 1992, the Labour Party led a major parliamentary attack on the government, following the events of 'Black Wednesday'. In the debate Gordon Brown was challenged on Labour's policy. He stated unequivocally that: 'The difference between the parties has become clear ... Our policy is for managed exchange rates'.[16] Over 80 per cent of this sample would have no idea what he was talking about. This is why Labour is still making no impact on public consciousness. In October 1992, only 24 per cent of the population trusted Labour on the economy (ICM Poll, *Guardian* 14 October 1992). The bulk of the population can, however, understand that the economy must be rebuilt and that this may need radical government intervention. Indeed, they may well expect it since there is a widespread belief that it is the 'job' of governments to make the economy work well. There is also some general understanding of basic ideas on the need for efficient industries, for education, training and new technology as well as the development of transport, construction and communications. This is why the threatened death of the coal industry was so elemental and struck such a chord in public consciousness. It was symbolic of the decline of Britain and was understood in a way that the failure of the ERM is not. The collapse of the Conservative economic programme should have been good news electorally for Labour. But in practice, the public is now just confused because Labour did not develop a media strategy to highlight the key failures of the economy in the 1980s. Instead of using the media to establish key elements of popular understanding about what was going wrong and what should be done, they relied instead on the shallow science of imagistics.

Conclusion

There are important theoretical issues raised by this analysis. Media images of political life must be understood in relation to the inputs made by major political interests. In this sense it is not sufficient to account for Labour's failure by simply blaming the right-wing tabloid press. But none-the-less, the media can clearly have a major impact in some critical areas – for example in their routine recourse to the views of economic 'experts' from the City, and their presentation of these as the final arbiters of what is 'good' for the economy. Finally, we have to consider the crucial question of how the audience responds to political and economic messages. What people understand, remember and what they believe depends in part on the nature of the message. But understanding, memory and belief also vary with factors such as practical experience and knowledge as well as the political, class, and cultural histories of the different groups receiving the message.[17] New information from the media is interpreted through these complex patterns of pre-existing knowledge and belief. This is the importance of popular consciousness and received wisdom about the political and economic world. Politicians can sometimes successfully relate to such pre-existing knowledges and can develop or even insert new elements of political understanding into them. The Labour Party's failure to do this in the 1980s is a case study in the misunderstanding of the communications process. It has lessons for both politicians and social scientists.

Notes

[1] Thanks to Michael Cockerell, John Underwood, Andrew Gamble, John Eldridge, Bill Miller, Will Hutton, David Miller, Kathleen Davidson, Cathy Irvine, Chris Pond, Paul Convery and Roger Simon for their help and advice in this work.

[2] Michael Cockerell, *Live From Number 10*, Faber & Faber, London 1988.

[3] We put this point to John Underwood as a former Labour Party director of communications. He agreed and said that the only 'Labour phrasing' he could think of was terming the 'Community Charge' as the 'Poll Tax' and referring to health service reform as 'privatising'. But as he noted, the tangential nature of these phrases actually confirmed the general point.

[4] By 1989 Japan was investing $250 billion a year in machinery and equipment overall compared with $54 billion in Britain. See 'The Slide to Skid Row' by Hutton and Story in *New Statesman and Society*, 13 October, 1989.

[5] See *New Review No 10*, Low Pay Unit, 1991.

[6] In the same period output rose by over 60 per cent in Japan and over 30 per cent in the USA and 25 per cent in the former West Germany. See Central Statistical Office February 1992.

[7] A CBI report of 1990 showed the limited impact of the privatisation programme on public attitudes to share-holding. More than 40 per cent of the public still did not know how or where to buy shares. Of those who did own them a majority did not know how to trade or develop their holdings. The report 'pours cold water on the idea that millions of people have been transformed into mini-speculators' (*The Guardian*, 2 February, 1990).

[8] Taking 1985 as the base year at 100, output in 1979 was 106.0. It dropped and then eventually returned to 106.6 in 1987 (Source, *Economic Trends*, Central Statistical Office).

[9] Bill Miller *et al*, *How Voters Choose*, Clarendon Press, Oxford, 1990.

[10] Michael Cockerell, *op cit*, p 323.

[11] It was certainly possible in theory – though in practice the rich would go to great lengths to avoid paying the extra tax. As we show later, the

prospect of a Labour victory occasioned many plans to move capital out of Britain.

[12] Fabian Society, *Qualitative Research Amongst Waverers in Labour's Southern Target Seats*, London, 1992.

[13] The Labour Party, *General Election Manifesto*, Walworth Road, London, April 1992, p 11. Labour's manifesto also contained positive policies in developing investment in manufacturing, in research and development and on skills and training. But such proposals remain as empty phrases unless they have a resonance in a strong popular understanding about what has gone wrong and what corrective measures need to be taken.

[14] Peter Golding noted of his own study of the 1992 election that 'a MORI poll last month showed that 90 per cent of top financial executives would be voting Conservative. Yet this particular group of analysts ... are called upon with increasing regularity as neutral analysts in election news'. (See *The Guardian*, 6 April 1992 and the work of Loughborough University Communications Research Centre).

[15] A study of 'floating voters' by John Curtice of Strathclyde University for the BBC1 programme, *On the Record*, showed a Conservative lead over Labour before the election of 18 points, on the issue of 'the party best able to handle the economy'. Just after the election, this lead was measured at 41 points.

[16] *Hansard*, Issue No 1596, 24-25 September 1992, p 98.

[17] Greg Philo, *Seeing and Believing*, Routledge, London 1990.

Unfinished Business: From Thatcherite Modernisation to Incomplete Modernity

MICHAEL RUSTIN

In an earlier contribution to the debate on New Times[1] I argued that the explanations of contemporary social changes being put forward within this new paradigm were in part mistaken. They looked, for their dominant logic, to the systemic or functional consequences of technological innovations – essentially the introduction of information technology and the flexibilisation and globalisation that this made possible. The models of Fordism and 'post-Fordism' being used inclined towards a 'socio-technical determinism' – in which a dominant technology, allied to an appropriate form of social organisation, was held to give shape to a whole social system. The intellectual power of these theories derived from the range of phenomena that could be included insightfully within their scope. Changes in modes of consumption ('nicheing'), in forms of organisation (from vertical to lateral structures, from command to devolved forms), in political ideology (from collectivism to individualism), and in the domains of culture and identity (from the binary conflicts of classes to the dispersed antagonisms of 'difference', whether of gender, generation, or ethnicity) all seemed to follow from this underlying change in the dominant mode of production and consumption. Descriptively there is no doubt that these models of 'flexible specialisation'[2] and 'disorganised capitalism'[7] draw attention to transformations of the social and political landscape which seemed to threaten established socialist politics with the fate of the dinosaur.

But so far as explanations were concerned, I suggested that the New Times theorists' emphasis on technological change as the main source of these developments was mistaken. Essentially, I argued, the motive force of the changes which were taking place lay in the sphere of class relations and class strategies, not technologies per se.[4] Technological innovations, globalisation, restructuring, attacks on collectivist ideology, took place as a solution to problems of capital accumulation and class security which had arisen as deep contradictions in the system of mature welfare capitalism. Increasing pressures to raise wages at the expense of profits, and to enhance worker power at the expense of management, produced concern and reaction among employers and the political and intellectual circles identified with them. Corporatist attempts[5] to regulate and moderate these conflicts, attempted in many advanced capitalist countries during the 1970s, were deemed to have failed, and more radical and reactionary strategies were adopted as the programmes of both Reagan and Thatcher. The concessionary aspects of earlier conservatisms of the centre-right were denounced by the New Right as fiercely as it attacked socialism itself, as the dangerous 'enemy within' the Conservative ranks.

Moves to the Right

The social conflicts to which the radical right had reacted manifested themselves in sustained demands during the late 1960s and 1970s for increased social expenditures: on health, education, housing and income support programmes. And also for political intervention, by means of nationalisations and tougher regulatory structures (e.g. for employment protection, health and safety legislation, environmental protection), in the workings of the market. Data for the whole OECD zone[6] shows rising rates of public expenditure during much of the post-war period up to 1980, with a remarkably uniform pattern in the upward trend of growth, even if significant national variations of relative rates and levels of social expenditure remained. Those committed to the values and interests of capitalism came to conclude, not without reason, that if these trends were extrapolated forward for a further decade or two, capitalism would itself be in serious danger of being supplanted by, at best, a state-regulated social democratic system, and at worst, anarchy or communism. Of course these anxieties were exacerbated by the more dramatic manifestations of trade union power and socialist ambition; for example, the successive defeats of British governments in 1970, 1974 and 1979 directly or indirectly at the hands of trade unions, demands for industrial democracy in Britain, for wage-earner funds in Sweden and Mitterrand's wave of nationalisations after 1981 in France. These high points of social democratic ambition were moments of rising alarm for the advocates of capitalism. The conflicts over class subordination, or as Ralph Miliband put it in a telling phrase, 'desubordination', had their analogues in the spheres of sexuality and 'family values', ethnic justice, and generational and sub-cultural expressiveness. Such 'moral' (or immoral) threats to the conservative social order also played their part, especially in America and Britain, in promoting a conservative reaction.

The relentlessness and cold fury of the radical right's programmes in office during the 1980s cannot be understood without recognising what the right perceived as a class threat. (It is hardly material that this danger might now seem to be an exaggerated or wilful caricature, so limited was the actual grasp of the left on power or of the resources and competencies its exercise requires.) There was a considerable output of academic work in this period justifying the view that a deep crisis had indeed occurred, formulated in terms of 'ungovernability', 'political overload', 'fiscal crisis', 'crowding out' (of private investment by public expenditure) etc.[7] The dominant priority of Western policy-makers shifted from the goal of stable economic growth, to that of controlling inflation, as innumerable OECD publications and national government publications stated. 'Controlling inflation' has become a proxy-term for the imperative need to suppress all redistributive pressures within society. The concomitant of counter-inflationary strategies has, of course, been high unemployment, demoralisation and loss of social solidarity, and fiscal crises, brought about by declining tax revenues, which then justify further contractions in public expenditure budgets.

Measured as a strategy of class *revanche* alone, Thatcherism has been a signal success, as has its equivalent in the United States. Trade unions have lost membership dramatically, both in absolute numbers and as a proportion of the employed workforce. Legal regulation has severely weakened their capacity to engage in bargaining, and especially to seek wider support for their struggles. Incomes have been redistributed, against earlier post-war trends, in favour of the propertied, and a culture has developed in which wealth has been celebrated and rendered apparently free of guilt or responsibilities.

The privatisation of the nationalised industries has been largely at the expense of workforces who have lost the protection of highly institutionalised industrial relations systems. It has also removed, from key sectors of the economy, public organisations who were on the whole committed to large-scale government investment, planning and regulation, and who tended to stand apart, as the natural supporters of corporatism, from an adversarial approach to class relations. Public services of all kinds have been subjected to a penetrating process of marketisation, requiring their managers to change themselves from public service bureaucrats or professionals, into new kinds of public service entrepreneurs. To manage a budget and to achieve the public sector equivalent of profit, has become the central concern of a whole social stratum who previously thought of themselves as committed mainly to providing a social service. Seducing and cajoling the public sector middle class into the embrace of the market has been a key objective of public service reforms, potentially dissolving social democracy's core constituencies among professional workers as the attack on trade unions and public housing has sought to dissolve its larger mass base. The specific citizen roles of passenger, audience-member, patient, pupil are all being redefined in the market terminology of 'customer' or 'client'.

The better-off have been able to escape the dire consequences which this regime has for the growing ranks of the poor by geographical self-segregation. The enforced reduction of the public housing sector will, in due course, reinforce these tendencies to social segregation, producing more uniform gradients of income-level in each urban neighbourhood. Council house tenancies become converted, through the 'right to buy', into another form of monetised property, and housing that would have been allocated formerly by housing departments or passed on through families of tenants, becomes accessible only at its purchase price. Housing becomes commodified, though of course its lifeworld meanings for its occupants remains more complicated. Large-scale unemployment has the intended effect of keeping the poor in their place, a silent reminder of the risks that go with unconventionality, resistance and failure under the regime of the market.

The Balance Sheet of Thatcherism

Thus, conceived solely as a zero-sum distributive game of who has what, Thatcherism can be acclaimed a triumph. Only the continuing high levels of public expenditure and thus of public sector deficits seem to qualify this 'success', in the balance-sheet of what one might have expected from a market-oriented government. One explanation of this difficulty is the scale of unemployment, and the costs of income-maintenance – on however pinched a scale – for many millions of 'unproductive' people. Mandatory social expenditures have thus risen at the very point when the tax base has been reduced. This can be seen as the continuing residual cost to the market system of democracy, whose voters do not expect their fellow

citizens to have to starve because jobs are not available to
them.

It is one thing to triumph in a zero-sum conflict between
capital and labour, the propertied and the unpropertied,
and another to create a social world in which even the
better-off want to live. Capitalism is dedicated to the
accumulation of wealth, not merely to its distribution to
the advantage of the successful and to the disadvantage of
the rest. Markets which might be quite effective at
achieving a distributive benefit to the rich, in their own
terms and in the absence of political restraints, might also
fail to achieve stable growth in the production of goods
and services. They may thus generate less absolute wealth
than a more interventionist and socially-regulated system.
In fact the aims of trade – maximising gains within a given
system of exchange – and the goals of accumulation within
a functioning system of capitalist production – are far
from identical. It is confusion between the two –
reinforced by the Adam Smithian and somewhat
anti-productionist ideology of the Thatcherite intellectuals, and possibly also by Thatcher's own shopkeeping
origins – which has now brought the Thatcher experiment
to its prolonged crisis.

Britain in Decline

This crisis is evident in the failure of the British economy
in the years since 1979 to maintain even the average levels
of growth of the strife-torn 1970s. The economy is now in
chronic external trading deficit, as a consequence of the
erosion of its productive base during the years of deflation
and restructuring. A demand reflation which brought
unemployment down to even two million would produce a
catastrophic balance of payments problem and a further
enforced devaluation of the currency. Britain has never
before faced a balance of payments crisis at the point when
it is barely emerging from recession, with 3 million
unemployed.

Although inflation is currently at record low levels, this
is the result of economic depression, not of a reformed

and well-functioned labour market. Any expansion whatsoever would soon threaten the UK economy with levels of wage inflation higher than that of most of its competitors, despite the severe damage inflicted on trade unions over fourteen years.[8] The reason for this is that labour militancy and wage inflation were always symptoms more than causes of the underlying problems of skill shortages in Britain. Where there is scarcity of appropriate labour, there will be high prices whenever demand for production rises. A large reserve army of the unemployed does not affect this as much as might be expected, if the unemployed do not possess the skills which are needed, or live in the 'wrong places' anyway. Far from being sources of disruption and conflict, trade unions may even help employers to regulate the labour supply, and ensure that long-term interests take precedence over short-term gains when scarcities develop. This was the argument for corporatist systems of industrial relations in the 1960s, the assumption being that conflicts in the workplace needed some normative, not merely coercive resolution.

Limits of the Market

It is now also clear that markets, left to themselves, do not automatically provide an environment in which capital accumulation will occur. Modern systems of production and exchange involve very large externalities and investments which need to be committed in large amounts over very long periods. Economic activities are often most efficiently clustered into interdependent sectors, and firms may succeed best only when they are part of such clusters, able to benefit from the 'competitive co-operation' of similar firms.[9] The fiasco of the Canary Wharf development on the Isle of Dogs, when huge property investments were made in the absence of an infrastructure of transport, shows the dependence of even the most modern markets on appropriate boundary conditions being in place. It is in the interest of all firms that large infrastructural investments should be made, but not in the interests of individual firms to take the burden of these on themselves if their competitors escape them. Thus firms are rationally reluctant to subsidise public transport, from which others will benefit without paying their share of these costs, and correctly argue that public provision will be fairer and more efficient. But a market-oriented government, denying the very existence of externalities which are a commonplace of every textbook, did not see it that way, and has brought some of the largest property companies in the world to the brink of ruin. Similarly, there is no sense in firms investing in schools or colleges, if free-riding competitors across the street can recruit the pupils without having to add the costs of their education to the price of their goods and services.

The theorists of post-Fordism,[10] did perceptively grasp the systemic conditions of capitalist accumulation, as some shrewd theorists of the welfare state had done previously.[11] Mass production presupposed mass consumption, and therefore regulatory measures which ensured a stable long-term rise in consumer demand would benefit producers as well as consumers. Labour had to be reproduced, educated and trained, and could not meet the full costs of its own reproduction. In any case, it was dysfunctional as well as unjust to penalise the children of those less successful in the labour market by denying them education. The enhanced supply of skilled and educated labour was to the long-term benefit of the economy as a whole, and it would therefore be beneficial to provide it in excess of the demand of those who could afford to pay for it. Some forms of production are so integrated, in terms of their optimum technologies, that it is best to operate them as planned systems, rather than by internal market exchange. Railways are a prime example, where the likely 'transaction costs' of requiring negotiated exchanges between owners of track, trains and stations rather than operating a unified system, will exceed efficiency gains from competition.[12] The well-established proclivities of private monopolies to exact excess profits in return for insufficient volumes of production, largely ignored in the Thatcher government's privatisation programme, are another instance of market dogmatism overruling the facts of life of real economies. Environmental regulation, costly as it may be to particular firms or individuals, may also be necessary to the collective interests of capitalists or peoples, since pollution threatens everyone's well-being.[13] It is increasingly clear that cities cannot attract investment unless they offer high environmental standards which depend on public investment and regulation. It is curious that in a commodified world it seems to be *social* and not merely economic factors which determine whether capital investment will take place or not. Attractive locations for individual and collective consumption have become preconditions of production.[14]

There are obviously complex trade-offs to be made, even from the point of view of capital itself, between the disciplines of competitive markets, and the countervailing benefits of planning and co-ordination. Corporations make these trade-offs in different ways within their own organisations. They create different levels of devolution and internal marketisation according to technology and environment, but they do not abandon an essential capacity to regulate, standardise, and plan from the centre.

The higher the level of planning and co-ordination within a system of production, the larger the potential for 'voice' and for resistance to policy goals by peripheral units. Marketisation has the advantage of forcing sub-units to confront 'natural' constraints, no longer transparently the consequence of particular decisions. Disciplinary or normative – that is persuasive or consensual – kinds of co-ordination have to replace the disciplines of the market where 'planning' is deemed functionally appropriate, as it sometimes is. Where incentives of individual economic gain cannot be provided, people have to be given a reason to follow rules or commit themselves to shared values. It is for this reason that corporations worry about corporate morale, take trouble over staff selection and development and cultivate sensitive management. Industrial relations in some industries aims to include trade unions in this system of regulation of good functional reasons. It may be well worth paying the price of allowing members voice, to be listened to and treated with consideration within an organisation, if to do so generates economies of scale, capacity to control the environment, and ability to operate over the long-term.[15] Casualised workforces, operating on the most short-term calculations of economic self-interest, do not necessarily generate the highest levels of profit in the long-term.

These considerations apply also at a societal level. Higher levels of infrastructural investment, provision of high-quality education, training, and health care programmes, urban planning regulations, and planned labour market policies, all restrict the freedom of markets. Collective consumption allows scope for political voice, and provides an opportunity for consumers to organise themselves in order to influence the quality and quantity of what is provided. The 'new social movements', as many social theorists have pointed out, are in large part the product of 'collective consumption' in the same way that the labour movement was the product of 'collective production'.[16]

Full employment and rising incomes, even with significant levels of inflation, generate more buoyant demand for goods and services, and thus stimulate more investment, than a regime of deflation adopted in order to suppress the power of labour. It may be more to the benefit of capital to 'contain' social conflict by normative means, than to rely mainly on dire economic or coercive sanction to do so. Capital may accumulate faster, not slower, under these 'regulated' conditions, than in circumstances which ostensibly might appear tailor-made for profit. The fact is that only certain kinds of profitable activity flourish in laissez-faire environments, and there are not enough of these kind of activities to make Thatcherism work.

The Thatcher experiment, motivated by class anxieties arising from the social turbulence of the 1960s and 1970s, subordinated all these modern, systemic considerations to the goal of regaining powers lost by the owners of property and capital, and the social strata identified with them. The chief benefit that marketisation seemed to offer was to outflank those who had resisted the disciplines of production and the unequal distributive outcomes of markets, and to undermine their resistance to these.

Governments subsequently found that circumventing the resistance embodied in the nation state itself left them without power too, throwing the nation state, like all other institutions of the post-war 'class truce', into crisis.

The Contradictions of Thatcherite 'Modernisation'

The analysts of New Times shifted from an insightful, though unduly culturally-determined, analysis of Thatcherism, to a more positive charting of the new landscape of 'postmodern' capitalism. The connections between these two phases of analysis were never fully clarified. Was Thatcherism an agent of this 'modernising' process, or a mainly reactionary force, holding modernisation back? What theoretical framework could make sense both of the conservative class offensive that was obvious within Thatcherite dogma *and* of the apparent emergence of a new, differentiated, semi-classless order of post-industrial production and consumption? What role might one expect the state to play in the construction and regulation of a postmodern social order? Policies cannot be coherently formed without some analysis of what is materially and functionally appropriate to a system of production and consumption. The Labour Party's flounderings through this period are the result of its not having an adequate way of addressing these issues.

Let us attempt to answer these questions by returning to the crisis of the Fordist class compromise. Firms responded to the problems of 'resistance' to profitable operation by strategies of 'restructuring', making use of dispersal, relocation, and technological transformation to reduce their wage budgets and to increase profitability. They also sought greater economies of scale by merger, transnational operation, and by support for the internationalisation of the economy, via European economic union, tariff reductions through the GATT mechanisms, and free movement of capital. The globalisation of consumption patterns, extending demand for new products and establishing international demand for products with particular market niches was pursued by firms whilst they at the same time internationalised their systems of production.

The effect of these corporation-led developments was severely to diminish and weaken the bargaining power of the 'traditional' industrial working class, closing or relocating the factories, mines and shipyards by which it had been constituted, and exposing producers and employees to intense competitive pressure. At the same time, modern consumption patterns diffused by the mass media, invaded the previously relatively segregated and inward-facing social spaces of working class life, eroding various kinds of class solidarity in the process. There is no doubt that the social environment of production and consumption has been transformed by these processes, and pre-existing conceptions of standardised 'mass' agency have to be abandoned as major social forms.

Welfare systems have been subjected to a similar process of evolution, in part because the habits of mind evoked by more individualised and segmented forms of production and consumption lead to impatience with standardised and authoritarian forms of social provision. People expect, reasonably enough, to find the same degree of differentiation and self-expression in public spaces and amenities, as they look for in the private sphere. This is the reason for the ideological appeal even of such toothless initiatives as the Citizens' Charter, which would be desirable if it fulfilled promises and conferred voice and remedy upon citizens instead of relying on empty rhetoric.

Many local authorities have realised long ago the need to offer services which are comparable in quality and diversity to those of the market. Much contemporary public housing design, conservation and pedestrianisation schemes in cities, and the quality of the 'new amenities' of sports centres and country parks by those councils that can afford them, show that there need not be any unfavourable contrast between public and private provision.

If differentiated and responsive forms of public provision are to exist, then more flexible and entrepreneurial forms of organisation are also going to be needed to provide them. Where standard mass facilities and services are all that is wanted, then a minimum level of professional competence by civil engineers and an insistence that rules be followed by employees may be sufficient. But if design, sensitivity, innovation, and responsiveness to the wishes of consumers or citizens are wanted, then quite different kinds of institutional practices are necessary.[17] To this extent, the devolution and partial 'marketisation' of public services, holding individuals and sub-units responsible for specific performance and quality and allowing some measure of competition in provision, may, in principle, be a beneficial development, once it ceases to be dictated solely by considerations of budget-reduction.

An enlarged system of market exchange is only one element of this transformed system of production and consumption. Economies of scale do generate wealth, and the extension of capitalist production to India, Brazil or China frankly has to be welcomed as the best hope of bringing improvements of living standards to the majority of the world's population. 'Internal marketisation' within western economies can also, as we have suggested, achieve new flexibilities and innovations at the level both of production and consumption.

But there has been a deep confusion in the project of the radical right between the technical or functional objective of realising the potential benefits of an expanded system of market exchange, and the social objective of strengthening the power of the propertied class and defeating the social forces resistant to it. There has sometimes seemed to be convergence between these projects – the greater the sense of 'system crisis' or 'class emergency', the harder it has been to separate them. However, they are different, for the reason that some of the measures taken to reinforce the rights of property and the market system which is seen as their main guarantor, contradict the needs of a dynamic system of accumulation.

We can say, following Marx, that there is both an ideological and a rational content in the New Right's argument for markets. Its rational basis is obvious, and has been detailed above. Its ideological basis is the fetishistic assumption that all regulation, redistribution, public investment, and democratic control, are *ipso facto* damaging unless proved otherwise. This assumption mistakes the short-term interests of particular property-owners or capitalists with the long-term interests of capitalists and even property-owners in general. Capitalists and the capitalist system appear to need extensive regulation, a co-ordinated system of international currency management and trade regulation, a banking system that furthers investment, large government investments, and guarantees of rising demand. The larger and more interdependent the system of production and consumption, the more need there is for such regulatory and steering systems. The reason that this necessarily complex relationship between government and capital is so poorly perceived by the Thatcherites and their American equivalents is because the perspective from which they view the world is remote from that of the managers of the most advanced sectors of the economy. The overriding concern of these politicians, and their intellectual allies, has been with social conflict – mainly the memories and scars of the social conflicts of the 1970s. The rage that has fired them has propelled them to redress the damage done to threatened middle class and lower middle class status-groups by the welfare compromise of the post-war years, symbolised by its most insurgent and 'wild' moments. The dead-weight of the English class system (in which the resentment of the *nouveaux riche* and the status-anxious has had an unprecedented weight) has been the largest determinant of social existence and development in Britain.

Thus, the programmes of the radical right have conflated and confused the immediate interests of the propertied, with the long-term interests of capitalism as a system. This might seem to be an unimaginable form of conflict, since capital *is* or depends on, property. But property has many forms and roles. The meaning of property as a source of wealth, status or upward mobility, and its functions within a complex, modern system of production and exchange, are distinct from one another. The long-term development needs of corporations, as the institutional 'containers' of property rights, are not necessarily identical with the needs of the individuals and status groups who depend on their operations, though many social mechanisms operate to maintain their convergence.

This is not simply the distinction between owners and controllers, or shareholders and managers, so important to 1950s and 1960s debates about the nature of capitalism. Rather, it is the distinction between the requirements of systemic stability of an institutional structure, and the social demands being made of it by social actors. One way of explaining social crises within a neo-Marxist framework is to see these systems of integration as chronically disarticulated from one another. There is social stability when the conflicts of social actors are rendered positively functional for a system – the Fordist class compromise was arguably such a condition. There is instability when social conflicts exacerbate tendencies to crisis.

The theory of Thatcherism was that welfare capitalism had come to such a crisis condition by the end of the 1960s, and that demands from its subordinate classes were threatening its destruction. The paradox is that this may now have become the crisis condition of post-Thatcherite Britain, and indeed of a world capitalist system locked in cumulative recession after a decade of reaction. Not, that is, because of a class struggle being initiated from below, but rather the reverse, because of a class struggle being waged from above. The aims of short-term conditions of profitability, reduction of tax burdens, the suppression of labour through unemployment, the paranoid displacement of conflict on to ethnic minorities, the overriding priority of anti-inflationary policy and the defence of the value of currencies, may now be chronically incompatible with the needs of a dynamic system of capital accumulation.

This distinction between the rights of property and the system needs of capitalism can also be clarified by noting that much of the capital being swished electronically around the world and invested internationally 'belongs' in fact to ordinary citizens in their roles as pension fund beneficiaries or holders of insurance policies. The pursuit of the profits on which pension funds depend may lead companies to destroy the employment base from which the entitlement to pensions derives in the first place.

Towards a Socialism Without Class

A potential beneficial outcome of the Thatcherite programme is that in attacking what it saw as vested interests and privileges, it invoked, in individualist but nevertheless extremely assertive terms, claims to justice and universal rights which it will not necessarily be easy to contain. Even the attack on identifications of class and class-membership, though intended as a weapon against the left, may also be seen as a form of 'modern-ising' revolt against inequalities of status whose real origin is feudal.

Socialists made the most of the inherited inequalities of class for their own purposes, turning weakness into a form of strength, and attempting to generalise the subordinated working class as a universal class of equals. This enabled powerful defensive solidarities to be constructed, looking backwards for their cultural and moral sustenance as radical utopias have usually had to do, but nevertheless constructing some vision for the future. This was always a fraught undertaking, since the hidden and not so hidden injuries of class have always deprived most working class citizens of potential capacities (for example those which require prolonged education, or which are fulfilled in autonomous labour.)[18] It was never convincing to construct the image of an entire new social order from the lifeworld of its least advantaged members – its visions of mutuality and solidarity apart – and when in practice social revolutions had to be attempted on this basis, substitutionalism was the unavoidable result. The idea that

class might be part of the problem, not the ultimate
solution, and that we have to try to construct a 'socialism
without class' may yet turn out to be a positive outcome
from this disastrous period.

Similarly the Thatcherite insistence on the rights of
individuals and 'consumers', although anti-collectivist and
anti-social in their intentions and main effects, may have
the longer-term consequence of raising citizens' levels of
aspiration. The new wave of irreverence towards the royal
family, now being vigorously fanned by the Murdoch
press, is another erosion of forms of class and status
subordination which have ultimately limited democratic
aspiration in Britain. The face of this aggressive
individualist populism is not an attractive one, but nor
were social deference and acquiescence such desirable
states of mind.

The Post-Thatcherite Vacuum

Thatcherism intended itself to be the destroyer of the
post-war welfare compromise and its social democratic
ideology. It was to be the means of restoring an earlier,
'purer' form of market society. But like other attempted
'restorations', its ultimate meanings and effects may not be
those which it intended. The damage done by the
Thatcherites to various forms of collectivistic and
'traditional' regulation of life in Britain may have cleared
away some of the legacies of the class system of the past,
and inflicted severe social injuries in the process, but that
does not mean that its own 'utopia' is viable as an
alternative social system.

It is because Thatcherism is so maladapted to the
functional needs of late-industrial capitalism that there is
now an ideological and theoretical vacuum in which a
programme which better corresponds to modern necessities could be evolved. This requires the redefinition of
rights – political, social and economic – in universalistic
terms. Such a programme should depend on legislative
guarantees as the justice-seeking underpinnings and
regulators of a capitalist system of accumulation. The

operations and mechanisms of capitalism have to be separated from individual entitlements to its profits. Entitlement to profit from capital – whether this is assigned to individuals or institutions – needs to be seen as a right of citizenship no less than freedom before the law or the right to vote. This is why arguments for basic income rights are now fundamental, since they stake universalist claims to shares in the ownership of the means of production, that is to say, in the products of capital as well as labour.[19] Capital and labour should be defined as complementary 'functions' in the system of material production, not constructed as the resources and powers of distinct social classes. Socialists have misread their collective means of class organisation and defence as the social forms of a future society. A means of defence and an architecture of the future are analytically distinct from each other, and the route to a society of equal citizens may ultimately lie through the dissolution of class society rather than through organised class struggle.

The New Times analysts correctly grasped the potency of Thatcherism as an ideology of transition. They saw, too, that in the values of individualism, difference, autonomy and choice, there might be something of positive democratic potential. They insisted that a merely defensive or reactive politics, attempting to conserve the institutional defences and forms of mass provision of the welfare compromise, would not succeed in this changed climate.[20]

The New Times analysts did not altogether avoid, however, the dangers of over-identification with their object of study, and of becoming drawn into the polarised struggle between Thatcherism and the left, which their real aim was to analyse and transcend. The attempts to find an independent platform – neither left traditionalism nor market individualism – foundered, to some degree, in a superficial optimism based on themes of 'difference', consumption, and life-style which reflected only minority opportunities in a broader context of impoverishment, both public and private.

I have tried to identify in this chapter the issues that are central if this debate is to continue fruitfully. These include, first, the recognition that Thatcherism was a potent ideology of power, a means of destroying or at least badly damaging a particular class configuration, but nevertheless does not provide the basis for reconstructing even a viable democratic capitalist order in Britain. The imperatives of social conflict, and the imperatives of dynamic system stability, point in different directions. Second, a perspective of 'modernisation' and 'modernity' is required, in which Thatcherism can be seen as a transitional moment only. Transitional, that is, in the sense that it has attacked forms of power (including working class and state power) which derive too much from the inherited order of social deference and arbitrary authority to be defensible in the long-term. The aspirations expressed by Thatcherite politics, for freedom and equality of citizenship, though not the form in which they have been advanced, need to be recognised as potentially positive. Third, the organisation of production, not merely consumption and the distribution of consumption entitlements, must remain central to any socialist perspective. That is to say, a key problem of achieving a democratic form of 'modernity' is to distinguish the necessary functions of capital in generating wealth, from its unequal and arbitrary distribution as a form of power. Acknowledgement of the former – and the consequent acceptance of the necessities of markets and of a capitalist labour process – should not lead to the obscuring of the injustices and unacceptability of existing forms of ownership. Finally, there is need to formulate social goals in universalistic terms, and to base these on a framework of democratic law-making, now, in a globalised economy, extending beyond the boundaries of the nation state. Radical programmes which merely attempt to aggregate the claims of particularistic interest groups without a universalistic framework threaten to damage the concept of the shared social good on which they necessarily must depend.

Notes

[1] Michael Rustin, 'The Politics of Post-Fordism: Or the Trouble with New Times', in *New Left Review* 175, May–June 1989.

[2] See Charles Sabel and Michael Piore, *The Second Industrial Divide*, Basic Books, New York, 1984, and Bob Jessop(ed), *The Politics of Flexibility: Restructuring State and Industry in Britain, Germany and Scandinavia*, Edward Elgar, Aldershot 1991.

[3] Scott Lash and John Urry, *The End of Organised Capitalism*, Polity, Cambridge 1987.

[4] Robert Brenner and Mark Blick's critique of Aglietta and the French 'regulation school', one part of which has so far been published in *New Left Review*, has a similar implication regarding the primacy of explanation by the social agency of class over functional imperatives of structure. See, Robert Brenner and Mark Blick, 'The Regulation Approach: Theory and History', in *New Left Review* 188, July–August 1991. My own argument in this chapter suggests that in fact both kinds of argument, from the functional imperatives of late industrial capitalism and from the class interests of its dominant class, are necessary to explain these changes, each accounting for different (and contradictory) elements of them.

[5] See John Goldthorpe (ed), *Order and Conflict in Contemporary Capitalism*, Clarendon Press, Oxford 1984.

[6] See A. Maddison, *Phases of Capitalist Development*, Oxford University Press, Oxford 1982.

[7] See for example, Samuel Brittan, *The Economic Consequences of Democracy*, Temple Smith, London 1977; Jürgen Habermas, *Legitimation Crisis*, Heinemann, London 1976; James O'Connor, *The Fiscal Crisis of the State*, St James Press, London 1973; James O'Connor, *Accumulation Crisis*, Blackwell, Oxford 1984 and Claus Offe, *Disorganised Capitalism*, Polity Press, London 1985.

[8] Inflation levels had, in fact, already begun to rise by the autumn of 1993 and the government threatened a public sector pay freeze in response.

[9] See Michael Porter, *The Competitive Advantage of Nations*, Macmillan, London 1990.

[10] For example, see Alain Lipietz, *Towards a New Economic Order*, Polity Press, Cambridge 1992, and Robin Murray, 'Life after Henry (Ford)', in *Marxism Today*, October 1988.

[11] See Ian Gough, *The Political Economy of the Welfare State*, Macmillan, London 1979.

[12] See O.E. Williamson, *Markets and Hierarchies*, Free Press, New York 1975; O.E. Williamson, *The Economic Institution of Capitalism*, Free Press, New York 1985; O.E. Williamson, *Economic Organisation*, Harvester Wheatsheaf, New York 1986.

[13] On this topic see especially, Ulrich Beck, *Risk Society*, Sage, London 1989.

[14] David Harvey, *The Condition of Postmodernity*, Blackwell, Oxford 1989.

[15] The concept is from Albert Hirschman's, *Exit, Voice and Loyalty*, Harvard University Press, London 1970.

[16] On these issues of new social movements and collective consumption see M. Castells, *The City and the Grassroots*, Edward Arnold, London 1983; Patrick Dunleavy, *Urban Political Analysis: The Politics of Collective Consumption*, Macmillan, London 1980: Alberto Melucci, *Nomads of the Present*, Radius, London 1989; P. Saunders, *Social Theory and the Urban Question*, Hutchinson, London 1985; and A. Touraine, *The Return of the Actor: Social Theory in Post-Industrial Society*, Minnesota University Press, Minneapolis 1988.

[17] Arguments for more lateral and decentralised forms of organisation were one of the most interesting aspects of the *New Times* perspective. See for example, 'The Power of the Weak' by Geoff Mulgan in Stuart Hall and Martin Jacques (eds), *New Times: The Changing Face of Politics in the 1990s*, Lawrence & Wishart, London 1989.

[18] See R. Sennett and J. Cobb, *The Hidden Injuries of Class*, Cambridge University Press, Cambridge, 1977.

[19] See P. Van Parijs, *Arguing for Basic Income: Ethical Foundations for a Radical Reform*, Verso, London 1992.

[20] See Stuart Hall and Martin Jacques (eds), *New Times: The Changing Face of Politics in the 1990s*, Lawrence & Wishart, London 1989.

Nostalgia Isn't Nasty: The Postmodernising of Parliamentary Democracy

WENDY WHEELER

Modern democratic political practice no longer answers to the lived experience of contemporary life in British society. The old political languages speak to fewer and fewer people and no new radical and progressive democratic, political languages are heard which appear capable of calling forth a popular political response.[1]

This chapter addresses the question of the contemporary insistence of nostalgia as a central feature of postmodernism and asks what the implications of this postmodern nostalgia might be for contemporary parliamentary political practice. The chapter argues, paradoxically, that an understanding of what is at stake in the nostalgic impulses of contemporary culture in Britain requires a modernizing response from the political 'centre'. It also argues, however, that, in order to take full account of the subjectivities which postmodernity articulates, this 'modernization' can be most helpfully thought through as a *post*modernization.

The chapter argues that postmodern nostalgia can most usefully be understood as a culturally significant expression of popular desire. This is not necessarily regressive and sentimental, but is the affective expression

94

of the desire for community.

Understanding the characteristic features of postmodernism – the nostalgic concern with past, place, space and images of 'home', the hybridization and pastiche of earlier forms and discourses – can be a way both of beginning to make sense of the contemporary failure of the politics of modernity, and also of exploring the kinds of languages and practices in which a progressive postmodern politics might be possible.[2] Rather than seeing the intensification of nostalgia in postmodernity as a regressive sentimentalism, or as a symptom of the loss of any sense of history as real,[3] it is perhaps more useful to view it as an intense cultural expression of the desire for social forms capable of representing what is 'lost' in the experience of Enlightenment modernity.

Offering an answer to the question 'What is Enlightenment?' in 1784, Kant described Enlightenment as an exit from immaturity and from the uncritical acceptance of the tutelage of others.[4] Enlightenment modernity is thus a kind of entry into a different, more 'mature' subjectivity. This is political inasmuch as it begins to produce a new notion of the subject as a mature and critical citizen who refuses the childlike condition of allowing others to do his thinking for him and asserts instead the right to critical, and by implication and eventually, political freedom. Kant is no revolutionary. He insists that, as a private citizen, one must still pay one's taxes and perform one's civic and professional duties, but he also insists on the individual's right to the public exercise of critical thought. This insistence, on private capitulation and public freedom of debate, forms the political basis of modern, bourgeois, democratic societies.

Modernity thus replaces an uncritical and unreflective acceptance of traditional beliefs and ways of life with the obligation to aspire to critical autonomy and the hope of political freedom. Its impulse is utopian. In unenlightened, or premodern, societies, social and political justification is limited by the acceptance of tradition and belief. Enlightenment modernity also imposes limits upon the acceptable but these are no longer described in terms of faith or tradition but consist, instead, in the exercise of rational thought. Critical thought and knowledge can only count as such if it is rational. In this way Enlightenment modernity sets limits upon what counts as Reason, and also constitutes a certain kind of 'rational' critical and political subject. Against this, other categories of thinking (affective thought, visionary thought) and certain categories of people (women, children, madmen) are constituted by processes of exclusion as 'other'.

Enlightenment modernity thus buys the possibility of critical freedom and the project of political freedom at a certain cost. This cost is the radical exclusion of all that seems to threaten an 'adult' and rational consciousness. This radical exclusion of Reason's 'other' forms the basis both of the major distinctions upon which modernity is founded (reason/unreason; maturity/childishness; masculinity/feminity; science/art; high culture/mass culture, critique/affect; politics/aesthetics etc.) and of modern subjectivity itself. In relation to the experience of modern subjectivity one is justified in talking of exclusion as repression here. Modern subjectivity is constituted on the basis of a repression which re-emerges as a sense of uncanny (*unheimlich*), unhomely, self-estrangement and alienation.[5] As Mladen Dolar has pointed out, 'It seems that Freud speaks about a "universal" of human experience when he speaks of the uncanny, yet his own examples tacitly point to its location in a specific historical conjuncture, to the particular historical rupture brought about by the Enlightenment. There is *a specific dimension of the uncanny that emerges with modernity*.'[6] Postmodernism is the return of repressed contents with a particular insistent intensity. Since it is modernity that troubles us, what comes 'after' modernity is to be found written upon the features of our contemporary cultural life as the return to those things which are excluded, lost or repressed as a condition of modernity and of the subjectivity it produces.

Modernity as Alienation –
Postmodernity as Longing to Come Home

Since an authentic, affective experience of life and relatedness is specifically what is apparently 'lost' or repressed within modernity and the processes of technological and critical/scientific modernization, there may be good – or at least comprehensible – reasons for the social attraction of forms which seem to offer an appeal to affect. Much deploring of sentimental inclinations, 'conservative' literary and visual realisms, pastiches of pastness, and the absence of critical facility may be done but, where it is done without serious attention to the power of the social desire thus expressed, it will be done without critical effect.

Contemporary nostalgia is a symptom of the desire to return to a non-alienated condition, understood as something we have left behind us in the past.

If nostalgia is understood in this way, there will be no difficulty in understanding the postmodern as an intensification of modernity's sense of itself as expressing 'consciousness of the discontinuity of time: a break with tradition, a feeling of novelty, of vertigo in the face of the passing moment'.[7] In this understanding, nostalgia and the nostalgic image arises in postmodernity as an almost unbearably intense and uncanny yearning for the homely comforts of a settled way of life.

But this understanding of nostalgia is not yet sufficient. First, it does not allow us to reflect deeply enough, either upon the inevitability of postmodernity, or upon the specific ways in which what is repressed within and by Enlightenment modernity *must* return, both socially and politically, to haunt modern reason. Second, this understanding fails to address the ways in which the nostalgic experience is imaginary and culturally consti-tuted. This is not simply to say that there never was any fixed past or any such plenitudinous place as 'home', but is to argue, paradoxically, that it is precisely because nostalgia is imaginary and culturally over-determined that, its utopianism points towards a potentially political community of interest.

In reality everyone knows that nostalgic feeling is for a past which is imaginary. Nostalgia is not, in fact, the yearning for experience which continues through time. What is nostalgic is not what really happened over a period of lived time, but something more like the affect we experience *in the present* from a collection and distillation of images. But, importantly, nostalgia is not simply individual. Nostalgia is fragmentary; a collection, under the sign of the subject, of fragments of images, sounds, smells and textures. But these images – which become nostalgic – are fixed in our imaginations in the first place because they crystallize events and meanings which are already a party of our shared cultural symbolizations.

Nostalgia both returns us to the affective images of the place (or places) in which we think we have been, immediately present to ourselves in experience – to a sense of 'being-in-place' – and also connects us to other subjects. Its fragments are the constituent pieces of what Buñuel called 'That Obscure Object of Desire' and what Lacan called the *objet petita*. In nostalgia it is not simply our own pasts which constitute this imaginary realm, but also those fragments of our culture which in some way articulate with the identity we experience ourselves as being. That these are commodified images in no way lessens their effect.

In this way we can also understand that nostalgic affect, whilst it coagulates under the sign of the subject, is *not* purely personal. We might all have our personal nostalgias – a particular smell, a particular sensation – but it is evident that a significant feature of nostalgia is its sharedness. Its mode is not arcane or formal but realist. The nostalgic scene or episode always contains social fragments and elements of pastiche which it invites us to share in and which even compel our recognition. It offers no barriers to our understanding because it does not appeal in the first place to critical understanding but to experience and affect.

The strength of affect in the experience of nostalgia lies in the way in which it, first, seems to present a moment in which one experiences one's self in immediate sensual relation to reality, and, second, that this moment is not simply private but is culturally overdetermined and thus communicable. Third, in this retrospective recognition one understands the extent to which the nostalgic memory is, in the Lukácsian sense, a shared 'type' which joins one to others and which, thus, becomes one of the means by which subjects overcome their experience of alienation and loss.

Nostalgia, then, turns us towards the idea of the individual as non-alienated, as knowing and being known by others in the commonality of the community which is identified as 'home'. Nostalgia both reminds us of the pain of alienation and also of the utopian ideas of finally being 'at home' with oneself and others. As Marianna Torgovnik, writes: 'Home is the utopian ideal. Home is what we have to believe is safe, where we have to carry on as though it will be safe. Home is the last frontier.'[8]

A Postmodern Politics

Thinking critically about nostalgia, it will be clear, as Doreen Massey argues, that the fixity of identity and place symbolized by notions of home is imaginary. Not only is it the case that 'the past was no more static than the present' and that the privileging of 'some particular moment/location in time-space' is generally a claim to power on behalf of one group/identity or another, but it will also be clear 'that the identity of any place, including that place called home, is in one sense for ever open to contestation.[9] Whilst postmodern 'time-space compression has produced a feeling of disorientation, a sense of the fragmentation of local cultures and a loss, in its deepest meaning, of a sense of place',[10] and although reactionary and defensive ideas of 'home' are 'attempts to fix the meaning of places ... [and to] construct singular, fixed and static identities for places',[11] it is nevertheless still the case, as Angelika Bammer argues, that these nostalgic gestures of postmodernism are 'the recuperative gestures of our affective needs'.[12] One of the questions which postmodernism poses to politics is that of a response to 'affective needs', to the desire for communal identifications.

Democratic politics is not simply about 'rational' thought and material needs but is also about desire. Nostalgia presents us with an imaginary configuration which represents significant elements in the desiring experience of the contemporary subject. The success of Thatcherism lay almost entirely in the ways in which it managed to mount an affective address to the question of personal and social desire. Its actual economic performance was patchy to dismal, and its market theory profoundly intellectually flawed,[13] but it is clear that Thatcherism was able very successfully to address nostalgic desire and the anxieties which it signifies. This was expressed most clearly in the continued emphasis upon a return to the values of the past, in its appeal to the idea of the nation as one community and in its pursuit of the idea that everyone should be able to own their own home and to exert some influence upon the servicing of their own community. Although, in practice, Thatcherism's emphasis on the 'private' served to increase a sense of social alienation, its promise, including its continual emphasis on law and order, was that social and self-alienation would be ended.

The success of New Right conviction politics (now somewhat shaky under Major) has remained, in the main, anathema to the left. This is because, whilst the left sees quite clearly the economic disarray caused by Thatcherism, it is unable to grasp the extent to which the establishment of political hegemony is a question of addressing imaginary desire rather than simply of addressing need. Needs can be met (and even, *viz*, Thatcherism, not met) but desire, and the promise of its satisfaction, remains central and crucial to any political project.

The Labour Party may now attempt to win popular consent, but its grasp of what this means does not appear to have extended to the idea that appropriate action can only flow from an ethical understanding of what might constitute a new 'common sense'.[14] In the main, the left still continues to think of imaginary desire at the very superficial level of the media image. The images which have been projected do not flow in one continuous and uninterrupted line from the hearts and minds of a united and convinced movement, but consist of ad-man's stuff pasted onto attitudes and habits of mind which remain wedded to a past few people care to remember. Everyone knows this and the frequency with which opinion pollsters have recorded public conviction that 'Labour hasn't *really* changed' bears eloquent testimony to this knowledge.

For a time, socialism, and its communist variant, really did seem to offer the promise of an answer to modern alienation. It cannot, however, be said often enough nor strongly enough that this particular articulation of modernity's utopian impulse has failed miserably. It is a utopianism – an imaginary answering of desire – that nobody wants any longer. Its distinctions have lost their significant imaginary purchase. As Geoff Mulgan has said recently, 'Most people trying to reform politics are still working within divisions which were appropriate a century ago.'[15] This is not to say that such distinctions and divisions do not remain but that the ways in which these differences can be effectively addressed politically have changed.[16]

These changes in political possibilities are one aspect of social and cultural changes which go wider. They range from the global extensions of capitalism to the related penetration of aestheticized images into almost every sphere of modern life.[17] Changes in work patterns impact upon the family and meet the critical articulations of feminist critiques of gender roles. Both gender and class-appropriate roles and identities shift, break down, and temporarily recoalesce in response to changes in spheres as diverse as marketing and education, politics and aesthetics. It is in the context of all these changes in social and cultural life in Britain that the idea of postmodernism first begins to have an explanatory purchase in contemporary debate.

The British Context of Postmodernism

The word postmodernism first enters the vocabulary of the British left-liberal intelligentsia during the 1980s, most notably via the pages of *Marxism Today* and *New Left Review*.[18]

Although the meaning of the term is complex and much debated, in Britain use of the term 'postmodernism' in a political context emerges largely as the attempt to 'name' the socio-cultural effects associated with New Right policies and the rejection of the post-war consensus.

In place of any root and branch political modernization in the form of the bourgeois revolutions experienced by many western societies during the eighteenth and nineteenth centuries, this consensus marked a renewed attempt to democratize a country which, up until the Second World War, remained sharply divided along traditional class lines in terms of access to political, educational and cultural power.[19] Beneath the surface of British politics at the end of the war lay a real establishment fear of the kind of revolution experienced in Russia in 1917. The post-war consensus of greater social and cultural inclusivity was intended to avert this.

One of the central planks of the consensus was the idea that broadened access to what Alan Sinfield calls 'good culture'[20] would provide an ideological basis upon which far greater numbers of ordinary people might come to appreciate the good life previously limited to the leisured classes; thus forestalling any mounting pressure for a resort to revolutionary change. Wider access to education (including, importantly, higher education) and culture (meaning high culture as formulated in Britain largely via the institutionalization of the academic study of English Literature and History towards the end of the nineteenth century) was seen as one of the central means of achieving this increase in democratization and socially harmonious community. Providing greater access to 'good culture' still meant, at the end of the Second World War, providing access to this nexus of English 'good culture'. This was founded upon the idea of a 'great tradition' which exemplified an authentic, national genius. It included not only, and inevitably, Shakespeare, but also other examples of 'natural' English genius from Wordsworth, Austen and

George Eliot to the expressive genius of English folk music.[21] This was not merely a device of the high bourgeoisie but was equally subscribed to by the middle class dissidents of the left.

It was not until the 1960s that disaffection with this view of good culture as high culture began to set in. Whilst there was an 'immediate consequence' in 'profound dissatisfaction with the dominant English tradition, with the role of literature and with Leavisism,[22] the left-liberal intelligentsia was still able to argue that the commitment to 'good' culture for all which had been promised by consensus and the welfare state should be met in the provision of greater resources for 'good' education and culture. Nevertheless, in the 1960s 'the moment of left-culturalism was also the moment of its supercession and of the distintegration of the assumptions about "good" culture which it had inherited and developed.' By the mid-1970s, the continued breaking down and challenging of earlier cultural and social distinctions, the effects of technological and social change called forth a mainstream political response in the form of the rise to influence of the New Right within the Conservative Party. By the 1980s, and especially in the face of Thatcherism's evident ability to intervene *politically* in the dispersal and reconstitution of political, social and cultural subjectivities, left critics began to confront the idea of 'postmodernism'. They began to deploy the term as a means of understanding not only these profound changes themselves but also the ways in which a new political articulation of change and changing identities had proved possible.

It is, then, in this context of social and critical argument and rethinking that the term postmodernism first comes into significant usage in Britain as a way both of naming profound changes in the cultural terrain, and also of identifying problematic changes in the possibility of cultural identifications. In other words, the ethos governing the ways in which both private and public, and individual and collective identities had been 'mapped' since the end of the nineteenth century became less and less tenable in terms of the lived experience of large numbers of people.

The New Right were the first to grasp this in terms of the articulation of a political agenda. They undertook this on the basis of the characteristically postmodern gesture of the turn to the past – in this case formulated in a most reactionary fashion via the attempted reaffirmation of national identity and national culture, and by the articulation of an imaginary 'Victorian' golden age of virtuous and hard-working individuals in 'proper' families. They were, however, neither able to fix this adequately to contemporary economic conditions, nor were they able to address the new fluidity in contemporary identifications nor the underlying demands of postmodern nostalgia for the constitution of political collectivities appropriate to contemporary experience. The New Right 'common sense' articulation of the subject remained fixed and at the level of the individual, with no reciprocal *political* representation in which these identities might be 'mirrored' as active and multiple 'us's'.

Centre-left politics has, to some extent, responded to and taken up the postmodern questions of changes in culture and subjectivity. These questions are posed by what might be called the 'first phase' of identity politics – i.e., the implicit questioning of Reason as singular, unified and normative which finds expression in the affirmation of the legitimacy of affective experience as a source of knowledge. However, it has done so without, perhaps, realizing the full implications of this response. Identity politics seemed reasonable on the grounds of social justice, but its initial insistence on the legitimacy of different, and affective, rationalities marked a crucial change in the ways in which subjects could be thought about and addressed politically. It certainly marked a radical departure from the universal reason and subject predicated by Kant. Needless to say, the 'checklist' politics of the left – which tacked 'difference' on to what basically remained a normative Enlightenment modernity conception of subjectivity – has offered an inadequate response to such 'first phase' articulations of different identities, communities and desires; and no response at all to the pressing questions of postmodern identities currently being addressed in the 'second phase' of a politics of identity explicitly challenging ideas of identity as stable and fixed. Criticism on the margins continues to pursue this 'second phase', and to question and problematize the usefulness of ideas of identity as pre-given, authentic and fixed in defensible spaces.

Political (Post)Modernization

The postmodern question consists in asking 'What can count as rationality *now*?' Precedents have already been set for the ways in which it might begin to be answered. One might say that the contemporary politics of difference, whose initial positions are predicated upon appeals to the specificity of different affective experiences give voice to political languages which express a hybridized ethos of both affectivity and critique in which Enlightenment's idea of a unified, exclusive (and normatively 'masculine') Reason no longer holds.[23] Precisely because these identities are marginal, plural, displaced and non-normative, they have not been amenable to the kinds of assimilation to mass positions and oppositional politics available to an earlier, class-based politics.

Part of the challenge which a radical and emancipatory parliamentary democratic politics now faces is, first, that of acknowledging a plurality within reason and identity, second, that of understanding that popular expressions are symptomatic, and third, that of finding ways of making a political response to the nostalgic desire for communalities. This means articulating a politics capable of constituting a 'we' which is not essentialist, fixed, separatist, divisive, defensive or exclusive. Clearly, the structures and forms of such a politics must be capable of representing both the diversity and the desire of contemporary identities.

Common experience, should be understood as a political commonality: blackness does not name skin colour so much as the socio-political experience of

colonialism. The loosely affiliated group Queer Nation
have identified as 'Queer' any socio-political identification
with non-normative sexualities. The attempt here is to
acknowledge the force of affective experience and to lift it
into the sphere of rational discourse in which identity,
including affective experience, is represented and
understood as socially and politically constituted. Such a
move does not ignore the great pain, anger and longing of
those whose identities have been constituted as non-
normative and marginal, but it addresses this as an
historical and political question.

The political challenge now consists in persuading
'normal', 'ordinary', people that their unquiet hearts can
be set at ease by the recognition of a *political* commonality.
At one time, and especially when the working class was
excluded from the bourgeois norm, this political
commonality took the form of a revolutionary, anti-
capitalist, class consciousness. The contemporary problem
is to constitute a commonality of the political imagining of
identifications through which a wide, but no longer class
based, commonality might be established, but without
resort to the dangers of national or religious fun-
damentalisms.

Arguing against an essentialist expressive politics,
Andreas Bjørnerud suggests that this political imagining
might take the form of giving up 'the quest for a
normative notion of identity',[24] Bjørnerud suggests that
'identity is never authentic, never fixed once and for all,
but [is] always only an imaginary identification ever ready
for loss and displacement.'[25] But, as I have argued,
postmodern nostalgia does not affirm any essential
identity. Rather, it configurates a culturally constituted
experience of the desire for an intersubjective sense of
being-in-place. Nostalgia may seem like a desire for what
was but it is better understood as the desire for collective
identifications. To date, only feminism has come
anywhere near to a widely successful articulation of such
complex identifications. As Bjørnerud argues, the political
task consists in recognizing that this 'we' is never prior to
its political constitution.[26] The 'first phase' of a wide and

radical, democratic politics must consist in recognising the expression of cultural symptomologies. Nostalgia is such a central symptom. Reading it ethically means understanding that, rather than being regressive and sentimental in the worst sense, it poses a real question to democratic, parliamentary political forms about how a 'we' can be constituted.

Tom Nairn has argued that British parliamentary democracy is badly in need of modernization.[27] It might be more accurate to say that it is in need of postmodernization. As an institution, British parliamentary politics has arguably never quite caught up with modernity. Any progressive politics attempting to work within such a system must be disadvantaged by this.

It seems likely that British political life will remain in a condition of appalled paralysis and dismay until significant parts of the centre-left recognize the need both to reconnect politics to contemporary life and also to recast it along lines which answer, in spirit and in practice, to contemporary desire. Modernization might suggest constitutional and electoral reform. Postmodernization suggests the need to recognize that, in order to be popular, the pursuit of such reforms must, in the first place, catch at the desire for the constitution of social 'places' of identification which postmodern nostalgia expresses. The task of a progressive postmodern politics is that of a double enunciation in which reforms of political structure are at the same time articulations of the communal 'spaces' in which personal and social desire can be addressed and new identifications can be constituted.

Utopia means, literally, 'not a place'. Popular politics always needs an element of utopianism. But perhaps the contemporary insistence of nostalgia suggests the need for a shift in which the emphasis in hopefulness falls upon 'topos' and upon a sense of being-in-place, in which the constitution of new political, social and economic places, spaces and identifications makes more and better common sense.

Notes

I would like to thank Carolyn Burdett for helpful and careful comments in an earlier draft of this essay.

[1] This question, of the possibility of the articulation of a radical and progressive democratic politics, is the task addressed in Ernesto Laclau & Chantal Mouffe, *Hegemony and Socialist Strategy: Towards a Radical Democratic Politics*, Verso, London 1985.

[2] The intensity of postmodern nostalgia and the longing for a non-alienated sense of 'being in place' has recently been addressed in the essays gathered together in a special issue of *New Formations* entitled 'The Question of Home', *New Formations 17*, Summer 1992. The identification of postmodern practices as hybrid is argued in relation to architecture by Charles Jencks and in relation to literature by Linda Hutcheon. C. Jencks, *What is Post-Modernism?*, Academy Editions, London 1986. L. Hutcheon, 'Beginning to theorize postmodernism', *Textual Practice 1*: 1 Spring 1987, also appearing as Chapter 1 in L. Hutcheon, *A Poetics of Postmodernism: History, Theory, Fiction*, Routledge, London 1988. Homi Bhabha has also developed the term as a way of describing subversive identifications in the context of post-colonialism. See Homi Bhabha, 'Signs Taken for Wonders: Questions of ambivalence and authority Under a Tree Outside Delhi, May 1817' in H.L. Gates, Jr. (ed.) *'Race' Writing and Difference*, University of Chicago Press, Chicago 1986.

[3] Fredric Jameson, 'Postmodernism, or the Cultural Logic of Late Capitalism', *New Left Review 146*, July-August 1984 and also in F. Jameson, *Postmodernism or, The Cultural Logic of Late Capitalism*, Verso, London 1991. See especially, Section II. 'The Postmodern and the Past'. Jameson's view of postmodern nostalgia is that it is something like a 'schizophrenic' compensation for the contemporary subject's inability to articulate an historical grammar.

[4] Immanuel Kant, 'What is Enlightenment?', *On History*, ed. Lewis White Beck, Bobbs-Merrill, Indianapolis 1956.

[5] For Freud's understanding of the uncanny as an instance of the return of the repressed, see Sigmund Freud, 'The Uncanny' in Pelican Freud, vol 14: *Art and Literature*, Penguin, Harmondsworth 1985 and in *SE Vol. XVII*, Hogarth Press, London 1955.

[6] Mladen Dolar, ' "I Shall Be with You on Your Wedding-Night": Lacan and the Uncanny', *October*, no 58, Fall 1991, p 7.

[7] Michel Foucault, 'What is Enlightenment?' in Paul Rabinow, (ed.), *The Foucault Reader*, Peregrine/Penguin, Harmondsworth, 1986, p 39.

[8] Marianna Torgovnik, 'Slasher Stories', *New Formations* 17, Summer 1992, p 145.

[9] Doreen Massey, 'A Place Called Home', *New Formations ibid.*, p 13.

[10] Massey, *ibid.*, p 7.

[11] Massey, *ibid.*, p 12.

[12] Angelika Bammer, Editor's Introduction, *New Formations* 17, p xi.

[13] During the 1980s, one of the clearest and most consistent British explicators of the major intellectual flaws of the Free Market has been Will Hutton's regular column in the *Guardian*.

[14] Perhaps it is necessary to say that by 'ethical' I do not mean subscription to this or that morality, but mean the sense in which what is ethical now is that which flows from thorough contemplation of the ethos of modernity and its failure.

[15] See 'The Sunday Review', *Independent on Sunday*, 24 January 1993.

[16] The Spring 1993 founding of Demos – a non-party aligned 'think tank' with Geoff Mulgan as its director and an Advisory Council drawn from diverse social, commercial and political groupings – marks an attempt to provide a site for the development of policies directed towards this need for changed political articulations. See Demos's Inaugural Statement, *Demos: Why?*. Demos, 9 Bridewell Place, London EC4 6AP.

[17] Massey *op cit.*, esp. pp 6-7.

[18] *Marxism Today*, special issue on Postmodernism, January 1989 and Jameson, *New Left Review, op cit* 146.

[19] See Tom Nairn's thesis on the British failure of political modernization in T. Nairn, *The Break-up of Britain*, New Left Books, London 1977.

[20] See Alan Sinfield, *Literature, Politics and Culture in Post-war Britain*, Blackwell, Oxford 1989, esp. chapter 6 – 'Freedom and the Cold War'.

[21] F.R. Leavis's *The Great Tradition* provides an exemplary instance of the constitution of a 'tradition' of (moral) English genius. F.R. Leavis, *The Great Tradition*, Peregrine/Penguin, Harmondsworth 1962. For essays detailing the wider constitution of English cultural identity, see R. Colls and P. Dodd, (eds.) *Englishness: Politics and Culture 1880–1920*, Croom Helm, London 1986.

[22] Sinfield, *ibid.*, p 271.

[23] For a discussion of the gendering of Reason in the thinking of Enlightenment, see Jochen Schulte-Sasse, 'Imagination and Modernity: Or the Taming of the Human Mind', *Cultural Critique 5*, Winter 1986-87, especially p 42.

[24] Andreas Bjørnerud, 'Outing Barthes: Barthes and the Question of (A Gay) Politics', in *New Formations* 18, winter 1992, p 137.

[25] Bjørnerud, *ibid*.

[26] Bjørnerud, *ibid*.

[27] Nairn, *op cit*.

Section Two: Crossing the Border – The Postmodernism of Global Times

Feminism, Postmodernism and the Real Me

ANGELA McROBBIE

A three way split has developed recently around postmodernism. There are those who refuse to acknowledge that postmodernism engages with anything that modernism is not better able to explain and who also defend the values of modernism as they relate to both intellectual work and political analysis.[1] This grouping has established itself as a counterbalance to those others who from such a 'reasonable' standpoint display what are viewed as the excesses of postmodernism.[2] Allowing even for predictable negative typecasting in a debate which has become as heated as this, the image of these postmodernists remains particularly flimsy and marked by what Judith Butler describes as a kind of slur of infantilism or, at least, youthful aberration.[3] The third path is occupied by the post-colonialists[4] and there is in this work both a notion of what Paul Gilroy, drawing on Zygmunt Bauman, labels 'counter cultures of modernity' and at the same time a remorseless critique of modernity and a looking to those accounts of postmodernity as a way of finding a place from which to speak and a space from which to develop that critique of the places and the spaces of exclusion inside modernity.

The question which will be asked in this chapter is what does this three-way divide mean for women? And how does feminism define itself in an intellectual world now characterised by shifting borders, boundaries and identities? To begin to answer this question it is necessary to look first at how two prongs in this debate, the pro-modernist and the post-colonialist, put on the agenda quite separate issues as central to our understanding of contemporary society. These usefully set a framework for going on to consider the place of feminism in this new conceptualisation of the social. But, in engaging with the feminists who have taken up a strongly postmodernist position, the reader should be warned that these writers have been criticised for 'taking leave of their senses'. To enter their discourse is therefore to display a willingness to explore consciously the other side, the underneath side of contemporary critical theory, a realm of thinking which is frequently charged with the abandonment not just of reason, but also of the subject, good sense, politics and almost every other heinous crime that can be imagined. In this process of searching around in the landscape of post-feminism, as well as postmodernism and post-coloniality, the question of who 'we' intellectuals are these days and what role we have to play in feminist politics is constantly forced to the front.

Postmodernists: Guilty of Playing with Politics

My starting point is to suggest that the provocative stance adopted in relation to language by a figure like Jean-François Lyotard,[5] which results in him being charged with playfulness, is a deliberate strategy, 'strategic disrespect' as Judith Butler calls it, a way of positioning himself within a certain kind of rhetorical mode which allows him to develop his critique.[6] Gregor McLennan has recently expressed his antipathy to this way of thinking as follows, 'The contemporary world, in spite of patches of surface civilisation remains too ravaged by oppression, ignorance and malnutrition for privileged intellectuals to trade in seriousness for the sparkling interplay of language games'.[7] Contrary to this position it can be argued that postmodernism represents neither an absence of seriousness, nor a kind of political immorality or irresponsibility. It works as a critique because it forces precisely this kind of response, either to urgently (and perhaps defensively) redefine and defend the political and intellectual formation of modernity or else, having subjected to scrutiny the great pillars of thinking which have supported the project of modernity, stand back and ask 'what's going on'? (as the great soul singer Marvin Gaye put it.)

Postmodernism is a concept for understanding social change. It seems feeble to suggest it, but maybe the reason for the hostility to the concept in Britain lies at least partly in the absymal fate of social science research, and intellectual work in general, in the UK during and after the Thatcher years where there were such constraints that political and intellectual responses were inevitably defensive. Sociology as well as 'society' itself were such redundant categories that there was little opportunity to investigate what the new theoretical vocabulary might look like in practice. Thus, while there has been a debate about 'news ways of living' and about post-Fordism as well as one on fragmentation and identity, there has been little opportunity to examine in any depth the lived 'condition of postmodernity'. As a result, the really engaged debate on how best to understand this re-figuring of society was never able to take place. What happened instead was either a rejection and retrenchment, which nonetheless involved re-examining the premises and the assumptions upon which the intellectual edifice of modernity was based, or else there was a process of translating some of the categories of French or American postmodernism into the cultural politics of contemporary Britain.[8] This latter can best be seen in the emergence of New Times politics in the late 1980s and early 1990s with its interest in consumerism,[9] identity, ethnicity, and with the critique of essentialism, be it in relation to gender;[10] class;[11] or ethnicity.[12]

Finding the 'Real Me'

The 'real me' which is part of the title of this chapter alerts the reader to the fictive unity of the self and the essentialism entailed in the search for such a person. It is a

Stuart Hall phrase, and what is being questioned is the possibility of a 'real me'.[13] One of the questions that will be explored here is what remains when we do away with the 'real me'. How do we construct what I would define as a sufficiently focused 'social self' in order to be effective in politics? And who can such a politics now claim to represent? Who therefore is the discursive 'I' which speaks or writes, to whom and with what purpose? This question will be returned to in the final part of this chapter. But, for the moment, I would want to signal postmodernity as marking a convergence of a number of discourses each of which open up new possibilities for positioning the self.

What is distinctive about the discourses considered in the following pages is the respect for difference which they display, not, as some might see it a 'simple' celebration of difference, but rather a rigorous thinking through of what living with difference might entail. In addition I think there is a brave and necessary inclusion in the new intellectual agenda of difference, a different kind of language, one which insists on the interplay between intellectual boundaries and borders and also one which recognises the importance of what have been the hidden dimensions of subjectivity, those which arise from positionalities which within modernism had no legitimate place, ie that of the black woman, that of the mother, the daughter, that of the feminist intellectual, the feminist teacher.

This kind of work is reflected is Carolyn Steedman's *Landscape For a Good Woman*[14] which pulls together strands of social history and personal psychoanalysis, producing a remarkable text where the oblique search for 'the real me' through the joint guidance of history and psychoanalysis produces instead a layered, mysterious, unresolved self, a fictive daughter, whose positionality as daughter within a particular configuration of class, culture and family, has required that 'she' produce 'this' book. Feminism, in Steedman's case, also requires a necessary interdisciplinarity of intellectual work which problematises its own foundations. It may well be that it is this which makes such work, as well as that produced by post-colonialist writers including: Trin T. Min- Ha, Homi Bhabha and Gayatri Chakravorty Spivak,[15] appear unruly and truculent and poetically disrespectful of the boundaries which have guarded and guaranteed the old rules of academia. It is partly this 'game' of academic convention and the defense of disciplinary boundaries as guarantors of academic authorship and identity, which underpins recent alter-cations between those who defend modernity and those who move in some 'other' direction.

In the recent volume which is part of the new Open University social science course 'Modernity and Its Futures' we find an interesting version of the debate for and against postmodernism being played out by Gregor McLennan and Stuart Hall.[16] Neither author wholly defends one against the other. But as McLennan veers towards modernity, Stuart Hall, boldly explores frag-mented subjectivity. In the following pages a reading of these debates will be suggested as a means of establishing a framework for considering recent work in feminist theory.

Critical Embrace: Modernity and its Critique

In some ways the embracing of modernity as a critical concept in contemporary political thinking is a way of decentring Marxism by showing it to belong to a broader, philosophical project. Thus, while Stuart Hall shows how modernity and its focus on 'man' and the unified subject was itself undermined by Freud (the unconscious), by Marx (production and labour rather than exchange, the market and free will), later by structuralism (which opposed the transparency of meaning), and more recently by the social movements (including those of gender, sexual identity and ethnicity); so also could we say that the interest in modernity can be seen as a way of both re-locating Marx in a less universalistic mode, (a kind of process of downgrading or relativising) and of looking to find something in modernity which can be used to ward off the encroaching chaos of postmodernity. Feminist intellec-tuals (with a few exceptions) have tended either to argue for the necessity of some of those great modernist values; truth, objectivity, reason;[17] or else they have argued against the assumed invisibility of women found in much of the recent writing on modernity.[18]

Gregor McLennan reminds us that the Enlightenment gave rise to the idea of social betterment, of improving and making better the society in which we live. The development of the social sciences was part of this project. Are these 'foundations of modern thought' now obsolete? Or do they only need to be revised? The first of these questions implies that postmodernity blows everything away, the second that the existing vocabulary merely needs updating. McLennan opts for modifying modernity. He pitches the 'overhauling' Lyotard against the more 'reasonable' Jürgen Habermas.[19] For Lyotard the Enlightenment promised science as pure knowledge and as narrative-free practice, but that picture of pure knowledge was in itself part of a very powerful story which helped legitimise capitalist exploitation. Therefore beware of the meta-narratives. Knowledge is not pure or in the mind but moves around like a game. Habermas, in contrast, sees the Enlightenment as an ideal not a reality. It poses questions of morality, science and art as separate from myth and primitivity. To abandon the commitment to reason and rationality and to the validity of asking certain questions is to embrace despair, and ultimately conservatism. We can retain hope of objectivity in universals (the good life, the better society) without having 'naive expectations'. Thus we arrive at the theory of communicative action/reason.

For McLennan relativism is the issue. Does cultural relativism lead to cognitive relativism, that is, we cannot understand therefore we give up and go home? Relativism encourages indifference, he suggests. It means arguments about what is good and true cannot be engaged in and across cultures. Critics of this position (the rest, the others) would, McLennan agrees, say that what is being defended here 'is the culture and society of Western science and philosophy'. He says, in defense of this position, that some values can be shared cross-culturally. And if this is not possible, and if knowledge has such little import, then why carry on doing academic work at all? Modernity did not promise one kind of progress but many. There was always a radicalised strand within modernity.

McLennan argues his position on the grounds that there is communicative action across cultures. There are still universals, for example, the possibility of democracy.[20] One problem with McLennan's argument is that he takes the postmodernity critique as a kind of intellectual earthquake. He responds truculently. It is one or the other. If there is no logic, no reason then we all shut up shop or embrace mysticism or unreason or madness. But this mode of argumentation, based on pitching binary opposites against each other, need not always be the most useful way of proceeding. The tendency is to feel the necessity of coming down strongly in favour of one or the other, or, as McLennan does in a later piece, more measuredly, bringing together the 'better elements of Enlightenment sociology' with 'the undoubted insights of "post" currents. Not … in order to form some bland and convenient theoretical convergence but rather to generate a series of productive and taxing tensions'.[21] What this restrained mode cannot afford to do is to look beyond the 'reasonable' frame of reference within which the debate is conducted. Why not? What happens when we challenge this kind of management of reason, when we suggest that the tensions are more usefully explored when they remain aggressively outside and deeply uncomfortable with this kind of 'convergence'?

Stuart Hall: Working in a World of Shifting Boundaries

Stuart Hall travels down a different road. What he is interested in exploring are the new world identities which have come into being to sweep away, as capitalism itself does, the old nation states which were the bearers of modernity and the givers of identity and 'nationality'. Instead we live in a world of moving boundaries. Borders which are crossed, new sub-nationalisms which are embraced, transnationalisms which are also embraced. For Hall it is the struggle to explain which is important. What he turns his attention to are those aspects of modernity which incorporated subjection and subordination in the language of social advance, exploration, development, civilisation. This more open-ended approach avoids the either/ors which define the terms of McLennan's argument. Instead it adopts a strategy of unsettlement and an embracing of the idea of difference and hybridity. What is also unsettled and differentiated is the 'real me'. This approach is also quite different from Fredric Jameson's,[22] as well as McLennan's, in that we see no sign of a return to the values or ethics of modernism being proposed. It is focused instead around the 'new ethnicities' and it looks out for the connections among subjugated people which emerge from within the cracks of the meta-communications networks of the new global order.

Hall's contribution is significant, also, in that it does not prioritise an exclusively academic mode as the means of producing knowledge and understanding. Post-colonialist writing recognises the knowledges found in, and produced by, the intersection of art and popular culture. Culture is a broad site of learning, and perhaps we learn best and are most open to ideas when the barriers between the discipline and the academy and the experiences of everyday life are broken down. There is a sense in which Stuart Hall is here speaking from the other side, from the space of difference. Where those who espoused modernity and its ideals saw vision and order and reason and achievement, he sees turbulence and savagery.[23] Included in Hall's essay is a quote from Salman Rushdie responding to the review of his book *The Satanic Verses*, 'A bit of this and a bit of that is how newness enters the world. It is the great possibility that mass migration gives the world'.[24] If, therefore, post-colonialist experience shares anything in common with the postmodern experience, then it must be a postmodernism which is much more than an overstylised posture adopted by those who can afford to abandon politics. Instead it is a way of marking out a new set of convergences and divergences round certain critical questions about the society in which we live.

Towards a Feminist Postmodernism

In her contribution to *Beyond Equality and Difference* Rosi Braidotti[25] rejects the defence of theoretical reason, the unity of the subject and even of equality (equal to whom, she asks?) as 'domination' Enlightenment concepts which have been part of an apparatus of regulation and subordination, hidden under the great achievements of rationality and knowledge. This marks her out immediately as a postmodern feminist. The question that has to be asked, she suggests, is that of how we think, what is it to think? What does it mean if reason and truth are unsettled from their secure places in the foundationalist discipline of philosophy? She thus opens up for debate not only the possibility of other ways of thinking, but also the question of on whose behalf do we think as critical, feminist intellectuals? What is the responsibility of the feminist intellectual? Is it not, in part, to think about thinking and thus to unveil some of the power relations caught up in the category of knowledge?

These questions, which she is asking from a feminist viewpoint, happen to coincide with the critique of western thinking by subaltern discourses. So the whole status of thinking and of thought is called into question. Let us move out of a dualistic logic, she continues: male versus female; women equal to men. 'Feminists propose that reason does not sum up the totality of, or even what is best in, the human capacity for thinking'.[26] Do we therefore learn to think differently as a 'female feminist subject'? The postmodern subject, argues Braidotti, is a subject in process organised by a will to know and desire to speak. The crisis of subjectivity posed by postmodernity 'offers many positive openings'.[27] This crisis emerged in the dying moments of modernity through Freud,[28] for example with his insistence on the non-coincidence of the subject with consciousness and then later with Foucault's account of the self as the product of discourse.[29] Much thought, she reminds us, following Freud is pre-rational, unconscious matter. Rationality itself rests on premises about thinking which are themselves non-rational. And desire 'is that which being the *a priori* condition for thinking is in excess of the thinking process itself'.[30] For Braidotti, the enunciation of a philosophical stance rests, therefore, on a non-philosophical disposition to represent the self, to inscribe the subject in language. How then do we re-think subjectivity and the body as an 'interface of will with desire',[31] that is the will to know and the desire to say?

Such an emphasis on desire inevitably runs the risk of positing desire as the source of a new essentialism. This is particularly the case when desire coincides not just with language but also with sexuality which is then taken, as Foucault has pointed out, as representing the truth of the body and of the self.[32] Or is it, as Braidotti argues, rather that in western culture the sexed body dominates over other levels of experience. It is how we are known, how we come to know. In language we are sexed and this process of being sexed is one of the key modalities of power inscribed in each of our bodies. 'Sexuality is the dominant discourse of power in the West'.[33]

It is, therefore, a point of contestation. What, might the feminist critic ask, *is* the female body, what is it for, for whom? And to follow in this vein, the feminist cultural critic might ask, is it because Madonna constructs herself exactly along this axis of *all body* that she unnerves and disrupts the axis of power which prefers to remain hidden? She pulls it all off the top shelf of the newsagent and brings it; sex, power, pornography, the body, to the surface and leaves us to respond. It could also be suggested that by placing her body on precisely those lines of classification, for example as the site of sex, as the truth of femininity, and also as the property of the female self, something which can and does give pleasure, quite autonomously from the regulative discourses within which it is more traditionally placed, that the image of Madonna is disruptive. It is too much about sexuality to exist comfortably within the commercial machine, even where that machine is already linked with excessive sexual imagery (ie pop), or where it is licensed to shock. Instead of simply rejecting the essentialism which equates woman with body, Braidotti argues that (like Madonna) we must revisit the sites of assumed essentialism and work through them. We should explore the boundaries by going back to them.

But if we no longer know what woman is, if we are all good anti-essentialists, and if we take into account the critique by black feminists of white feminism's universalism, how do we move from analysing the implications for power of the borders and boundaries, to actively re-defining the bonds through which a politics remains viable? Like all of the postmodern feminists being considered here, Braidotti puts the possibility of a communicative bond between women as the basis for politics, on the agenda. This takes the form, for feminist intellectuals, of a kind of accountability. A recognition of the relations of responsibility between the writer and her readers and, it could be added, between the teacher and her students. Feminist thinking should then attempt to represent and analyse what it is to be female. In one decisive way, this breaks down the barriers between art, fiction, culture and the academic disciplines in much the same way that Stuart Hall suggests. By far the most visible example of this force for breaking down barriers is the success and achievement of black women's writing over the last few years, not just for the community of women it brings into being as readers, but also because it *is* simultaneously: art, history, literature, sociology, politics, biography, auto-biography and also popular culture.[34] At the opposite end of the same spectrum, but 'doing' in her own theoretical work very much the same kind of thing, we could also place Gayatri Chakravorty Spivak. Coming from the high end of deconstruction, and bringing to this practice a feminist post-colonialist critique, Spivak works within the discourse of theory, but so transforms it as if to make it an entirely different kind of practice. Theory becomes a series of interrogative, interweaving, reflective poetics. For Spivak the community of women can only come after the recognition of difference between women, and after the raising of some key questions about who is talking to whom, and why, all points which she returns to in her contribution to *Feminists Theorise The Political*.[35]

This is a similar position to that described by Judith Butler who also engages with a notion of the community of women. In articulating women, from a feminist perspective, such a category is immediately broken and it is the breaking that is the important point.[36] Who is not spoken to in feminism? In addition who was the 'subject' of feminism, but is no more? How is it that feminism has opened itself out to speak to many female subjects and yet still engages with only a few? Butler sees these as crucial questions and illustrates them by referring to the old centrality of the mother as one of the primary, stable subjects of feminist discourse. But this figure of the mother is not a biologically defined and stable category. She herself shifts and changes, just as feminism does. As her children grow up and move away, she no longer defines herself primarily through that particular mode of subjectivity. So as the subjects of feminism change, feminism itself changes, particularly as it becomes the focus of criticism by black women, and, as the society within which feminism exists, also undergoes quite dramatic changes. We could also add to Butler's questions the important one of how under such conditions feminism, or what remains of it, can hope to reproduce itself among a generation of young women? What space away from feminism do young women need in order to disconnect from the historical experience of their mothers or their teachers and then find their own way towards feminism, redefining it in the process for themselves? These questions of how feminism continues and seeks to extend itself while recognising different histories, experiences and identities is therefore crucial. Can it continue, can it still call itself feminism? What must it do to be able legitimately to address women?

Judith Butler also takes issue with the slightly ridiculing tones frequently adopted to make light of postmodernism. As though in direct engagement with Gregor McLennan, she disputes the assumption that there 'must' be a foundation and a stable subject to have a politics. She sees this as authoritarian, the use of the 'must' clause. Postmodernism does not mean that we have to do away with the subject but rather that we ask after the process of its construction. The value of postmodernism therefore is that, like deconstruction, it shows clearly how arguments bury opposition. Its disorderly force is rude and impertinent in that it shows where power resides; hidden, quiet and displeased at being exposed. Demonstrating these ruses does not mean descending into unruly chaos. Rather, it allows for open debate and dispute about boundaries and disciplines and what constitutes a study, what is knowledge. 'A social theory committed to democratic contestation within a post-colonialist horizon needs to find a way to bring into question the foundations it is compelled to lay down.'[37]

Thus even minimal foundations need scrutinizing. Within feminism there is a need to speak as and for women. But no sooner is this done than it is objected to. This is the point at which things move. The category, women, then becomes 'an undesignatable field of wills'. The dispute is the ground of feminist theory. The category has to be released from the anchoring which feminism felt it needed. As Judith Butler puts it: 'What women signify has been taken for granted too long ... We have to instead break from the list of meanings and expand the possibilities of what it is to be a woman'.[38] In a similar way, sex imposes a uniformity on bodies for the purposes of reproductive sexuality. This is also an act of violence. Therefore there must be a re-defining, an invention of new categories. (We could add to this the question of whether this is already happening, with the emergence of the 'single mother' as a sign of these expanded possibilities of being female. A category which marks a changed society and a changed mode of familial organisation.)

Jane Flax completes the assault on the male modernists who defend reason by saying how comforting it is to believe that reason will triumph and bale us all out.[39] How often has it? Admittedly, it is frightening to think that without truth, pure power might prevail. Feminists are as prone to this wishful thinking that reason will win through as anybody else. But Flax asserts that this failure to face up to the limits of reason, truth and knowledge is predicated on a fear of letting go and of thinking outside the safety of inherited assumptions about thought. 'They fear what will emerge in disrupted places if they are not in feminist control. They believe innocent clean knowledge is available somewhere for our discovery and use'.[40] Flax prefers desire, fantasy and power. 'What we really want is power in the world not an innocent truth'.[41] Many feminists are fearful of losing what they have gained by embracing or being seen to embrace postmodernity. But this being made insecure is productive and it coincides with being made insecure through critiques from women of colour. At its best postmodernity invites us to 'engage in a continual process of disillusionment with the grandiose fantasies that have brought us to the brink of annihilation'.[42] Feminist postmodernism does not eliminte the subject or the self but finds it in operation as a series of bit parts in the concrete field of social relations. Politics must therefore imply subjectivities in process, interacting and debating.

This idea of, as Stuart Hall puts it, 'becoming rather than being',[43] continues the mode of argument that all of these feminist writers adopt, which is to avoid binary oppositions and to dispute the value of terms like equality, and relativism, as a discourse of absolutism which they are committed to questioning. What emerges from this work is a desire to hold onto the notion of a meaningful, feminist politics by interrogating rather than assuming the relations between who is talking to whom. In subjecting some of the big questions and concepts to critical scrutiny these feminist writers are not taking leave of their senses, but rather they are asking questions about how we learn, how we think and write. This has the effect of re-aligning the disciplines, re-arranging the furniture of intellectual life. It allows for a certain inter-disciplinary licence.

In the absence of a 'real me', what I would describe as a social self (the female, feminist subject as Braidotti labels her) nonetheless emerges, marked by a set of constraints and dispositions. This social self participates in intimacy, in communality and communication. She also uses desire and will in order to understand the process of subjection. The feminist social self, it might be suggested, is an amalgam of fragmented identities, formed in discourse and history, and called into being both by the experiences of femininity and by the existence and availability of a feminist discourse whether that comes in the form of books, education, mass media, or through friends, politics and community. This I think, is what Butler and other feminist writers discussed here mean by the communicative aspect of female experience.

Unmasking the 'Real Me'

But while little work has been done on what is left behind when the myth of the 'real me' is revealed, deconstructing the 'real me' has involved showing it to be a social and political requirement, a form of enforcement, a means of regulating legitimate ways of being, legitimate ways of understanding the self and the world. The real 'respectable' me is also the product of a certain kind of psychoanalytic violence where desire is also constrained and endlessly legitimised in culture around the tropes of heterosexuality. Not being at one with this 'real me' has produced much pain and suffering, and has required, particularly on the part of gay men and lesbians, an enormous effort to construct different kinds of subjectivity. But if the 'real me' is a mask, a fiction which transcends discourse as an essence, how then, once we have dislodged this kind of self, can we talk about women, identity, or indeed of feminism as mobilising political categories? Once again Gayatri Spivak shows how, for white western feminists, there is still an instant recourse to a language where feminism is pursued, insensitive to the limits of its effectivity and unwilling to be constantly interrogating who is the subject of its address. It is her attentiveness to the consequences of being designated a subaltern subject, as she moves with her passport through the boundaries and barriers of nation states and is inevitably questioned as to her professional status as teacher, as a person 'here' to give a paper, that makes her

ever alert to the question of power. In her contribution to
Feminists Theorise the Political Spivak asks 'What is it to write
for you? What is it to teach? What is it to learn? What is it
to assume that one already knows the meaning of the
words "something is taught by me and something is
learned by others"?'[44]

The value of the work of these feminist writers lies in
their interrogation of the ground rules, the boundaries
and the barriers which define feminist theory and politics
and which simultaneously have to be broken, have to be
trespassed. In this postmodern field what we find is not,
however, a scene of catastrophe, the cost of questioning
reason, the punishment for risking rationality. Instead,
the riposte to white feminists that they were not speaking
and could not speak on behalf of 'all women', has
prompted a reassessment of the feminist self and who she
is, and was, speaking to and about. At the same time this
particular fragmentation of the feminist subject is
confirmed through the global and postmodern critique of
the European Enlightenment. It is not so much a question
of what is left behind, what fragments of the disassembled
self can be picked up and put together again, but rather
how might the continual process of putting oneself
together be transformed to produce the empowerment of
subordinate groups and social categories. This might
mean living with fragmentation, with the reality of
inventing the self rather than endlessly searching for the
self. But abandoning the 'real me' need not mean
resignation, despair, or simply being reconciled with the
loss of wholeness.

Living along the fault lines of the postmodern condition
might also give us some reasons to feel cheerful. We might
modestly be aware of our limited successes, in putting
feminism (with all the limits that word implies) into the
webs of popular discourse about gender and sexuality.
The appearance of new feminist discourses, not just in the
academy but also in women's magazines, for example, and
in some other spaces within the commercial mass media,
tells us that feminism now has some control over
constructions of the feminine, as Charlotte Brunsdon has

recently suggested.[45] But this fact should not be viewed as an unproblematic success. There remains the question of what sort of feminism is found in these spaces and to whom is it speaking?

This kind of question challenges, by necessity, the process of reproducing feminism. Just as a feminist 'real me' was perhaps a necessary fiction in the early 1970s, so also was it necessary then to believe in the reproduction of feminism as part of the process of politicisation. That such an attempt can backfire is not just about 'backlash' but more productively about other, younger women and black women disputing their being represented by older, white, feminists, just as much as they might take issue with their being represented in advertising, or in popular culture or in the tabloid press. Thus, once again, politics occurs in the act of breaking away from the claim to be represented, in that new or emergent or otherwise excluded identities emerge from this discourse of rejection and repudiation. 'This is not us' they are saying. And in saying so there is also a question of who indeed 'they' are.

While this might create a crisis for the (white) feminist movement and for the feminist intellectuals who came into being in the 1970s, such a crisis is no bad thing. Indeed, it is entirely healthy. In the process of being challenged, older feminist identities are also revised. And what remains is remembered, perhaps even in a *Passion of Remembrance*.[46]

The passage of feminism into the 1990s should not be seen, in conclusion, as a process of political dismemberment, leaving behind a sadly dispersed band of individuals dotted about the globe but found mostly in the universities of the western world and defining themselves as 'feminist writers' or 'feminist intellectuals'. Nor should it be understood, after postmodernism, as a politics of difference based simply on pluralism, on everyone going their own way. In short, the strength of feminism lies in its ability to create discourse, to dispute, to negotiate the boundaries and the barriers, and also to take issue with the various feminisms which have sprung into being. The value of the contributions to new feminist theory reviewed

here lies, first in their rejection that there could be or
should be 'one voice', second in their willingness to take
risks by exploring the relatively unnavigated political
continent which lies 'beyond equality and difference',
third in their engagement with the politics of difference as
characterised not by pluralism but by lines of connection
and of disconnection, and fourth by their abandonment of
the search for the 'real me' in favour, to use Judith Butler's
words again,' of expanding the possibilities of what it
means to be a woman.'[47]

Notes

[1] There is an enormous body of work which comes into this category. In
a sense, in the politics of intellectual work in Britain in the 1990s, it is
this approach which has become dominant. See for example P. Wollen,
Raiding the Ice Box Verso, London 1993. For the purposes of this article
I am concentrating on G. McLennan's 'The Enlightenment Project
Revisited' in S. Hall, D. Held and D. McGrew (eds), *Modernity and Its
Futures* Polity Press, Cambridge 1992.

[2] The two names who attract the greatest degree of criticism are of
course the French writers and philosophers J. Baudrillard and J.F.
Lyotard.

[3] J. Butler, 'Contingent Foundations: Feminism and the Question of
"Postmodernism" in *Feminists Theorise The Political* (eds) J. Butler and
J.W. Scott, Routledge London; New York 1992.

[4] See for example P. Gilroy, *The Black Atlantic* Verso, London 1993, and
also S. Hall, 'The Question of Cultural Identity' in S. Hall D. Held and
D. McGrew (eds), *Modernity and Its Futures* Polity Press, London 1992.

[5] J.F. Lyotard, *The Postmodern Condition*, Manchester University Press,
Manchester 1984.

[6] J. Butler *op. cit.*

[7] G. McLennan, 'Sociology After Postmodernism' *Inaugural Address*
Faculty of Social Sciences Occasional Papers, Massey University, New
Zealand 1992.

[8] Two examples of this can be seen in R. Boyne and A. Rattansi (eds)
Postmodernism and Society Macmillan 1990 and also in the new feminist
collection edited by M. Barrett and A. Phillips *Destabilising Theory* Polity
Press, Cambridge 1993.

[9] S. Hall and M. Jacques (eds), *New Times: The Changing Face of Politics in
the 1990s*, Lawrence and Wishart, London 1989.

[10] D. Riley, *'Am I That Name?'* Macmillan, London 1988.

[11] E. Laclau, *New Reflections On The Revolution Of Our Times*, Verso,
London 1991.

[12] G. Chakravorty Spivak allows for the 'strategic use of essentialism' in

A. McRobbie, 'Strategies of Vigilance: An Interview With Gayatri Chakravorty Spivak' in *Block* No 10, 1985.
[13] S. Hall in 'The Question of Cultural Identity' *op. cit.*
[14] C. Steedman, *Landscape For A Good Woman*, Virago, London 1985.
[15] See, for example, T.T. Min-Ha, *Woman, Native Other* Indiana University Press, Bloomington and Indianapolis 1989. Also H. Bhabha, *Narrating Nations*, Routledge, London 1991 and G. Chakravorty Spivak, *In Other Worlds: Essays in Cultural Politics* Routledge, London 1988.
[16] G. McLennan, 'The Enlightenment Project Revisited' *op. cit.* and S. Hall, 'The Question of Cultural Identity' in the same volume.
[17] L. Nicholson (ed), *Feminism and Postmodernism* Routledge, London 1990.
[18] R. Bowlby, *Still Crazy After All These Years* Routledge, London 1992. J. Wolff, *Feminine Sentences* Routledge, London 1990. M. Nava, *Changing Cultures: Feminism, Youth and Consumerism*, Sage, London 1992.
[19] J. Habermas, 'Modernity; an incomplete project' in H. Foster (ed), *Postmodern Culture* Pluto Press, London 1985.
[20] C. Mouffe 'Feminist Citizenship and Radical Democratic Politics' in G. Bock and S. James (eds), *Beyond Equality and Difference; Citizenship, Feminist Politics and Female Subjectivity*, Routledge, London 1992.
[21] G. McLennan, 'Sociology After Postmodernism' as above.
[22] F. Jameson *Postmodernism Or The Cultural Logic of Capital*, Verson, London 1991.
[23] S. Hall, 'The West and The Rest' in S. Hall and B. Gieben (eds), *Formations of Modernity*, Polity Press, London 1992.
[24] S. Rushdie quoted in S. Hall, 'The Question of Cultural Identity' *op cit.*
[25] R. Braidotti, 'On The Female Feminist Subject or From She-Self to She-Other' in *Beyond Equality and Difference: Citizenship, Feminist Politics and Female Subjectivity* as above.
[26] R. Braidotti *ibid.*
[27] R. Braidotti *ibid.*
[28] S. Freud, *The Interpretation of Dreams* Penguin, Harmondsworth 1991.
[29] M. Foucault, *The History of Sexuality*, Vol 1, Penguin, Harmondsworth 1984.
[30] R. Braidotti as above.
[31] R. Braidotti *op cit.*
[32] M. Foucault *op cit.*
[33] R. Braidotti *op cit.*
[34] See for example Toni Morrison, *Beloved* Picador, London 1988 and Alice Walker, *The Colour Purple* Women's Press, London 1983.
[35] G. Chakravorty Spivak, 'French Feminism Revisited: Ethics and Politics' in J. Butler and J.V. Scott (eds), *Feminists Theorise The Political, op. cit.*
[36] J. Butler, 'Contingent Foundations: Feminism and the Question of 'Postmodernism' in J. Butler and J.V. Scott (eds), *Feminists Theorise The Political op. cit..*
[37] J. Butler *ibid.*

[38] J. Butler *ibid*.

[39] J. Flax, 'Beyond Equality: Gender Justice and Difference' in G. Bock and S. James (eds), *Beyond Equality and Difference op. cit.*

[40] J. Flax, 'The End of Innocence' in J. Butler and J.V. Scott (eds), *Feminists Theorise The Political op. cit.*

[41] J. Flax, 'The End of Innocence' *ibid*.

[42] J. Flax, 'The End of Innocence' *ibid*.

[43] S. Hall, 'The Question of Cultural Identity' *op cit*.

[44] G. Chakravorty Spivak, 'French Feminism Revisited; Ethics and Politics' *op cit*.

[45] C. Brunsdon, 'Pedagogies of the Feminine: Feminist Teaching & Womens Genres' in *Screen* vol 32, no 4, 1991.

[46] *Passion of Remembrance* is the title of a film directed by Isaac Julien and Maureen Blackwood for Sankofa Films.

[47] J. Butler, *op cit*.

Postmodernism: The Highest Stage of Cultural Imperialism?

DAVID MORLEY

'Okay, you Limey has-been, I'm gonna give it to you country-simple. You have been taken over, like a banana republic. Your royal family is nothing but a holograph projected by the CIA.' (William Burroughs)[1]

'Good evening, fine people. Welcome to humble show. We were just bought by Sony.' (Johnny Carson)[2]

'Hollywood is a place you can't geographically define. We don't know where it is.' (John Wayne)[3]

It has become a commonplace to note that we live in a condition described as 'postmodernity'. One of the distinctive characteristics of this period, it is often argued, is that we live in a period of 'space-time compression', in which we move towards an increasing sense of global interconnectedness and simultaneity of experience. More specifically, under the influence of Foucault's[4] remarks to the effect that, if the great obsession of the nineteenth century was history the present epoch will perhaps be obsessed by, above all, space. There has been, in the recent period, a flowering of work in the area of what is increasingly described as 'postmodern geography'. In this work, the dimension of space and spatial analysis, has begun to get the kind of attention which it deserves. However, as soon as we begin to proceed in this way, a whole new set of difficulties emerge. In the first place, to speak of postmodernity is to speak of a period. The

133

difficulty is that events have not only a temporal but also a spatial form. In speaking of a period of postmodernity, if we are not very careful, the temporal marker overrides the spatial one. That is to say, quite apart from the notorious difficulties in giving a temporal delimitation to the period of postmodernity, we must also supply it with a spatial delimitation, if we are not to presuppose that everyone, everywhere, simultaneously lives in this era of postmodernity. We might ask: Where is postmodernity? As soon as we insert the qualification, we raise the possibility that postmodernity may be a suitable periodisation for contemporary experiences in western industrial societies, but not necessarily a suitable characterisation for experience elsewhere on the globe. While the inhabitants of Los Angeles may perhaps experience postmodernity, it would be foolish to presume that the inhabitants of rural areas of India or Uganda necessarily also experience the same era in anything like the same way.

The difficulties here are manifold. Postmodernity presumes a temporal sequence in which postmodernity supersedes 'modernity'. However, it is not at all clear that modernity itself is simply a temporal concept. It could well be argued that 'modernity' is as much a geographical as a temporal concept. Modernity is usually equated, somewhat unproblematically, with the history of the societies of the industrial West. The correlative of that, of course, is that the societies of the Orient are equally equated with the realm of tradition and of the past. As Kevin Robins and I have argued elsewhere,[5] the West is not, in any simple sense, a geographical category, rather it is a name always associating itself with those regions that appear politically or economically superior to other regions. Onto the geography of East and West is directly mapped the distinction between the pre-modern and the modern. The category 'West' has always signified the positional superiority of Europe, and later of the United States, in relation to the rest of the world.

Modernisation has long been equated with Americanisation. Contemporaneously, in the writings of Fukuyama[6] *et al*, we see a rerun of the arguments of the modernising sociologists of the 1960s, for whom the modernisation of the 'underdeveloped' world was held to depend on the spreading of 'modern' attitudes, which would release the energies of the poor from the barriers of tradition.[7] As we know (and as the quotation from Johnny Carson above dramatically illustrates) things have changed. In the contemporary period, the hegemony of America in the world system is in question. Specifically, the rise of Japanese economic power and, again most dramatically, Japanese investment in Hollywood, the symbolic home of the American dream, is seen to threaten America's position. Indeed, Japan's rise to world power status raises a fundamentally problematic question for the West. If the West has always been modern and the East, by definition, traditional or pre-modern, the question arises now (at the point at which Japan 'overtakes' America,) of whether we are entering a period in which the world may need to be read from right to left, rather than from left to right – a period in which They (the peoples of the presumed backward East) have become more modern (or indeed postmodern perhaps) than Us (the peoples of the supposedly advanced West).

As Doreen Massey[8] has noted, contemporary writing on the question of postmodernity makes much of the fact that this period involves some supposedly new sense of dislocation. The problem which Massey raises is the sense in which this perception is, in fact, very much a First World take on things. As she notes, the assumption which runs through much of the literature, is that this is quite a new and remarkable situation. Her basic point is that, for the inhabitants of all the countries around the world colonised by the West, the experience of immediate destabilising contact with other alien cultures has a very long historical resonance. What is new is simply that this experience of dislocation is now returned, through patterns of immigration from the peripheries to the metropolis. Ulf Hannerz puts it another way when he remarks that 'it may well be that the First World has been present in the consciousness of many Third World people a great deal longer than the Third World has been on the minds of most First World people'.[9] In a similar sense, Anthony King remarks that

> the culture, society, and space of early twentieth century Calcutta or Singapore prefigured the future in a much more accurate way than did that of London or New York. 'Modernity' was not born in Paris but rather in Rio. With this interpretation, Euro-American paradigms of so-called 'postmodernism' have neither much meaning nor salience outside the narrow geographical confines of Euro-America where they developed.[10]

For all these reasons, as Massey notes, to characterise 'time-space compression' and the consequent sense of dislocation as a problematically new and dramatic development, is very much a western colonialist view, insofar as this sense of dislocation, as Massey puts it, 'must have been felt for centuries, though from a very different point of view, by colonised peoples all over the world, as they watched the importation, maybe even used, the products of the ... European [and later American] colonisation ...[11]

There are also a further set of questions which we must address, which concern the tendency of theories of postmodernity to fall into a kind of formalist, post-structuralist rhetoric, which over generalises its account of 'the experience of postmodernity' so as to decontextualise and flatten out all the significant differences between the experiences of people in different situations, who are members of different social and cultural groups, with access to different forms and quantities of economic and cultural capital. The point is simply that 'we' are not all nomadic, fragmented subjectivities living in the same postmodern universe. For some categories of people (differentiated by gender, race, and ethnicity as much as by class) the new technologies of symbolic and physical communications and transport offer significant opportunities for interconnectedness. For those people, there may well be a new sense of postmodern opportunities. However, at the same time, for other categories of people, horizons may simultaneously be narrowing. Many writers have referred to the contemporary dynamic of the simultaneous globalisation and localisation. However for some people the globalising aspect of that dynamic is the dominant one, while for others it is very much the localising aspect which is increasingly operative, as their life-chances are gradually reduced, and they increasingly remain stuck in the micro-territories in which they were born. To give but one example, the film *Boyz n' the Hood*[12] dramatises the sense in which, for many of the most deprived Black and Latino Americans, locality is in fact destiny, where the horizon, far from being global, extends only as far as the boundary of 'the hood'.

All of that is to suggest that we must be very cautious when applying any abstracted notion of postmodernity, and must resist the temptation to generalise our theories in such a way as to ignore the continuing significant differences in the experience of this era, by people in different social and geographical locations. However, there remains the fundamental claim that there is something significantly new about the period. While not wanting to deny such significant changes as have occurred, and are continuing to occur, it would seem that we should be cautious in accepting too readily any claims that our contemporary experience is so significantly new and different from all that has gone before. Some of the claims that have been made for the distinctiveness of postmodernity are not, in fact, so very new. I refer, in particular, to the claims that the era of postmodernity is distinctively characterised by an increasing tendency to the 'mediation' and global interconnectedness of social experience. The first claim, concerning 'mediation' is largely associated with the work of Jean Baudrillard.[13] However, it can readily be argued that Baudrillard's work depends on, and draws on, in an unacknowledged way, a rather old tradition in American social psychology. As long ago as the mid-1950s, the American social psychologists Horton and Wohl[14] were arguing that our social experience is increasingly subsumed, and indeed supplanted, by forms of para-social relationships which media viewers develop with the characters they watch on the screen. Indeed, it is

Horton and Wohl, not Baudrillard, who originate the
concept of the 'simulacrum' and its key place within the
field of contemporary social relations. The second claim,
that postmodernity is characterised by an increasing sense
of global interconnectedness, can equally be seen to have
quite long historical roots. Thirty years ago Marshall
McLuhan was already claiming that the effects of modern
communication's technologies were such as to lead to a
position in which we all effectively live in a 'global village'.[15]

The issue on which I wish to focus concerns the extent to
which the global village is, in fact (and despite some of the
recent developments, to which I will return below), an
American village. Contemporary commentators such as
Fukuyama[16] suggest that the contemporary world, the
post-Cold War world, is not simply the postmodern world
but also represents the 'end of history'. The first problem is,
of course, that all societies tend to believe that history is
simply that which has led up to and culminated in their own
existence. My contention will be that, in fact, a historical
approach to the questions at stake here is our best guide to
understanding the position in which we find ourselves.

The Media are American

One of the fundamental facts of our postmodern era, as
Jeremy Tunstall noted some time ago, is that, of course,
the media are American.[17] Someone, somewhere, is
watching a Hollywood film at every minute of the day and
night. This contemporary dominance has long historical
roots. In the 1920s, as President of Trade, Herbert
Hoover was quick to notice the potential of the American
motion picture industry as a form of export-led
advertising for American consumer products and the
American way of life. To that extent, the American
government was involved, from a very early period, in
encouraging the export of American movies, and the
American movie subsequently became, according to the
claims of the Motion Picture Association of America 'the
most desired commodity in the world'.[18]

In his book *The American Century* (1941) Henry Luce,

one time editor of the American magazine *Life*, argued that 'we must accept wholeheartedly our duty and our opportunity, as the most powerful and vital nation in the world, to exert upon the world the full impact of our influence, for such purposes as we see fit and by such means as we see fit ... it now becomes our time to be the powerhouse from which ideas spread throughout the world'.[19] Herbert Schiller claims that Luce, as the controller of one of the most powerful communication complexes in the United States (the Time, Life, Fortune magazine conglomerate) understood earlier than many people, that 'the fusion of economic strength and information control, image making and public opinion formation was the new quintessence of power, international and domestic'.[20] That is to say that Luce understood that the very availability of a developed international communication system, which the USA had at the close of World War Two, was a unique instrument of power, which had simply not been available to would-be expansionist states in previous eras. American governmental strategy in this connection developed fast. The strategy was founded on a combination of economic and communications power, in the furtherance of what was understood as the project of 'the American century'.

American strategy depended on the defence and expansion of 'freedom' – crucially freedom of trade and freedom of speech. The problem of course is that, in a free or unregulated exchange between the strong and the weak, the strong tend to do better and get stronger. Thus, in Schiller's view, freedom of speech has meant the opportunity for the American mass media to disseminate their message throughout the world arena. As he puts it, if free trade is the mechanism by which a powerful economy penetrates and dominates a weaker one, then the free flow of information is the channel through which the life-styles and values of America have been imposed on poor and vulnerable societies. Schiller demonstrates, quite simply, that these were matters of conscious American policy, at key points in the post-war World War Two period. Thus, he quotes from the congressional committee, set up in

1967, to consider 'modern communications and foreign policy'. The committee produced a paper called 'Winning the Cold War: The American Ideological Offensive' which argues that 'to a significant degree, what America does will shape the emerging international communications system ... to a very large degree, other countries will imitate our experience and will attach themselves to the institutions and systems we create ... given our information technology and information resources, the USA clearly could be the hub of the world communications systems.'[21] This was also, straightforwardly, a matter of military concern. America had taken over the role of 'world policeman', and the military desperately needed effective international communications to coordinate their forces – out of which conjuncture emerged the very strong links which Schiller points to (and which still persist) between the American military and the big American communication companies. However, beyond this concern with their own international communications needs (to coordinate military forces abroad), the same committee also saw, very clearly, the potential use of international communications as a means of influencing foreign populations.

> Certain foreign policy objectives can be best pursued by dealing directly with the people of foreign countries, rather than their governments. Through the use of modern instruments and technologies of communications, it is possible today to reach large and influential sections of national populations – to inform them, to influence their attitudes ... to motivate them to particular courses of actions. These groups, in turn, are capable of exerting, noticeable, even decisive, pressure on their governments. [22]

The main issue here is the ability to bypass the control of national governments. At this point, the committee recognised that the very status of communications had changed, so that telecommunications had progressed from being an essential support of international activities to being itself a direct instrument of foreign policy.

Schiller argues that the contemporary situation exhibits two particular features of significance. In the first place, he argues we see a significant move towards a situation in which information itself becomes a commodity for sale, and towards a position in which the communications and information industries serve as the dynamo of contemporary economic development. In this context, communication ceases to be a merely secondary adjunct, facilitating business, and communications itself becomes big business. The second development to which Schiller calls attention is the extent to which this new 'heartland' of communication and information technology is itself increasingly controlled by a very small number of powerful transnational corporations, which may be based (as indeed a large number of them are) in the USA, but which operate simultaneously in many different countries around the world, on a global scale. In Schiller's view, the problem here is that the activities of these transnational corporations depend precisely on the overcoming of national boundaries and the opening up of the 'free flow' of information, across a world market. The concerns of national governments, to regulate communications in their own countries, therefore presents an obstacle to the transnational corporations, and these transnational corporations are increasingly concerned (and increasingly able) to override national government policies, to the extent perhaps of posing a threat to the very sovereignty of individual nations.

There are many dimensions to a question of media or cultural imperialism. As far as the world pattern of international television flow is concerned, the USA is indisputably the world's number one television exporter. The USA continues to export a far greater quantity of television programmes to the rest of the world than all the rest of the world in combination manages to do, while at the same time America imports only one or two percent of its own television broadcast output. Moreover, this pattern of American dominance is even more prevalent in important areas of television programming such as prime-time fictional programming and news programming. To take the second of these examples, to this day, 'world news' is largely supplied by a very small number of press and news agencies, all of which are Anglo-American.[23] These agencies clearly shape the international political agenda by the way in which they define news values. To that extent, it is in fact difficult to exaggerate either the direct presence or the indirect influence of Anglo-American materials and styles on television news throughout the world. However, it is not simply a question of the export of American programmes, as such. The influence of the American media extends far beyond that. In particular, its influence can be seen in the extent to which other countries' media, throughout the world, have either bought franchises from or literally copied American formats. There are, for example, national versions of the television programme *Blind Date* in many different countries of the world. It is not simply that America exports a lot of television programmes – beyond that, America has written the 'grammar' of international television – the formats of television developed in America have literally set the frame for the production of television in most other countries.

But Does the Subaltern Listen?

In recent years, the cultural imperialism (or media imperialism) thesis has in fact come under some criticism, and a number of revisions of the basic thesis have been advanced. These criticisms are various, but among them there is the point that the media imperialism thesis was originally developed by writers such as Schiller *et al* at the high point of American cultural hegemony, a point of predominance from which America has most certainly declined in the recent period. In the same sense the thesis tends to focus exclusively on the pattern of American television exports, without paying sufficient attention to non-American forms of cultural imperialism involving, for instance, the continuing export of cultural materials by British and French agencies to ex-colonies in Africa, or in another context, the strength of Mexico as a television exporter to other Latin American countries, or the position of Brazil and its export of Telenoveles back to the

Catholic countries of southern Europe. All of these factors must of course be taken into account in any adequate version of the thesis of media imperialism.[24]

Most fundamentally, critics of the cultural imperialism thesis argue that the thesis presumes a hypodermic model of media effects. That is to say that it assumes that the affects of viewing American televisual material on audiences across the world can be automatically predicted. The issue here is that such empirical work as has been done in this field demonstrates, in fact, not so much the direct effects of America media material as the capacity of audiences in different situations to re-interpret the American-produced material which they view in a way which is influenced by their local circumstances. Armand Mattelart[25] gives the example of the frequency of American-produced series featuring Aryan heroes being subject to a process of 'reverse identification', when viewed by Third World populations, who will more often identify with the 'bad guys' in the story. In their work on international decodings of *Dallas*, Elihu Katz and Tamar Liebes[26] demonstrate the significant variations in the way in which people with different cultural backgrounds interpret the same series, *Dallas*, in quite different ways. Most dramatically, perhaps, in his work on Australian aboriginal interpretations of *Dallas*, Eric Michaels supplies fascinating accounts of the ways in which the Warlpiri aboriginals with whom he was working, re-interpret Hollywood narratives, in ways never imagined by their producers, because, in order to make sense of them, the Warlpiri necessarily read into the text their own cultural understandings of kinship and morality – understandings of a quite different kind than those of the culture in which *Dallas* was originally produced.[27] That should not suggest to us that cultural power does not exist, or that the American dominated international media have no effect whatsoever – rather it should alert us to the complexity of the modes in which cultural power is both exercised and resisted.

If the position of America and American hegemony is not as secure as it once was, and if we must now pay attention to the increasing strength of new powers – especially around the Pacific ring – within the context of global geopolitics, nonetheless it will not do to treat the question abstractly, and to speak only of some general question of 'globalisation'. The issue remains who controls the flows of information and communication, and who controls the networks which constitute the grid of globalisation. In the crude version of the cultural imperialism thesis, the worldwide dominance of the American media is seen as evidence of the threat posed by American commercial culture to all authentic indigenous national cultures and identities.

Identities: America, Europe and Little England

Identity is, of course, one of the obsessions of the period in which we live. We see, all around us, resurgent forms of nationalism and racism. Identity, it seems, is increasingly defined by a process of cultural, if not ethnic, 'cleansing'. We can only be defined by reference to 'Them', those who are not us, those who are excluded by the boundary which we draw around ourselves. We see this at many levels. If we address, for a moment, the problem of European identity, we see that Europe has long defined itself against America. The history of anti-Americanism has dominated discussions of European identity throughout the last century. Nowadays, of course, it is not only the Americans who are seen as the threat to European identity. The fear, again and again, is of being overwhelmed by a foreign, materialist, vulgar culture, washing over and washing away authentic, aesthetically sophisticated, European culture. The very project of the single market in Europe in large part emerged as the brainchild of Jean-Jaques Servan Schreiber's analysis of the 'American Challenge'.[28] Schreiber's point was that unless Europe developed its industries, and specifically the crucial industries of the twenty-first century – the communication and information industries – on a European-wide scale, it would prove impossible to compete in the international market with firms based on the economies of scale available in the

American and Pacific-Asian markets. Nowadays, the European Commission increasingly takes the view that culture is indeed central to the success of the single market, not least because the continuing pertinence of national cultural differences within Europe vitiates the possibility of the development of pan-European cultural and communications industries.

However one of the problems with this 'defensive' model of resistance to foreign cultural imperialism concerns the fact that the 'foreign' does not necessarily always play a regressive cultural role. It can be argued that 'foreign' materials often play a subversive (and potentially progressive) role, by undermining the certainties of established national or local cultural hierarchies. The point can be explicated perhaps by reference to the history of the debates about the Americanisation of British culture. A number of the key cultural institutions of British life, such as the British Broadcasting Corporation and the Arts Council, were explicitly set up to defend the great English cultural tradition from the seemingly unstoppable flow of American popular culture. In this paradigm, the great Satan of American popular culture is counterposed to all those values and traditions by which 'we' have understood and identified ourselves, as cultured and civilised. The guiding slogan here was perhaps expressed most pithily by Lord Keynes, the Chairman of the Arts Council, in 1945, when he issued the rallying cry 'death to Hollywood'.[29] Of course, if these institutions were to defend British culture, there remained the question of how British culture was to be defined. British culture was, in fact, effectively defined by these institutions as English culture, and even more specifically, as the white English culture of the upper-classes of the home counties. As Geoff Mulgan and Ken Worpole put it 'the BBC ... by its refusal to engage with anything other than the cultural tradition of the southern English upper-class, left a vast, vacant, cultural space, which the early entrepreneurs of ITBV were only too happy to fill.'[30] Of course, what they filled it with was, in some large part, either American imported programmes or British-made programmes modelled on American formats. The problem, from the point of view of the defenders of the great British tradition, was that the working-class audience seemed in fact to find these American-style products *less* 'foreign' to them than they did the established cultural forms of the British tradition, which their betters were busy defending.

Elsewhere, in his investigation of literary tastes among the British working class Ken Worpole has explored the pleasures of working class British men discovering American detective fiction writing in the 1930s. Thus Warpole quotes an ex-docker explaining why, to him, this American literature had a greater appeal than the writers of the English literary tradition: 'I read the English writers, H.G. Wells, Arnold Bennett ... but they weren't my kind of people ... you always have the edge of class there ... what intrigued me about the American writers was that they were talking the way we talked.'[31] What these British working-class readers seemed to find was that the portrayal of the modern city, for instance, and of urban working-class life, offered by American crime fiction, was *less* foreign to them than the portrayal of English life offered by the English writers of the period. The question is one of *what* is, experientially 'foreign' to *whom*. 'Foreignness' is not necessarily a matter of nationality – it can be as much a matter of class or gender or race.

There is, of course, in British cultural analysis, a long tradition of work (originating both from the right and from the left) which bemoans the homogenising impact of American culture on British life. Thus, in *The Uses of Literacy* Richard Hoggart deplored the extent to which British working-class life was being destroyed by the 'hollow brightness', the 'shiny barbarism', and 'spiritual decay' of imported American culture, which he saw as leading to an aesthetic breakdown, in which traditional values were being undermined and replaced by a 'candyfloss world' of 'easy thrills and cheap fiction' which were in his view 'unbending the springs of action' of the British working-class.[32] But the problem with Hoggart's analysis, is that these 'vulgar' American products, streamlined, plastic, and glamorous, appealed to a

substantial sector of the British working class as constituting a space in which oppositional meanings (in relation
to dominant traditions of British culture), could be
negotiated and expressed, in opposition precisely to the
paternalism of the upholders of 'traditional British values'.
By breaking away from traditional, class-based notions of
'good taste' these American cultural products made
genuine connections with the actual tastes and desires of
large numbers of British working class people. For them,
these cultural products represented positive symbols of a
massive improvement in the material quality of their lives,
and for them 'America' was a positive symbol, functioning
by opposition to what they perceived as the dead hand of
traditional English culture, as defined by the cultural elite.

As Bigsby put it,[33] some time ago, in a world where the
modern experience has often been equated with that of an
'imaginary America'[34] 'opposition to popular culture and
complaints about Americanisation have often amounted to
little more than laments over a changing world … where
'Americanisation' frequently means little more than the
incidence of change, and change, especially in new
cultural forms, provokes established patterns of negative
reactions. The new is characterised as brash, crude,
unsubtle, and mindless and destructive of taste and
tradition. 'America' is thus mobilised as the paradigm of
the traditionless; the land of the material, counterposed to
the cultural.'[35] British identity has long been defined in
opposition not only to America but also to modernity
itself. As Chambers remarks, it seems that, for many
traditionalist cultural commentators, the very syntax of
modern urban life is somehow antithetical to a British
culture.[36] As J.B. Priestley put it 'the modern world is alien
to the English temperament.'[37] In that slide, from the
'British' to the 'English', we also see a process in which not
only is Britain equated with England, but the actuality of
Britain as a modern industrial country is denied, and the
image of English identity is, again and again, a *rural* image,
of a cottage in the imaginary landscape of 'Constable
country'. 'Englishness' always seems to be located in the
countryside, within the stable logic of tradition and

community; within the terms of an anti-industrial
pastoralism, in which the natural and the national are very
deeply entwined.

The contemporary resonance of all of this lies in the
significance of Thatcherism's project of mobilising a
certain image of the English past as the keystone for the
construction of a defensive identity for 'Little England' in
the contemporary world. This is a complex process, which
operates simultaneously at many levels, from the boom in
the heritage industry in Britain and the rapid growth in
the membership of the National Trust, to the dominance
of British television's export trade by costume dramas set
in the glorious past, to the valiant struggle to 'save' various
archeological remnants of the past from the ravages of
modernisation. The point, as Raphael Samuels argues it, is
that what we have here is a process in which a romantically
sanitised version of the English past is being visibly
recreated, in a form of born-again cultural nationalism,
operating across a number of fields.[38] It is not only a
question of a boom in the conservation and heritage
movements and the re-evaluation of English landscape
painting; not only the educational reforms aiming to
return us to traditional standards. It is also registered in
the return to fashionably 'old-fashioned' styles, in the
realm of design, in the rise of a reinvented classicism in
architecture, and in the use of 'traditional materials' in
building construction and in furnishing – as Habitat
replaces its Scandinavian pine with 'traditional English
kitchen furniture' and Covent Garden's shopping piazza is
gradually transformed into a (Dickensian) walk down
England's memory lanes, past shops offering 'traditional
fare' in 'traditional styles'. The point, as Samuels argues, is
that what we have here is a reactionary defence of national
tradition, a kind of upper-class revenge for the American
modernisations of the 1950s and the European modernisations of the 1960s.[39] What we also have, as Paul Gilroy
argues, is a morbid celebration of some of the most
reactionary and regressive forms of white Englishness.[40]

If I have stressed the reactionary and regressive aspects
of these defensive forms of contemporary identity

building, this is not to say that the questions that they address do not have a profound cultural resonance. The very appeal of these backward-looking, traditionalist rhetorics is precisely that they resonate, in their stress on the sanctity of the individual, the community, the place, and the past with that vast constituency of people who feel themselves to be, in Prince Charles' words, 'ignored or pushed aside' by the forces of modernity. If our contemporary period is marked by these forms of nostalgia and by the urgency of the desire for roots, for a sense of home, of *heimat*, of belonging, this clearly is because many people experience the pressures, and uncertainty of this postmodern period as threatening and disturbing.[41] In this confusion, to turn to the certainties of past tradition is a perfectly understandable response. The difficulty concerns the question of whether, in fact, it can ever be an adequate response.

The Geography of Postmodernity

The work of postmodern geographers, such as Edward Soja[42] or Joshua Meyrowitz,[43] alerts us to the sense in which contemporary developments in electronic forms of communication and transport have necessarily, and profoundly, transformed our understanding of place. At its simplest, these writers suggest that we now live within the terms of a postmodern geography, which is a geography of image spaces and communication networks as much, as if not more than, a geography of physical boundaries. Here, perhaps, is the rational kernel in the postmodern argument about 'time-space compression'. At its simplest, the key point, as argued by Meyrowitz, is that what has happened is that the relationship between community and place has been transformed by these developments. As he notes, on the one hand, we are simply no longer 'in' places to the same extent, insofar as communication and contact with others is no longer necessarily premised on physical contiguity. To that extent, to live next to others is not necessarily to be part of any effective community with them. Conversely, given the ways in which many people use the telephone to stay in regular contact with family members or friends in far distant places, their physical distance does not preclude their continuing, effective participation in some forms of community. A growing number of writers, among them Marie Gillespie[44] and Eliut Flores,[45] have begun to research the specific ways in which migrant communities utilise new communications technologies, such as video-recorders and video-conferencing facilities, to recreate and sustain their own senses of identity and community, across the geographical spaces of their dispersion and migration. This work, on the role of communication technologies in the creation and sustenance of diasporic identities, is of profound significance.

Doreen Massey has argued that places themselves should no longer be seen as internally homogeneous, bounded areas, but as 'spaces of interaction' in which local identities are constructed out of resources (both material and symbolic) which may not be at all local in their origin, but are nonetheless 'authentic' for all that.[46] In a similar sense the anthropologist Danny Miller has argued that it is unproductive to think about the question of cultural imperialism as a process in which a set of external or corrupting forces impinge on the pure sphere of the local, which must then be protected from their ravages. Rather, what he suggests is that we must understand the ways in which people in particular places make their identities out of things (including American television programmes) that have come from somewhere else, but which are then, in Miller's phrase, subjected to a process of 'indige-nisation', so that the products ingested from the external world are, in the process of their local 'digestion', transformed, so as to function as cultural resources, the effects of which, he says, should be assessed in terms of local consequences, not local origins.[47]

The conventional model of cultural imperialism presumes the existence of a pure, internally homo-geneous, authentic, indigenous culture, which then becomes subverted or corrupted by foreign influence. The reality, however, is that every culture has ingested foreign elements from exogenous sources with the various elements gradually becoming 'naturalised' within it. The notion that there are geographical spaces with indigenous, radically different inhabitants who can be defined on the basis of some religion, culture or racial essence, proper to that geographical space is a highly debatable idea.[48] As many authors have noted (for example Appadurai Bhabha, Hall) cultural hybridity is increasingly the normal state of affairs.[49] In an anthropological context, James Clifford takes up the same issue, noting that villages inhabited by natives and conceived of as bounded sites of residence, which then stand as metonyms for a whole culture, have long been the focus of anthropological fieldwork.[50] Against this traditional model, Clifford argues that cultures are no longer 'in' places in any simple sense, that the focus on rooted, authentic or native culture and experience fails to address the wider world of cultural import-export relations in which these processes are always already enmeshed.[51] Clifford supports Appadurai's contention that 'natives, people confined to and by the places to which they belong, groups unsullied by contact with the larger world, have probably never existed'.[52] Rather, Clifford suggests, we should work, not only with a model of 'ex-centric' natives, conceived in their multiple external connections, but with a notion of places as sites of travel encounters, as much as sites of residence. He suggests that we should be attentive to a culture's furthest range of travel, while also looking at its centres; to the ways in which groups negotiate themselves in external as much as internal relations; to the fact that culture is also a site of travel for others, and that one group's core is another's periphery.[53]

The Foreign, the Cosmopolitan and the Local

It is worth restating, in conclusion, some of the possible misinterpretations of my argument against which I would want to urge caution. I have argued that the 'foreign' is a problematic category, in a different sense than is normally presumed and that the question of what is 'foreign' to whom has to be posed as an experiential question. 'Foreignness' is by no means necessarily a matter simply of nationality. I have also argued that 'foreign' elements can frequently have progressive functions, within any given culture, insofar as they destabilise local hierarchies of local taste and power. However, even if the commanding position of America, in terms of its dominance of the world's media, cannot be so taken for granted as it once was, it remains deeply problematic that the 'foreign' is represented still, in so many places, by the American. That is to say, if it is formally possible for foreign elements to function progressively to destabilise local hierarchies, it remains problematic nonetheless if, in place of the local hierarchy, all that we get, again and again, is the American alternative. There remains the problem that America, referred to by some as the paradigmatically postmodern society, imports a smaller quantity of 'foreign' material into its own media than does any other country in the world. In this sense, the supposedly 'postmodern' society of America is perhaps still more provincial and more 'localised' than many places on the so-called periphery of the American Empire. The second point of caution relates to my argument concerning the relations of place and culture. I would support very strongly James Clifford's comments when he argues 'that we need to be very wary of a "postmodern primitivism" which, in an affirmative mode, discovers non-western travellers ("nomads"), with hybrid, syncretic, cultures, and in the process projects onto their different histories of culture contact, migration and inequality a homogeneous (historically "*avant garde*") predicament.'[54] Stuart Hall[55] has argued that, in developing our analysis of postmodern and diasporic cultures, we need to differentiate ourselves from fashionable postmodernist notions of 'nomadology' – the idea that 'everyone simply goes everywhere', nowadays. This would simply be to romanticise the figure of travel, hybridity and movement, in a generalising manner, which would be just as inadequate as contemporary ideologies of tradition and nostalgia, in all their reactionary and regressive formations. The question is one of understanding the relationship between place and travel, between the indigenous and exogenous, between the processes of indigenisation and the dynamics of globalisation and localisation. Of course, in our attempt to develop that analysis, we must recognise that we are not, by any means, all 'postmodern' in anything like the same way. It makes all the difference in the world whether one's migrancy or 'cosmopolitanism' is a matter of choice or necessity. We must also be attentive to the extent to which the multinationals increasingly recognise the necessity to present themselves as having local, user-friendly identities, rather than appearing as faceless external forces. Coca-Cola, for instance, has recently adopted a marketing slogan in which the company claims, 'we are not a multi-national, we are a multi-local'.[56] The dynamics of global localisation are a very complex matter. In this context, I end with a further note of caution. Some contemporary commentators foresee a prospect of increasing privatism, localism and 'cultural tribalism' within our postmodern electronic global village. Manuel Castells, for instance, foresees the bleak prospect of 'the coexistence of the monopoly of messages by the big networks and the increasingly narrow codes of local micro-cultures built around their parochial cable televisions'.[57] Thus, he argues, we must be attentive to the potentially negative aspects of the process whereby the spaces of cultural power are transformed into image flows over which we have less and less control, while the space of meaning available to many of us is reduced to that of the micro-territories of our newly tribalised and localised communities. Small (or 'local') is not necessarily beautiful: it can sometimes simply mean powerless.

The very final word should be given to the Latin American cultural critic Eduardo Galleano, here describing the 'postmodern predicament' from a Latin American perspective. As he puts it:

In Latin America we are still subject to the invisible dictatorship of the American media ... the people in power today relegate us to an absolute present, a historical

vacuum. Reality is reduced to the present as seen in
television news bulletins, and the news is becoming more
and more like a television soap opera. It's a way of cutting
us off from our history. If your past is erased and you don't
know where you're from, you can't know where you're
going to, or what other futures might exist; our present
dissolves our destiny, and it's a destiny in the style of a
television soap opera. Take the images of the Gulf War, for
instance. We all consumed the same images and heard the
same version of that television soap which had a million
extras, and surely was the biggest superproduction in
television history; the global village worshipping an
American massacre.[58]

Notes

[1] William Burroughs, 'What Washington? What Orders?', in *The Adding Machine: Collected Essays*, Seaver Publications, New York 1983.
[2] Johnny Carson, introducing his TV chatshow 5 October 1989, just after Columbia Pictures had been bought by Sony; quoted in McKenzie Wark 'From Fordism to Sonyism', *New Formations* No 15, 1991, p 43.
[3] John Wayne, quoted in Asu Aksoy and Kevin Robins, 'Hollywood for the 21st Century', *Cambridge Journal of Economics*, Vol 16, 1992, p 1.
[4] Michel Foucault, 'Of Other Spaces' *Diacritics*, No 16, 1986, p 22.
[5] David Morley and Kevin Robins, 'Techno Orientalism', *New Formations*, No 16, 1992, pp 136-157.
[6] Francis Fukuyama, *The End of History and the Last Man*, Penguin, Harmondsworth 1992.
[7] Daniel Lerner, *The Passing of Traditional Society* Free Press, Glencoe, Illinois 1964.
[8] Doreen Massey, 'A Place Called Home', *New Formations*, No 17, 1992, pp 9-10.
[9] Ulf Hannerz 'Scenarios for Peripheral Cultures', in Anthony King (ed), *Culture, Globalisation and the World System*, Macmillan, London 1991, p 110.
[10] Anthony King, 'Introduction' in King, *op cit*, p 8.
[11] Doreen Massey, 'A Global Sense of Place', *Marxism Today*, June 1991, p 24.
[12] *Boyz 'n The Hood*, Director John Singleton, Columbia Pictures, 1991.
[13] Jean Baudrillard, *Selected Writings* (ed. Mark Poster) Polity Press, Cambridge 1988.
[14] D. Horton & R. Wohl, 'Mass Communication and Para-Social Interaction', *Psychiatry*, No 19, 1956.
[15] Marshall McLuhan, *Understanding Media*, Routledge Kegan Paul, London 1964.

16 Fukuyama, *op cit.*

17 Jeremy Tunstall, *The Media are American*, Constable, London 1977.

18 Quoted in Thomas Guback, 'Film as International Business', in Armand Mattelart and Seth Siegelaub (eds), *Communication and Class Struggle*, Vol 1, International General, Paris/New York 1979.

19 Henry Luce, *The American Century*, Farrar & Rhinehart Inc., New York 1941, p 23.

20 Herbert Schiller, *Mass Communications and American Empire*, Beacon Press, New York 1971, p 1.

21 Quoted in Schiller, *op cit*2, p 9.

22 Committee on Foreign Affairs, Report No 2 on 'Winning the Cold War: the U.S. Ideological Offensive', 88th Congress House Report No 1352, 27 April, 1964, pp 6-7.

23 Anthony Smith, *The Geo-Politics of Information: How Western Culture Dominates the World*, Faber & Faber, London 1980.

24 Armand Mattelart et al, *International Image Markets*, Comedia, London 1985.

25 Armand Mattelart, 'Introduction' to Mattelart & Siegelaub (eds), *op cit.*

26 Elihu Katz and Tamar Liebes, *The Export of Meaning: Cross-Cultural Readings of Dallas*, O.U.P, Oxford 1990.

27 Eric Michaels, 'Hollywood Iconography: A Warlpiri Reading', in Philip Drummond & Richard Paterson (eds), *Television and its Audience*, B.F.I., London 1988.

28 Jean-Jacques Servan-Schreiber, *The American Challenge*, Penguin, Harmondsworth 1968.

29 Quoted in Geoff Mulgan and Ken Worpole, *Saturday Night or Sunday Morning*, Comedia, London 1985, p 37.

30 *Ibid.*, p 41.

31 Quoted in Ken Worpole, *Dockers and Detectives*, Verso, London 1983, p 30.

32 Richard Hoggart, *The Uses of Literacy*, Penguin, Harmondsworth 1956.

33 Christopher Bigsby, 'Europe, America and the Cultural Debate', in *Superculture*, Paul Elek Books, Amsterdam/London 1975, p 26.

34 Duncan Webster, *Looka Yonder: The Imaginary America of Populist Culture*, Comedia/Routledge, London 1988.

35 Bigsby, *op cit.*, p 6.

36 Iain Chambers, *Popular Culture: The Metropolitan Experience*, Methuen, London 1986.

37 J.B. Priestley, *English Journey*, Penguin, Harmondsworth 1984 (originally published in 1935).

38 Raphael Samuels, 'Exciting to be English', in his *Patriotism* (ed), Vol 1, Routledge, London 1989.

39 *Ibid.*

40 Paul Gilroy, *There Ain't No Black in the Union Jack*, Hutchinson, London 1987.

41 David Morley and Kevin Robins, 'No Place Like Heimat', *New*

Formations, No 12, 1990.

[42] Edward Soja, *Postmodern Geographies*, Verso, London 1981.

[43] Joshua Meyrowitz, *No Sense of Place*, O.U.P., Oxford 1985.

[44] Marie Gillespie, 'Technology and Tradition', *Cultural Studies*, Vol 32, 1989.

[45] Eliut Flores, 'Mass Media and Cultural Identity of the Puerto Rican People', paper presented to International Mass Communications Research Conference, Barcelona, July 1988.

[46] Massey, *op cit*, 1991.

[47] Daniel Miller, 'The Young and The Restless in Trinidad', in Roger Silverstone and Eric Hirsch (eds), *Consuming Technologies*, Routledge, London 1992.

[48] Ruth Frankenberg and Lata Mani, 'Crosscurrents, Crosstalk: Race, 'Postcoloniality' and the Politics of Location', in *Cultural Studies*, Vol 7.2, 1993.

[49] Arjun Appadurai, 'Disjuncture and Difference in the Global Economy', *Public Culture*, Vol 2.2, 1990; Homi Bhabha, 'The Other Question', *Screen* Vol 24.6, 1983; Stuart Hall, 'Cultural Identity and Diaspora', in Jonathan Rutherford (ed), *Identity*, Lawrence and Wishart, London 1990.

[50] James Clifford, 'Travelling Cultures' in Lawrence Grossberg et al (eds), *Cultural Studies*, Routledge, London 1992.

[51] *Ibid*.

[52] Arjun Appadurai, 'Putting Hierarchy in its Place' *Cultural Anthropology*, Vol 3.1, 1988, p 39.

[53] Clifford, *op cit*.

[54] Clifford, *op cit*, 1992, p 113.

[55] Stuart Hall, reply to James Clifford, in Grossberg et al (eds), *op cit*, p 115.

[56] Quoted in Duncan Webster, 'Cocacolonisation and National Cultures', *Overhere*, Vol 9.2, 1989.

[57] Manuel Castells, 'Crisis Planning and the Quality of Life', *Environment and Planning D: Society and Space*, Vol 1, 1983, p 16.

[58] Eduardo Galleano, interviewed by Miguel Bonasso, 'The Last Café', transmitted, Channel 4, London, 12 April 1993.

The New 'City States'?

KEN WORPOLE

When we talk or write about cities, we quickly get
enmeshed in different discourses and paradigms. For
there is 'the city', the singular historical and cultural
construct which has informed and inspired critical
thought and celebration from Plato to Walter Benjamin,
and from St Augustine to contemporary urban sociologists
such as Richard Sennett (and more recently Sharon Zukin
and Elizabeth Wilson),[1] and there are actually existing
'cities' (or the even more diminutive, in all senses, 'towns'),
the places in which people live today. At present it seems
that we have to choose between shadow and form,
metaphor and substance, grand narrative and quotidian,
messy, contingent, everyday life.

It is not easy to move from one level of meaning to
another. There are dangers of category errors. It is rarely
attempted. The discourse of the city that talks of
boulevards, of the *demi-monde*, the lifestyle of the *flâneur*,
the gossip of the *salon*, the human crush, the endless
parade of high fashion, the opera house crowds, the
teeming slums, seems wholly inappropriate when talking
about Aberdeen, Belfast, Brighton, Middlesbrough,
Swansea, for example, towns and cities that I know, have
worked in, and genuinely like and enjoy. Yet the search
for a common discourse, for common forms of critical
appraisal of urban forms, grows more urgent, even as the
current languages drift further apart. For where Richard
Sennett or Elizabeth Wilson quite properly and appro-

priately talk about sacred spaces, cosmopolitan identities, the carnivalesque and transgressive city, in contrast government policy makers, urban planners and real estate research departments talk about 'drive-time', 'floorspace yield', 'de-regulated labour markets', 'footloose capital', 'prime sites', 'tertiary zones', 'negative asset worth' and 'demographic upturn and/or decline'.

As a materialist, I feel some engagement should still be sought and explicated between economics and social outcomes, between historical and post-colonial explanations of population movements and the reality of contemporary urban social and spatial arrangements – in short, between cultural theory and lived experience. Not everybody lives in London, Paris, New York, Vienna or Prague. If there is a postmodern urban condition, how is it experienced in Liverpool, Barrow, Carmarthen or Inverness?

The Rise of the Urban Policy-Makers

There is, of course, a meeting point between theory and practice – it is called policy. Significantly one of the more benign effects of the enforced instrumentalism imposed upon higher education in the 1980s was the pressure to establish links with outside agencies, whether businesses, local authorities, development corporations, or through selling knowledge and expertise in the market-place. Colleges found themselves involved in joint ventures, or in partnership funding programmes, and had to learn to operate within other disciplines and economic understandings. They found themselves selling their research expertise in the market-place, or in alliances with consortia of public bodies who wanted to buy some independent thinking. Hence the rise of various urban policy studies units in universities and polytechnics around the country – CURDS (Centre for Urban and Regional Development Studies) in Newcastle, CURS (Centre for Urban and Regional Studies) and INLOGOV (Institute for Local Government) in Birmingham and Coventry respectively, the Centre for Urban Studies in Liverpool, being just a few among many – all of them doing invaluable work in the domain of public policy, but all, paradoxically, a product of the Thatcherite 1980s rather than any earlier, social democratic period.

Policy development has also been driven by the Europeanisation of British political culture, again largely in the 1980s, with very interesting connections being made by networks formed with funding from the EC. Jon Dawson has written:

> Economic interaction, the exchange of best practice policy and resource lobbying has, in recent years, led to inter-urban co-operation and an explosion of interest and participation in networks of cities throughout Europe. These institutionalised urban 'clubs' often aim to subdue the increasing intensity of city rivalry by stimulating collaboration rather than competition.[2]

Two major networks predominate in this field: the 'Eurocities' network, representing the major European 'second cities', and the 'Commission des Villes', representing a network of smaller towns and cities. Both have had the effect of exerting external pressure on British towns and cities to articulate their own development strategies and rationales, as a pre-condition for 'joining the club'. This has produced mostly positive benefits, as local authorities, often for the first time, have had to develop corporate policies and visions.

It may be surprising to some, but many local authorities have delivered services for decades without any written, negotiated or prioritised policy framework whatsoever, whether at a corporate or departmental level. For example, in the provision of library services, a recent study found that few library authorities had any fully developed set of policy objectives, and concluded that the main influence on policy was still the personal views and beliefs of whoever happened to be chief librarian.[3] A recent Audit Commission study on local authority arts provision found that the majority of councils investigated had no specific arts policy, no rationale for whether they spent all the budget on light opera, museums, or work with young people, no way of monitoring whether what they did was of any value or reached the people it was intended to, and no way of finding out if the money spent could have been more usefully spent elsewhere.[4] In fact, many good things happened, but they happened in a policy vacuum. In a recession, and in a world in which public financial resources will always be under pressure, policy matters deeply. After all, as Nye Bevan once famously said, 'socialism is the language of priorities'.

Urban policy is now a major testing ground of all political ideologies (as is environmental policy of course), and though in Britain local government elections are still fought publicly on largely negative, economistic grounds – Conservative councils cost you less, Labour councils do it better and still cost you less – behind the committee room doors and in the City Challenge and Development Corporation board rooms, the race is on to find out what can make anything work anymore within the exigencies of high unemployment, declining public housing stock, the collapse of many traditional community and collective support networks, the privatisation of leisure, rising crime and a palpable loss of hope in the future.

This last factor is perhaps most worrying. For one of the key qualities of city life has always been its ability to represent to its inhabitants and visitors, a contiguous sense of past, present and future, at every corner and every turn. Yet there is very little that currently seems optimistic, developmental or forward-looking in many British towns. The new towns, which once materially embodied a sense of a better future, are now as entrapped within the labyrinth of high unemployment, deteriorating housing stock and a dearth of cultural and leisure facilities (particularly for the young), as their nineteenth century predecessors. Basildon, Cumbernauld or Peterlee, for example, face immense social problems today. The vision has fled. Coventry, a symbol of post-war reconstruction, now seems to be embarrassed by the problems of its modernist town centre, and the focus once again is on the medieval 'heritage' of the city, rather than on a new world still yet to be won. Heritage is all.

Treasure-Houses of Cultural Capital

As Elizabeth Wilson has argued, towns and cities are the treasure-houses of our cultural capital – our public buildings, libraries, museums, schools and colleges, galleries, theatres, and cosmopolitan street life. That capital is disappearing fast in a *rentier* economy and political culture, one which fails to repair, rebuild or invent anew, but simply collects the short term gains from a dwindling and decaying portfolio passed on to it by earlier generations. I was talking to an architect recently who had designed a new public library in Maldon, Essex, and he mentioned that this was the first public building to be erected in that town this century. There are, of course, some new public buildings still appearing – big new libraries in Cardiff, Glasgow, Hounslow, Ealing, three hundred new library buildings in all in the 1980s, some new galleries such as the Tate at St Ives, the Sainsbury National Gallery extension in Trafalgar Square, the Burrell refurbishment in Glasgow, some new university colleges and city technology colleges – but significantly they have often been financed or part-financed as 'planning gains' on the back of a new shopping mall, or lavishly and conspicuously sponsored, or funded in the name of conservation, or as part of a national or European regeneration initiative.

The City as Social Organiser

There are many factors contributing to this new concern for urban life, but there seem to me to be two underlying, perhaps sub-conscious, impulses that have brought intellectuals in many countries rushing in recent years to contribute to urban policy debates. The first is that the renewed concern for the city is a way of displacing the unresolved aspirations of, or accommodating to, the two great failed social and intellectual experiments of this century: the implosion of modernism and the collapse of communism. Modernism and communism, sharing at times many of the same laboratories and even personnel,

for the first half of this century held out separate but
related promises of a bright and signal future, of a brave
new world of glass and steel, of light and air, heralding a
new realm of freedom and equality (beyond necessity),
where all would meet as equals and all the old antagonisms
of class, race, religion and gender would eventually wither
away. Le Corbusier drew plans for the 'radiant city'; the
Bauhaus School eschewed ornamentation and decoration
(with everything, preferably, painted white); communism
found in the clean, well ordered lines of modernist
architecture, the wide boulevards and great mon-
functional zones of housing, industry and recreation, a
planning regime and aesthetic entirely amenable to its
social project. Both were revolutionary upheavals 'starting
from zero'. The International Style and The Interna-
tionale at times seemed inter-changeable. Many of those
ideals, and achievements, are now in ruins. Both
experiments have conspicuously failed.

Yet because many of the aspirations they embodied –
equality, justice, material well-being, progress – remain, a
new form or over-arching metaphor has had to be found
to embody them. It is probably the city that now serves as
the key organising principle for social hope at the end of
the twentieth century, not just in the developed countries
but throughout the world. It is estimated that some 90 per
cent of the population will be living in cities by the middle
of the twenty first century. They won't all be the same
kind of cities. Some will be 'world cities', some will be 'edge
cities', some will be 'hundred mile cities', and so on. The
urban form will take on many new shapes and disguises,
but it will certainly be different from a nation, and it will
be different from a rural or peasant economy, society or
hinterland. It will need a new kind of political response.

The second point, equally compelling, is that in an era in
which the nation state is coming under intense pressure
from emergent, suppressed or irredentist local and
regional cultures, exemplified in the re-discovery of
federalism (in Europe the twentieth century was a great
anti-federal era, unlike Australia and the USA, for
example, which have a much longer tradition of federal

development), the city takes on a new importance as a focus for cultural identity and economic power. Neal Ascherson has recently described some of the current tensions in Europe, as different political formations manoeuvre to define the new Europe as either a *Europe des patries* or a *Europe des regions*.[5] Yet very recently a new model emerged from a gathering of European mayors in Istanbul: a *Europe des grandes villes*. A Europe of 'city-states' could be an effective bulwark against rising nationalist currents and political movements. National identity, it is believed, resides in the forests, lakes and mountains, rather than in the cosmopolitan streets, tenements and *quartiers* of contemporary European cities. The strength-ening of cities, and their success in negotiating successful cosmopolitan cultures, is possibly the best way of finding a route through the current nationalist and ethnic upheavals facing many areas of Europe and beyond. An interesting additional insight into the possibilities of this process comes from the world of football, where AC Milan's current owner, the media mogul Silvio Berlusconi, has argued that as football moves into the twenty-first century, the national team will decline in importance, and the multi-national, city club team will gain the ascendancy: 'The concept of the national team will gradually become less and less important. It is the clubs with which the fans associate.'

Second City Limits

The rise of the 'second' cities in Britain in the 1980s, particularly Birmingham, Cardiff, Glasgow, Manchester and to some extent Newcastle, cannot be separated out from the decline of London as the confident, elected, self-governing metropolitan centre of the UK. London's decline began in the 1950s, with gradual industrial and population losses, but the abolition of the Greater London Council (GLC) in 1986, effectively the ending of an interna-tionally famous local government tradition that began with – and for most of its life was co-terminous with – the London County Council, to all intents and purposes fatally

weakened London's organisational capacity to be taken
seriously on the world stage. Any new period of metropolitan renewal is not likely to make any impact until well into
the twenty-first century, as London continues to fracture,
fragment, lose direction, and find itself unable to respond
strategically to any new political, economic and social context that may develop. London today is like poor Lavinia in
Titus Andronicus: tongueless, maimed in every limb, helpless
and pitiable *in extremis*.

Many of the initiatives and new political alliances
developed by the GLC administration of 1981-1986 have
been admired and emulated elsewhere. The concern with
developing a detailed local economic policy (the GLC
Industrial Strategy) is now replicated through dozens of
local economic development units in towns and cities in
Britain and abroad. The opening up of the town hall
(literally) to voters, the holding of committee meetings in
public, the sponsorship of city festivals and forms of celebration of cosmopolitan life, again have all been taken up
elsewhere. On a visit to Australia in 1992, I was surprised to
find out how much Australian cities had learned from the
GLC, consciously copied and publicly acknowledged, particularly the sloughing off of the entrenched Morrisonian
paternalism, and a strong wish to get local government and
decision-making out of the city hall and into the communities. For Herbert Morrison, London's County Hall was a
fortress (he often slept on a camp bed in his office), a
Kremlin of benevolent municipal socialism from above;
under Livingstone it became an open house.

Into the London vacuum have stepped more than a
dozen quangos – the shape of things to come in what
increasingly looks like an era of British post-democracy –
including London Regional Transport, London Dock-
lands Development Corporation, the London Residuary
Body, the Housing Corporation, London First and
London Forum, nine Training and Enterprise Councils,
five City Challenge Boards, and various other non-elected
strategic bodies, some of which have no locally elected
council representatives on them at all, not even as a
minority. This is the 'new magistracy', the great and the

good whose honourable intentions do not somehow need to be tested at the ballot box, or through periodic re-election.

Yet London's loss has proved to be other cities' gain. Ironically, the abolition of the GLC and the subsequent decline of London as a metropolitan capital has inadvertently helped weaken the British nation-state, presumably not the intention of the Conservative government when it acted so decisively in 1986. London no longer dominates British politics and culture in the way that it once did. Britain today appears a more decentralised, regionalised and disaggregated culture, and London is no longer the jewel in the crown but the decaying centre of the *ancien regime*. Quality of life studies have helped focus attention on the many benefits which accrue to people the further away from London they work and live.

A number of British cities have not only established direct relations with Brussels and the EC, but have offices and full-time staff there. London is by-passed in the growth of the European networks, and in fact many of the most important regeneration projects that have helped British cities re-establish their new stand-alone identities – Glasgow, City of Culture 1990; Birmingham's Centenary Square development; Manchester's G Mex; Swansea's Maritime Quarter and proposed National Literature Centre – have been crucially aided by EC structural funds rather than by Westminster or the British Treasury.

Despite the very real diminution of local government powers over the past decade – the loss of housing responsibilities, local management of schools, the detachment of further education from local authority control, the tendering out of many kinds of services under CCT (Compulsory Competitive Tendering), the Unified Business Rate, rate-capping – there has nevertheless also been a parallel rise (symbolic perhaps in most part) of the notion of the new 'city-state', stressing each place's unique topography, demography, history and economy, which at least provides some of the intellectual and psychological groundwork for the notion of a *Europe des villes* rather than a *Europe des patries*, mentioned earlier. What we are witnessing, paradoxically, is on one level a globalisation of economies and trade relations, at the same time as an increasing localisation of urban identities.

Among the many factors which created this new era of self-definition by local authorities and city councils (a refusal at last to accept subordinate status always in relation to the dominant power of London), perhaps most important was the growth of unemployment, and a local wish to be seen to be doing something about it, in contrast to the national government attitude which was to accept high levels of unemployment as a fact of life as immutable as the weather, and for which nothing could be done outside the self-correcting processes of the market. In the early 1980s, perhaps for the first time ever, local authorities took upon themselves a role in local economic development, creating economic development units and commissioning studies of local employment patterns, trends, and areas of potential intervention. Analysis led to self-analysis. In a hostile environment, and with declining resources, it was imperative to act strategically and corporately, ensuring cross-departmental co-operation and becoming problem-oriented rather than service-oriented.

Pressures for Change

Nobody can, with hindsight, not believe that local government in many places needed a real kick up the backside. It had become inward-looking, obsessed with its own rituals, conditions of service, and creature comforts, and less and less responsive to real and often very distressing changes in local conditions. This was at its most extreme in London and some of the other big cities, where demographic and social change had produced new and very difficult patterns of local government politics, staffing, provision and administration, well analysed by Eric Hobsbawm in his essay on 'Labour in the Great City'.[6] For Hobsbawm the movement of the traditional inner city working class out to the suburbs in the 1930s and after the

Second World War, 'snapped the links between day and night, or between the places where people lived and where they worked, with substantial effects on the potential of the labour organisation which is always strongest where work and residence belong together.'

What happened in places like Hackney, a borough I have lived in, now, for twenty-five years, was that the borough was increasingly settled by ethnic minority groups, students, squatters or young professionals, who became the dominant residential population, but whose needs were serviced by a town hall staff of (relatively) well paid white working class officers and employees who commuted in from Essex and the outer London boroughs to the East, to which they had moved as new owner-occupiers. The ties between providers and users, between 'production' and 'consumption' as it were, were broken, often with quite disastrous political (and racial) results. Local government trade union consciousness inevitably became almost exclusively about pay and conditions, with little thought given to the equally valid social claims of the people who had to live in the council flats which remained unrepaired or who walked the unswept streets, as a result of various staffing disputes or procedural entanglements. The economic effect was also disastrous. Most of the salaries paid out by the council, the largest employer in the borough, were now spent in other boroughs, a result of which was that rates and poll tax charges increased as a result of the low rate base, and the Hackney local economy exponentially worsened. At its most paradoxical, council workers often campaigned in the daytime for their employing council to levy higher rates in order to protect jobs and wages, and in the evening returned home to vote against higher rates where they themselves lived.

The 'consumer-first' ideology of Thatcherism struck many local chords, even though many local councils had always been rightly proud of the services they offered to their electors. But in politics the weak link in the chain is the one the ideologists will focus attention upon, and top-heavy councils with unresponsive management systems, though perhaps in a minority, became the focus of a

new era of disempowerment and dismantlement. What
were the political arguments that could be made for
defending local government?

In Britain this is a problem (compared with many other
European countries which have much stronger city
traditions). Both the dominant twentieth century political
trajectories in Britain – Conservatism's 'family, church and
nation' or Labourist social democracy – have always
embodied an entrenched dislike of city life and urban
living. The Conservative Party, once the party of the
landed gentry and country house-owning *arriviste*
bourgeoisie, is now the party of the suburbs and the new
towns. John Major has, on several occasions in his short
premiership, evoked a 'lost England' of corner baker's
shops and small town virtues, and in a speech to the
Conservative Group for Europe in April 1993 assured his
colleagues that even within Europe, Britain would remain
essentially 'the country of long shadows on county
grounds, warm beer, envincible green suburbs.'[7] The
historic English socialist idyll (in its Labour and Fabian
variants) has invariably envisaged the good society taking
the form of a rural arcadia, in which strong-limbed men
and women bring home the harvest, wreathed in flowers
and singing down the lanes. Rather differently, Scottish
and Welsh socialist traditions have been strongest in the
industrial regions and have usually taken on an industrial,
often syndicalist, tinge.

At present socialist utopian visions are thin on the
ground, and maybe that is a good thing. Better and more
equitable social relations are likely to emerge in the
negotiated alliances, cultural fluidities, and impure
formations of the cosmopolitan city than they are in a
planned new world, even though the inner city remains
the site for most current dystopic visions of the future in
fiction or on screen. This raises another issue, too complex
to be dealt with here in any depth, to do with the way that
elite cultural forms such as the novel or the film
documentary continue to portray the inner city as a hostile
milieu, a corrupted and degraded locale, yet popular
cultural forms such as television sitcoms or soap operas

like *Desmond's* or *EastEnders* still manage to portray inner city life as capable of neighbourliness, warmth, humour, and of hope and aspiration. Which is closer to the truth?

Nationally, the Labour Party has always tried to keep its distance from the 'goings-on' of local government, and was clearly determined to learn nothing from many of the positive experiments of the GLC. The inner city – with its dissident, indigenous working class, its ethnic minority populations, its youth subcultures, its gay and lesbian cultures – has been demonised, rather than valued for its positive attributes. There seems to be a cross-party consensus that what the modern city needs is more top-down planning, more development agencies, more by-passing of local authorities, all in the interests of short term expediency and cosmetic achievement, rather than longer term development through strategy, organisational capacity-building, self-management and choice. The Liberal Democrats have attempted to take the political initiative in some inner city areas, in the name of 'community politics', but to little evident effect. All in all, this is not much of an intellectual base to start from in developing a more positive attitude towards urban living: but it has to be done.

For the continuing drift towards suburbanisation (or counter-urbanisation as it is now called) is becoming a serious problem: not on moral or aesthetic grounds but for environmental, social and economic reasons. Suburbanisation is predicated on the use of the car, on home or neighbourhood-based cultural identities (often racially divisive), on consumerism, and as such is neither sustainable nor responsive enough to new ideas, new social relations or economic innovation.

For example, the suburbs are deeply inflected with quite specific and narrow social identities. A young black person getting off at the 'wrong' bus stop and finding themselves in the 'wrong' neighbourhood in many British city suburbs becomes almost immediately an object of police suspicion. In the Comedia 'Out of Hours' study in which I was involved, this came out very strongly in every one of the twelve towns studied: the inviolable social boundaries of many suburban districts compared with the comparative democracy and spatial neutrality of the town centre. Black or Asian people in Liverpool, Middlesbrough, Luton, Gloucester or Preston – some of the multi-racial towns and cities studied – quickly learned where they could and could not go safely in the towns they settled in.[8] Spatial territorial forms which exacerbate social and ethnic differences are not likely to pre-figure the multi-cultural societies which should be one of the few sources of hope for the future, not just in Britain but everywhere else as well. In an era of great national and international population movements, urban forms are needed which can accommodate diversity and differences not serialise them and suppress them. At a time of enormous social and demographic change, the city is best placed to offer the flexibility to accommodate changing lifestyles.

Cities are also much more likely to be sources of educational and economic innovation, and this remains one of their great strengths. The recent rapid expansion of further and higher education in Britain (in 1979 1 in 8 people participated in higher education; by 1991 this had become 1 in 5, and by the year 2000 will be 1 in 3) is largely happening through the polytechnics (now universities) and the further education colleges which traditionally have been sited in the city centre, usually in very old (often ex-industrial) building stock.[9] This contrasts with the tradition of locating universities (especially the 1960s redbrick generation) in green field sites or on rolling downland, far from the taint of industrial or urban life, where students could lead a more cloistered and sequestered life. The urban polytechnics, without doubt, have been the true sources of cultural and intellectual innovation in recent years, and this owes as much to the greater social diversity of the student intake, the constant press of political realities and exigencies literally outside the poly gates, as it does to the syllabus and the professional interests of the tutors.

Forward-looking local authorities have welcomed the expansion of higher education as a real contribution to urban regeneration. Liverpool City Council has embarked on a programme of refurbishing empty city centre property as student accommodation, convinced that this can only lead to enlivening the city centre and in doing so making it safer for everybody else as well. The expansion of further and higher education as the leading edge of urban renewal programmes can clearly be seen in Hackney, in Southwark, in Luton, on Teesside and in many other places as well.

Economic innovation and development has also been successful in many urban areas, particularly in managed workspaces, enterprise workshops, and through sectoral development initiatives around particular constellations of industries in certain towns and cities. With new forms of post-Fordist manufacturing, depending on inter-linked networks, the city may well regain its older tradition of not only being a place of commerce and culture but also as an industrial workshop, as has been seen in Cardiff's re-emergence as a 'media city'. Towns and cities have also been at the forefront of new kinds of social economies, notably in the growth of LETS (local employment and trading schemes) which are local currencies based on barter schemes and exchanges of services and skills, particularly amongst the unemployed. Letslink UK is a national co-ordinating agency for these initiatives which are now operating in Norwich, Brighton, Swindon, Sheffield, Manchester and Bristol as well as a number of small towns. Barter schemes have their origins in the Green movement and in a 1960s concept of 'the alternative society', but today they are making in-roads into inner city districts, where the sheer wastage of skills caused by unemployment can find redress in non-cash-based networks. Not surprisingly, the Inland Revenue is beginning to take an interest. But plastic money already is making many traditional cash transactions redundant, and the prospect of new, electronically-based, local credit schemes geared to social objectives is now much stronger than it was in the early 1980s when certain politicians and economists fantasised about the GLC creating its own currency.

The debate about local taxes and local economies has been revived by the first pamphlet from Demos, written by Geoff Mulgan and Robin Murray, which argues for the reconnection of taxation directly with the services and provisions that taxation allegedly supplies.[10] While local authority spending is increasingly, directed, authorised and funded from national government, there is little opportunity for new local initiatives to emerge. The greater use of local referenda allied to local tax proposals, could bring voters back into the political arena, debating issues, making decisions – and paying for – better local services and new ideas. The principle of subsidiarity in decision-making and local expenditure is essential if towns and cities are to regain control of their political destinies again.

Cities are about citizenship, that is to say identities, loyalties and responsibilities forged by democracy rather than inherited and therefore either biological or divine. While the tenor of this chapter appears to be out of sympathy with rural, peasant or folk traditions and cultures, this is because the world is changing rapidly, and the change is towards urbanisation on an extraordinary scale. We have no choice but to attempt to respond responsibly and imaginatively to the massive population movements now currently underway across the world, mostly driven by economic necessity, and which only urban forms and cultures possess the flexibility to meet and satisfy. The city is sometimes a melting pot, sometimes a hiding place or refuge, and nearly always a place where new identities can be formed or old ones consolidated in new surroundings. It is a place in the modern world where time and space remain porous and fluid, so that parts of Bradford or Southall can be in the forefront of Indian musical development, even in world terms, or where Irish traditions and cultural forms in Boston are sometimes stronger than they are in Cork. It is also a place where generational conflicts within many ethnic minority cultures are likely to be stronger than between them. A walk on a summer's evening down Kilburn High Road, Atlantic Road in Brixton, or Stoke Newington High Street in north London, or in many parts of most cities in Britain today, is a powerful reminder that a place can be both local and international, a redbrick 'English' Victorian street as well as a bustling, cosmopolitan world.

Notes

[1] Richard Sennett, *The Conscience of the Eye: The Design & Social Life of Cities*, Faber, London 1991. Zukin, Sharon, *Loft Living*, Radius, London 1988. Wilson, Elizabeth, *The Sphinx in the City*, Virago, London 1991.
[2] Jon Dawson, *The Planner*, January 1992.
[3] Alistair Black, and Dave Muddiman, 'The Public Library Policy and Purpose', Comedia Working Paper, London 1993.
[4] Audit Commission, *Local Authorities, Entertainment and the Arts*, HMSO, London 1991.
[5] Neal Ascherson, *The Independent on Sunday*, 27 June 1993.
[6] Eric Hobsbawm, *Politics for a Rational Left*, Verso, London 1989.
[7] Quoted in the *Guardian*, 23.4.93.
[8] Ken Worpole, *Towns for People*, Open University Press, Buckingham 1992.
[9] Sir Christopher Ball, 'The Learning Society', *RSA Journal*, London, May 1992.
[10] Geoff Mulgan, and Robin Murray, *Reconnecting Taxation*, Demos, London 1993.

Mongrelisation is Our Original State: An Interview with David Dabydeen

KEVIN DAVEY

Introduction

Born on a sugar plantation in 1956, David Dabydeen originates from a minority Asian community in Guyana whose forebears were the indentured 'coolie' labourers from East India whom the British colony had pressed into service after the abolition of slavery. Dabydeen came to England as a teenager in the late 1960s and later studied English literature at the universities of Cambridge and London. He is now Lecturer in Caribbean Studies at the University of Warwick. He has recently been appointed Ambassador at Large for the Co-operative Republic of Guyana, a country he describes as putting 'socialism in action'.

History and cultural criticism formed the substance of his first two books, *Hogarth's Blacks*[1], and *Hogarth, Walpole and Commercial Britain*[2]. He has also written two prizewinning volumes of poetry: *Slave Song*[3] and *Coolie Odyssey*.[4] More recently Dabydeen has turned to the novel. *The Intended*[5] was a study of adolescence in the London Asian diaspora and *Disappearance*,[6] his latest work, is an exploration of the instability and corruption of Englishness and an explicit riposte to the cultural deference which characterises the work of the foremost Asian Caribbean novelist in England, V.S. Naipaul.

For Dabydeen, a black poet, novelist and historian living and working in England, the formation and reformation of identity is inevitably a reflexive positioning in language and global social relations. It is inescapably political, but also transforms what we understand as politics. His writing is highly attuned to the sexual dynamics of the colonial relationship (the troubled black masculinity to which this gives rise is the terrain of much of his poetry); to the experience of globalisation, migration and dislocation, in all its linguistic, cultural and personal consequences; to the assumed superiority of the English literary and visual art canons and the forms of scholarship and criticism that sustain them; and to the ingrained racist reflexes of European culture and politics. Simple celebrations of style and consumption fail to address the complex issues raised by this body of work. By exploring the tensions between language, desire, power and impotence in their global, national and personal settings, Dabydeen's writing maps out the much larger space which any politics of identity must inhabit.

Kevin Davey: Can I start by asking you about *Slave Song*? You wrote the poems in Guyanese Creole and then you provided translations into Standard English, plus a historical contextualisation and a critical commentary for each one. Was this merely a way of packaging the work for a western audience? Was it a joke? Or was something more complex – the impossibility of speaking from only one position or inhabiting one identity – being explored here?

David Dabydeen: I think there was a lot of intellectual play in that book. I was trying to prevent western criticism from approaching the poetry, even though the poetry was published in the west, and for the west. I still wanted to point to the fact that when 'Third World' literature is consumed and recolonised by western theorists – whether

it's deconstruction, postmodernism or more traditional
forms of analysis – some of the anguish and some of the
delight in the writing gets lost. In other words, a lot of
western criticism of 'Third World' literature tends to be
merely ideological. It can't see the ways in which the
language is complex, contradictory, and forged out of
particular 'Third World' experiences. Instead of looking
very closely at the literature, or listening very closely to it
when it's oral, western criticism tends to abstract from it
principles which serve its own causes and its own
radicalisms. As a result 'Third World' literature comes to
be used as a weapon of the West, against the West. To
prevent that I provided a number of spoof criticisms. I
parodied the role of the critic – the Cambridge educated
critic, with a western voice – and I also parodied certain
forms of criticism emanating from other academies of this
country. Of course, I was also playing with images. I've
always been interested in the relationship between the
visual and the verbal because the culture from which I
come is 'colourful', it's about colours! And I used a lot of
art history images. The poetry sometimes takes on the
form of art history. Writing *Slave Song* was like wearing a
series of masks – the poet from Guyana, original language,
the critic educated in the West, mimicking western
criticism, the genteel art historian – because art history in
this country is still a very genteel pursuit – and so on. And
of course, the translator, because all the poems have
translations, which were serious in the sense that they were
trying to draw attention to the difficulty of translating
from one culture to the next. It's not an easy matter. It's
not a literature that can be opened up just like that. It
demands effort.

**KD: You appear to wear fewer masks in the next
collection, *Coolie Odyssey*. Is the playfulness sustained
there?**

DD: Yes, I think it is in *Coolie Odyssey* itself, the long title
poem about the idea of folk. It was provoked by the death
of my own grandmother. Deaths in Guyana are marked by

talking about the dead. In my case I marked her death by writing about it. But I was writing about the dead in an English language, and it was being published in the West because this is where I live, largely for western consumption. Again I chose to play with the ironies in that position. So the poem asked two important sets of questions. First, what is this writing for? Who is it for? Who's consuming it? And secondly, when Westerners consume it, will they make a too easy correspondence between our folk and their folk? Hence the poem starts with a reference to Tony Harrison's 'northern folk', and to Seamus Heaney's 'potato-digging folk'. It goes on to ask questions about whether our folk can be slotted into these notions of folk that come from outside – and concludes they can't. So I had the dead grandmother attack the poet:

> *Is foolishness fill your head.*
> *Me dead.*
> *Dog-bone and dry well*
> *Got no story to tell.*
> *Just how me born stupid is so me gone.*[7]

She's saying that the poet is talking nonsense about her. She is emptiness but he wants to fill her out with concepts. The poem ends up by deflating all the attempts that the West might make to applaud it or receive it into a canon. Its last lines are:

> *See the applause fluttering from their white hands*
> *Like so many messy table napkins.*[8]

It objects to being consumed by the privileged, by the academicians. And so the poet is saying 'I don't want this to be a poem, and I don't want to write it, and I don't want to write it for you!' But it has to be written, because that's the language I've inherited, English. It's the only one at my disposal. English – or a Creolised version of it.

KD: In *Slave Song* your poetry offers a representation of the colonial experience in which power relations and subjectivities are highly eroticised. In fact Wilson Harris

once described your poetry as dealing with 'the pornography of Empire'.[9] In poems like 'The Cane-cutters Song', 'Slave Song' and 'Nightmare' it's almost as if interracial sex, despite the violence and humiliations that are imposed by unequal power relations, is actually based on complementary, utopian impulses. Encounters with the black body are shown to be offering a release from civilised restraint, with the white as a reaching out towards beauty and a better life. But perhaps these are actually sexual and racial cross purposes? In *Coolie Odyssey* and *The Intended*, your first novel, there's a lot more anguish.

DD: Yes, with *Slave Song* I was thinking of the idyll that black writers earlier than myself – Cesaire[10] and Senghor[11] for example – had created. They offered the idyll of a return and a utopian past which was in fact a black version of a white utopia. In *Slave Song* there are deliberate echoes of this. I use pseudo-romantic images of canaries singing and water flowing that could easily have come from the Negritude movement of the 1930s and the 1940s. This was a way of saying that although one can play with idylls, at the end of the day there is nothing to go back to. One has to make actual returns to actual places and the actualities are far more painful in Africa, or India, or wherever you originate, than the literary imagination will allow for, or confess. But I suppose *Slave Song* plays with, rather than debunks, an idyll which is, after all, still seductive. *The Tempest* was very much in my mind as it is for many writers from Africa, India and the old colonies. And the prospect of reconciliation at all levels between Prospero and Caliban, the possibility of a genuine romance, forgiveness and love remains seductive. And if not between Prospero and Caliban, certainly between Miranda and Caliban. So a lot of what I've written since has been about the potential, or the promise, of a relationship between Miranda and Caliban. But in my novel *Disappearance* I've moved away from that and into the possibility of a relationship between Prospero's wife and Caliban! I make the white woman in the relationship

68 years old. Now that's a tactic of revenge, I must admit, and probably occurs because I don't think it is possible to have a real unison between Miranda and Caliban, the relationship is much more troubled than literature will allow for.

KD: Is it inescapably tragic?

DD: It's certainly too rooted in history and historical memory to be an easy relationship. There can be a relationship, but not until there have been all kinds of catharsis between the people, the individuals, and the wider society, not until there have been many kinds of re-evaluation of where we come from and who we are, and a sense of the complexity and multiplicities of our identities and the way we've impacted on each other through the centuries. I don't think you can have a real relationship with the other, in my case the other being Miranda. It's possible if all those processes are lived through, but it's so damned difficult! You're always constructing. Instead of having an idyll based on the instant of love, and spontaneity, you're constructing the other, you're saying to her 'you are Miranda', while she has to say to me, 'and you're Caliban' so we're playing these complex historical games.

KD: In *The Sexual World* you refer to 'the repetition necessary for new beginning'. Can we explore that a little? Does it mean that the relationship between coloniser and colonised has to be re-enacted before it can be transcended?

DD: Well, in my own life I feel that I have to live through, I have to enact, the rituals of the past. And I have to enact them not just imaginatively, but physically, before I can feel free of that past. I don't want to live in a system of grievances, because I haven't got too long to live. As I don't want to be trapped in those grievances, I therefore have to live them through at a personal level. As a black person you live them through at a social level anyway, because at the end of the day you're a fucking nigger. You live it through socially but because I am not only a social animal, because I'm also an individual, I have to live these historical movements out in the sphere of the bedroom, or in my house, or in my workplace. Well, mostly in the bedroom in fact, because I do my romancing there. But I'm not talking about dressing up or role play. I don't mean the imperial relationship is actually restaged, just that you have to live it through, in some way, once again. There must be an acknowledgement that you are other and I am other. Again, I'm resisting being swallowed up by that other, by the traditional enemy – the people who colonised us. And in an attempt to recolonise us again they just suck up all my values, they just eat you in an easy consumption. What I'm trying to do is to reveal something of the difficulties of being what we are, and I don't mean difficulties in the sense of grievances. We're difficult because we can't just be penetrated like that. In the West I see all around me the ways in which our literature and art have been taken up and consumed, mindlessly. Everyone listens to Bob Marley, it's sub-cultural, its almost radical, the young people smoke their dope in their dark corners – and then they go to the beaches of Jamaica. And of course, they don't know Jamaica, they don't know where Bob Marley came from, or where that music came from. It came from anger and hatred and love and idyll. So you have to resist all that in your own body as well. In other words, don't think you can just fuck me. And that's where the personal and the intellectual have to engage, playfully, with history.

KD: Your poetry deals with difficult, political questions of identity. Are you looking to rediscover or perpetuate an older Guyanese identity in your writing? Are the tensions you describe generated by essential, unchanging identities embedded in different cultures? Or are the poems witnessing the creation of something new? It strikes me most of the writing is about the difficulty and, in many cases, the impossibility, of moving to any new or hybrid identity.

DD: Well, I think you're right. If I were still living in the Caribbean – I grew up there, but I've been living most of my life in England – I would be more celebratory of the whole process of hybridity, because I would have been in the very crucible of those processes in the Caribbean. But I've had enough experience of hybridity to understand that it means something very different in England. I understand how important it is that the future should be one of give and take, of exchange, of interculturations, of cross fertilisations. But as an individual living in England, amidst the piles of venerable stone that are Oxford and Cambridge and which everywhere surround me – I'm always aware of ancient and heavy traditions that resist and are impervious to any Creolising, transformative processes of change. I therefore have to be realistic and say that I think it will be almost impossible, in my lifetime, for there to be a genuine cross transference of values and emotions and languages. In England I feel most of the time that I'm living in a monoculture. That's partly because I live in a middle class, university environment, where language is standardised, where theologies are standardised – even if they're not believed in – and where there's liberal consensus and no real fight. If you exist in this kind of ambience, then all the things you have brought with you from the Caribbean, all the things that you really are deep down – drawn from the cultures of Africanised Indians, and Indianised Africans – you wonder whether they can actually survive in this country.

KD: Are you saying that the cultural effects of the Diaspora must be resisted? And that Salman Rushdie or Stuart Hall's celebrations of hybridity, are therefore premature?

DD: Well, they're prophetic. They identify processes that we will follow, and we have to follow, and that we can't avoid, unless we go back to a kind of fascistic division. At the same time you're right about the Diaspora. In my own life I feel that I have to keep discovering, and rediscovering, even refabricating, a notion of what was original. Western theories have often confused an interest in origin with a desire for purity and then connect that desire with fascistic movements and aspirations. For us the desire for originality is much more complex, it is in fact a sense of how complex and mongrel we have been – that India is mongrel, and that Africa is too. Mongrelisation is our original state. Consequently I don't want, at the moment, a mongrelisation that takes in the West. I'd rather spend more time rediscovering the hybridities of my past. Let white people make the effort to be mongrel!

KD: How does that argument differ from the voices of warning you adopt in the poems 'Brown Skinned Girl', 'Two Cultures' and 'Ma Talking Words'.

DD: 'Ma Talking Words' is my mother talking about the impossibilities of white people crossing over. And telling me that the burden is always on us to make the peace, to build the bridges, to create the magical impulses and the spark. And she's saying, that there's a kind of profound shallowness in the society in which I found myself in England. That I couldn't assume that my desire for magic would be understood. It might be tasted, in a voyeuristic way, it might be played with, it might thrill the society. And we often do. But she's saying don't be stupid, don't think your magic will be permanent, this country might erase you tomorrow.

KD: In *The Transparency of Evil* Jean Baudrillard speaks of Michael Jackson as a 'precursor of the hybridisation that is perfect because it is universal – the race to end all races. Today's young people have no problem with a miscegenated society: they already inhabit such a unvierse, and Michael Jackson foreshadows what they see as an ideal future ... an embryo of all those dreamt of mutations that will deliver us from race and from sex.'[12]

DD: That sounds rubbish to me. Technological, electronic puppetry, that's what Michael Jackson is – it's a manufactured, a media-based transformation, not a human transformation. It's plastic surgery, it's plastic – trust the French philosophers! Another abstract conceptualisation! I think this is the greatest danger that we face, the danger of a technology that we as people from Guyana don't understand – we don't understand the magic of their technology. We create sound systems and we don't understand how they work scientifically, and we play electric guitars and electronic jazz, all the time abandoning the source of our own music, which is the voice. I'm not saying we should just be singers, that we should remain oral. But we are too easily seduced by the electronic toys of Western culture. And that culture, when we play the toys well, first applauds and then like Baudrillard uses us as an image of transformation. Sometimes I think we're being used like monkeys.

KD: But what room will the globalising communications system leave for oral, face to face cultures?

DD: In Guyana, and I'm sure it's true of Jamaica, Barbados and other countries, we have as passionate a reverance for own native cultures as we have for Bob Marley and the global youth culture. To understand our reverence for our own, in a sense you've got to walk in the villages. You can't discover this as an armchair anthropologist, abstracting and generalising from media reports. I don't want to revel in the capacity of the society from which I come, which is debilitating in many ways – but you've only got to move through the villages and listen to how people speak to each other, how they curse each other, how they hate each other, how they gossip and rumour about each other, to know their music, and that the melody of their speech and the dissonance of their thoughts are music.

What I want to do is divest the environment from which I come – and the culture that thrives in these environments – from Western reverence, from escapism, from conceptualisations largely based on the unease that westerners feel about their own society. It's interesting that Derek Walcott in his Nobel Prize speech speaks of the burden of description, the way in which the poet from the West – himself, and myself – can so easily interfere with the actual processes of action, the actual processes of living, that go on in the Caribbean. I want to remove this burden of description from Guyanese people. Walcott sees Indian religious drama being played out by villagers in Trinidad, and at first he asks all kinds of impertinent poetic questions. Do these people know their histories? Do they really know what Rama means in relation to Sita? But then he suddenly realises that these people have actually been doing this for thousands of years. And that they mightn't know it in any conceptual way, but they're living it. And as a poet he's creating a distance between that actual life and himself coming from outside, equipped with intelligent words, or words that can be shaped into western metre.

KD: *The Intended* explicitly signalled the importance of Joseph Conrad to you as a writer. And *Disappearance* appears to be a multiple 'heart of darkness' in which at least three journeys deep into other cultures, and otherness, are undertaken. How consciously adopted is this figure?

DD: Very. I point to it by quoting Eliot quoting Conrad, to give a sense of the distance, and the distances which stretch back. The idea was not just to create an African character, but also to create a character who was not a recognisable West Indian. He can't dance and he doesn't have eloquence, because he's not from an oral culture. He could easily be a white man. Easily. And in fact he says things like 'I am not black, I am an engineer'.

KD: So he's the Enlightenment subject, centred, unified, scientific and reasoning?

DD: And he's got Prospero's books!

KD: But how sustainable is he?

DD: He could have been sustainable in the Caribbean,

where there is space for these eccentrities. But when he comes to England, paradoxically, he realises that he's what V.S. Naipaul called a 'mimic man'. And the agent for the revelation of this mimicry, again paradoxically, is an elderly white woman who had had some experiences, largely voyeuristic, of Africa. And she, in fact, is a much more Creole figure than him in her passions, in her outbursts, in her hatreds, self-hatreds and self-contempt. She is the Creole character, and he's not. So again, it's a question of putting different masks on different people, then taking those masks off and showing that people are more surprising than they appear on the surface.

KD: What is it that must disappear? History itself?

DD: The desire expressed at the end of the novel is a desire for disappearance from all history. It is a desire for amnesia, it's a desire for the pure escape from history, it's a desire for the total loss of memory, and for a different kind of idyll. How long can we let ourselves be plagued by Columbian legacies? There are new forms of slavery in the relations between North and South but, nevertheless, the slave trade ended in 1838. So how long will I go on being burdened by its pressures and its legacies? Forever, living in England. Here those burdens are inscribed in stone. If you walk around Parliament you will see how the place is hemmed in by monuments to murderers: *heroes* of the Morant Bay Rebellion, *heroes* of the Indian Mutiny. The latest is Bomber Harris. This country has a long memory. Do I want to be plagued all my life by these memories? No, I don't. So, since I can't remove myself physically – since there's nowhere else to go, this is home – you might attempt an intellectual amnesia. And you wonder whether if you blink, everything will disappear. And then what would you write about? What is there to write about once you don't write out of memory? Or out of history? That's the challenge, really, for the next millennium. Caryll Phillips, myself, Toni Morrison, Barry Unsworth – at the moment we are all still writing about the slave trade. We're still concerned about these moments of history.

I think the next project is to go beyond this. But not to the post-Columbian, not even to the non-Columbian. The word Columbus shouldn't figure at all in what it will be. And that's what the character wants to disappear from – history. He talks about new beginnings in an obscure country. It's almost a kind of Buddhist desire. And it's not nihilistic, in the western sense, it's not French nihilism, which was, at the end of the day, grounded in hatred and a desire to kill other people. Western nihilism really is a desire to abuse and murder others. This is a desire for a kind of emptiness from which one could emerge creatively. Derek Walcott calls it 'creative amnesia'.

KD: Can it be so easily done? For example, how easy is it to forget the intercommunical violence of 1964 in Guyana – the African pogroms of the Asian community which are commemorated in the poem 'For Mala' and recounted in *The Intended*?

DD: I think one of the most obvious things about the Caribbean is its social fluidity. This leads to an openness and a genuine democracy of mood and of practice in the region. The Anglophone Caribbean is one of the most democratic regions on earth, not just in terms of parliamentary structures, but in terms of people from different ancestries, from different cultures living side by side and, overwhelmingly, in peace. There has never been in my memory – in Barbados or Trinidad or Jamaica, or anywhere else in the Anglophone Caribbean, racial violence between black people and Indians and Chinese and so on. The great tragedy of Guyana is that it did happen. It was brutish, it was short and it was traumatic. And it happened because these differences were being manufactured into the weaponry of hatred. The differences are there, they've always been there, they've always been acknowledged, we've always lived side by side, and then, suddenly – in a period of destabilisation largely CIA-fuelled as we know from the records – the differences became sources of grievance and sources of hatred. And from being fluid in the way we lived with each other, we started closing off our identities, we started calling ourselves Indians and Africans – which we always had, but now we were naming ourselves aggressively. We were naming ourselves against each other. I think it's an un-Caribbean characteristic. It goes so deeply against the grain of our development, which has been one of mutualities. The African were there, they cleared the landscape; the Indians came, they reploughed the landscape; they lived next to the Africans in semi-poverty; the Chinese came, again as petty traders, as petty workers – everybody came to work. It was a commonality of experience, no matter what part of the world we came from. I think it's because of that humility, out of the humiliation of those migrations, and the humility of being a peasant and having very little – out of that was bred a humanism which made it possible for us to not kill each other.

KD: So 1964 was externally triggered, and exceptional?

DD: It was a tremendous exception. And to such an extent that nobody in Guyana talks publicly about it. It is an embarrassment to the Indians, who suddenly felt vulnerable and weak. Their own non-violent traditions became a source of vulnerability to them. And it's a tremendous embarrassment to the Africans because they behaved in highly indecent ways. But I would have to qualify that by saying that this was not entirely ethnic violence. The violence was not just simply manufactured by the Americans, but by groups of people within particular political parties. There were thug squads, there were agitators who went out to create trouble and murder. Three young girls who were very, very close members of my family, were protected from rape and brutality by a black neighbour who hid them under the bed and then went out on the veranda and shouted 'kill the Coolies, kill the Coolies', because she wanted to be seen to be on the right side. It was a much more complex thing than sheer ethnic violence.

KD: Did it make later identities – for example the black identity which emerged in the UK, as a consequence of the shared experience of exclusion – more fragile and tentative?

DD: A direct result of the race riots in Guyana was that Indians started to rediscover and rethink their history. An Indian renaissance took place. For the first time books were published on who the Indians were, and which part of India they came from. We were forced out of an easy Creolisation into a sense of difference. We tried to let those differences be a source of strength for us, and not a source of oppositional politics or aggression against the other – in this case, black people. At it's best this renaissance was a desire to find and understand our place in Guyanese society. We'd been cutting the cane and working the land for a couple of hundred years, so obviously we belonged to the place. But we didn't have a scholarly grasp of our history. The project was therefore a recovery of memory, a reaction against our sense of vulnerability, and an assertion of our citizenship. That is very different from the tribalisation that goes on in the West. West Indians are not tribal. We have all lost our tribes, we've lost our castes, we've been liberated into a new environment. If you live in the region, you are multi-cultural in yourself, with no sense of being Madrassi, Bihari or Mandingo. But when you come to the West you become black. You become tribalised. You become a Jamaican, or a Trinidadian, and you start remembering your history. It's not for the sake of self-understanding, or an assertion of citizenship. It's a way of saying this is what we are, as a reply to being told that we are nothing. The society in which we live here is far more tribal in terms of its class structures and work patterns. We are detribalised, free and democratic people, arriving in a tribal society which forces us into new tribalisations based on hatred. To me that is part of the pollution of the Diaspora which we have to resist. If West Indians have anything to give to this society it is a vision of democracy and the possibility of being plural within a singular character.

KD: What impact has that had on the choices you have made as a novelist? Will the idea of a unitary English literature also disappear?

DD: When I wrote *Disappearance* I wanted to have a go at writing an elegant, chiselled and restrained English prose. And it was definitely a novel addressed to VS Naipaul and his *Enigma of Arrival*,[13] the first major immigrant novel about the English countryside. I was writing my own novel about the English rural landscape, very much writing to Naipaul and imitating, as far as possible, his style. Mainly to distance myself from it, because my own views on the English countryside are much more troubled and much less nostalgic than Naipaul's. I wanted to write like Naipaul and undercut him with a series of disappearances and revelations of traumas that weren't there in *Enigma of Arrival*. *Disappearance* was a novel that rewrote *Heart of Darkness*, as we said, but actually I was rewriting Naipaul's rewriting of *Heart of Darkness*. To me that has radical potential. It means that we can develop the sense of our traditions of literature, that our traditions don't necessarily start with Chaucer, they might also start with Derek Walcott, or Edward Braithwaite, or VS Naipaul, or Jean Rhys. There is a younger generation of Caribbean writers who should be responding to and rewriting these masters – unfortunately they happen to be mostly male – and avoiding an obsession with *The Tempest* and Conrad and canonical texts which have encapsulated us in way which are negative or brutish. I wanted to acknowledge the master who had the original task of rewriting the canonical texts of the West. We must now rewrite their rewriting of those canonical texts. After a while, the canonical texts will disappear. They will cease to have relevance.

KD: Will it be a European literature, and a European identity, that finally succeeds them?

DD: Well, I don't think the British have coped well with the idea of a European identity. There is still an island mentality and an identity based on the various wars which have defined the British against the rest. Our situation as black people is even more intriguing. Although we are minorities in Britain, over the last fifty years or so we've negotiated space in the society. We've understood the language of the society, and we've used it to negotiate with the majority population. As the whole nation is plunged into Europe, I think the confusion which you get among the white majority is also reflected in our own confusions. We have not really thought about our European position. Its partly because a lot of us don't travel in Europe. I mean, I rarely see a West Indian tourist in Venice. To us Europe doesn't exist! And yet if you do go to Europe it's remarkable what you discover. There really are quite marvellous possibilities of connecting different points of the colonial process, of connecting up and recognising all kinds of bewildering strangenesses in our own condition. Recently I met a Dutch Indian like myself. He ended up in Holland and I ended up in Guyana. And we had both been given biblical names. He was speaking Dutch and couldn't speak English. And I can't speak Dutch. I marvelled at the fact that an Indian could speak Dutch. And when I go to Paris and I see Rastafarians, North African Rastafarians and non-English speaking Rastafarians. So I think for us Europe could be a place of adventure, a place where we can connect up to even more complex identities. But I also suspect it won't be, because of policies directed against refugees and immigrants. The fortressing of Europe will set limits, and tribalisms are flaring up everywhere.

Notes

[1] David Dabydeen, *Hogarth's Blacks*, Manchester University Press, Manchester 1987.
[2] David Dabydeen, *Walpole and Commercial Britain*, Hansib Publishing Ltd, London 1988.
[3] David Dabydeen, *Slave Song*, Dangaroo Press, Sydney Australia 1984.
[4] David Dabydeen, *Coolie Odyssey*, Hansib Publishing Ltd, London 1988.
[5] David Dabydeen, *The Intended*, Secker and Warburg, London 1991.
[6] David Dabydeen, *Disappearance*, Secker and Warburg, London 1993.
[7] *Coolie Odyssey*, op cit, p 12.
[8] *Ibid*, p 13.

[9] In an advance comment printed in *Coolie Odyssey, ibid.*

[10] Aime Cesaire, *Collected Poetry*, University of California Press, USA 1993.

[11] Leopold Senghor, *Collected Poetry*, University Press of Virginia, USA 1992.

[12] Jean Baudrillard, *The Transparency of Evil*, Verso London 1993, pp 21-22.

[13] VS Naipaul, *The Enigma of Arrival*, Penguin, Harmondsworth 1988.

Section Three: Faces to the Future – Towards a Twenty-First Century Left

Waking up to New Times: Doubts and Dilemmas on the Left

KEVIN DAVEY

Have no doubts
About the one
Who tells you
He is afraid

But be afraid
Of the one
Who tells you
He has no doubts

Erich Fried

Recent developments on the British left suggest that it will enter the new millennium in a state of exhaustion rather than anticipation. After its mid-century, reforming apogee under Clement Attlee, it has persistently failed to modernise and augment its project in a way that could generate viable, alternative models for social development. For a political force that still imagines it represents modernity, democracy and the dynamism for change in society, the left has been remarkably dilatory in acknowledging the new features of the social landscape which it inhabits. It has been even slower to revise, in the many places where it is necessary, its ideology, strategy, policy and organisation.

Despite a half decade of trauma, during which the state socialism that employed the language of Marxism to command and impoverish Eastern Europe has finally collapsed, and the electoral prospects of the western left have reached a nadir, the response of the Labour Party and its dependent left has been little more than a reluctant and uncomprehending accommodation to events. A puzzled, perplexed and bewildered left has been at best unable, and at worst unwilling, to recognise the recent and dramatic changes in the processes that structure contemporary life and shape the political opportunities which are available. Somewhat paradoxically, modern British Conservatism has been far quicker to discard the residual mental maps that had helped it to find its political way through the first half of the century. As the first to recognise that the post-war settlement was unsustainable, the right reaped the benefits in 1979 and has retained office ever since. In contrast, a left that has frequently argued 'no return to the 1930s' has, in its central themes, forms of organisation and perspectives, never forsaken the period.

In British politics, new ideas are generally suspect, unwelcome or disregarded. Where they cannot be overlooked, they are always and instantly challenged to justify themselves in electoral or instrumental terms. This is not necessarily a bad thing. Social theories are always contestable, must always be reflexive and will inevitably have strategic implications when they are linked to a political initiative. But the response of the left to the New Times analysis set in motion by *Marxism Today* was a combination of delusion, impatience and resistance so intense that it suggested a deeper appraisal was being forced. In fact, the short tempered retorts of the traditional left revealed its continuing dilemma: if it doesn't rethink, it will almost certainly become irrelevant; yet if it does, it will have to give up many of its certainties, practices and sinecures.

Once Upon a New Times

New Times is a shorthand phrase for the intellectual composite of Marxist and post-Marxist perspectives initiated in October 1988 by *Marxism Today*, the unruly, charismatic and highly subsidised offspring of a disintegrating British Communist Party. For eleven months the magazine ran a diverse series of analytic and polemical essays which, taken together, constituted an audit of economy, polity and culture that was both comprehensive and unique. As the main medium for Eurocommunist politics in Britain, it also insisted that a complementary transformation of the practice and thinking of the left was long overdue. Controversy raged and within a year the essays were anthologised in *New Times – The Changing Face of Politics in the 1990s*.[1] A *New Times Weekend* took place in October 1989 and the ideas later reappeared as a Manifesto agreed by the Communist Party in its twilight years. *New Times* persists as the title of the fortnightly newspaper of the Communist Party's successor, Democratic Left, and as the concern of the independent North London discussion group *Signs of the Times*, which generated this volume.[2]

The diverse issues raised by the New Times analysts cut the traditional left, already disempowered by an authoritarian and apparently irremovable government, to the quick. Contributors to the debate recognised, and in many cases celebrated, the numerical decline of the manual working class; the proliferation of cultural identities and the growing importance of choice, consumption and the new communications technologies; the irreversible globalisation of the economy and the appearance of new forms of economic organisation which threatened to make traditional forms of intervention redundant; the marginalisation and possible irrelevance of political parties; the simultaneous rise of the local and the transnational, tending towards the dissolution of nation states; the emergent themes of democratic citizenship, ecology, and feminism and the apparent obsolescence of left/right distinctions in politics.

The iconoclasm in part derived from the European utopian thinkers who, earlier in the 1980s, had been influential critics of social democracy and authoritarian smokestack socialism: Gorz, Touraine, Bahro and others. Generally speaking the British left was deaf to these prophets of post-industrial democracy and dismissed their work. In contrast, the New Times theorists domesticated many of their insights. The neo-Marxist economics of the French Regulation school were grafted onto Gramscian cultural analysis and important related voices on the European left–Napolitano, Glotz, Therborn – were acknowledged. And a disembedded feminism, surviving well beyond the lifespan of women's liberation as a movement, took up firm residence in the project.

This theoretical mixing and matching occurred in the context of, and in part drew on, a wave of non-foundationalist, philosophical thinking associated with French post-structuralist thinkers like Derrida, Lyotard and Baudrillard, and a redefinition of the way in which power operates, derived from Foucault, which are often casually summarily referred to as postmodernist. This direct challenge to historical materialism, the systematic theory of the Marxist left, also threatened many of the assumptions of social democratic political action. This put the grammatic elements of the New Times project at risk, and forced closer attention to post-Gramscian theorists of radical democracy – of whom Laclau and Mouffe were the most prominent – who had addressed the political implications of the philosophical critique of essentialist thought. The journal *New Left Review* hosted much of the ensuing debate while offering a rearguard defence on behalf of historical materialism.[3]

Derision, indifference and incomprehension have been the main response to this new body of postmodern work but an attempt to incorporate the main themes into more familiar, neo-Marxist frameworks has been made in the work of Lash and Urry on disorganised capitalism, Jameson on the postmodern as the cultural logic of late capitalism and in the powerful attempt at a synthesis offered by David Harvey.[4] In fact, the New Times analysis

itself was also an attempt to transform what had previously
been a fragmentary, cultural analysis into the refurbished
archetype of a post-Fordist base with a postmodern
superstructure.

The crowded interface between cultural theory and
Marxism was also the workplace of Britain's principal
Gramscian thinker. Stuart Hall had identified Thatcher's
hegemonic momentum as 'authoritarian populism' and
her government's achievement as 'regressive modernisation'. The crucial essays, which demonstrated that the
right had been quicker than Labour to acknowledge the
changed social, cultural and economic context for politics,
had first appeared in *Marxism Today* and they were later
collected in *The Hard Road to Renewal*.[5] Throughout the
1980s Hall's mode of analysis was frequently challenged
for the subordinate role it attributed to economics, for the
way in which he had characterised divisions in the
Conservative Party and for the lack of any empirical
evidence that the electorate had indeed become Thatcherite.[6] Since 1989 his work has also developed in ways which
suggest that it was in fact deeply troubled by the
philosophical challenge to realism and historical materialism, even in its Gramscian form.[7] Nevertheless Hall's
influential account of Thatcherism provided the foundation for the New Times theses, including the many
propositions and polemics whose antipathy to existing
political formations greatly exceeded his own.

In retrospect, 1988 should have been a favourable
moment for a hearing. It was a crucial year in the
evolution of the British left. Having lost its third successive
election, Labour, under Neil Kinnock's leadership, was
reluctantly considering a statement of aims and values
while also preparing for a comprehensive policy review.
And the non-Kinnockite hard left of the party, which had
recently lined up behind an ideologically intransigent and
highly unsuccessful Benn-Heffer leadership campaign,
largely based on Labour's 1983 Manifesto, had exposed its
own weakness.[8] An ambitious new series of Socialist
Conferences, initiated by the Socialist Society, the
Conference of Socialist Economists and the Campaign

Group, promised to act independently of the rhythms of electoral politics. The Socialist Conferences aimed to launch a twin track movement: based inside the Labour Party and outside.[9] In retrospect the year appears to be a political watershed.

The New Times initiative was therefore a striking and perhaps opportunist attempt to synthesise a number of developments in French philosophy and economics, Gramscian theory, British cultural studies and feminism. It appeared at a moment of difficulty and opportunity for the left in Britain as a whole while also serving as a further step in the ascendancy of the Eurocommunist tendency over the traditionalists in the British Communist Party.[10]

The British left's experience of defeat was compelling a full, if reluctant, remapping of politics. Neither of the traditional options for class struggle – syndicalist combat at the workplace or periodic electoral competition between democratic parties – had hindered Thatcherism in any way, and hybrid combinations of the two – the spirit of Bennism – had also been rebuffed. And all the old tools for intervention seemed blunter or threatened to be less productive. To many, the need for an expedition beyond the social democratic and Leninist perspectives which had long divided, confined and failed the left was becoming clear. Talk of 'dual tracks and third roads' was plentiful,[11] but in their breadth, aspiration and iconoclasm, only the New Times theses replicated and substantially extended the earlier post-war declarations by the left. 'Modern Capitalism and Revolution' by the Socialisme ou Barbarie group led by Castoriadis in France, the 'Port Huron Statement' of the American Students for a Democratic Society and the *1968 May Day Manifesto*[12] were three earlier attempts to break out of a related conceptual and political impasse. As texts these predecessors have become intellectual milestones for particular generational fragments of the political class which are aligned to the left. However, as movements, all were easily marginalised or eventually broken. The New Times analysis represents a recognition by the left, however contradictory or outspoken, of equally irreversible and parallel transformations in political culture

and social and economic activity. It too attempted to map a
path away from the disabling legacies of bolshevism and
social democracy. And although it also lacks sustained,
organised expression, its emphasis has persisted in two
subsequent manifestoes: Democratic Left's 'Renovation'[13]
and Alain Lipietz's *Towards a New Economic Order*[14].

There were and have continued to be many refusals to
look the new reality that was being documented in the eye,
and a number of counter-manifestoes and angry
denunciations were issued.[15] John Saville's response
repeated the main criticisms offered by the orthodox left
and can be offered as typical: the analysis had broken the
link between base and superstructure, it was obsessed with
ideology and consumption, it was intellectually subservient
to Thatcher and her success, and it had mistaken a
consumer boom for a successful hegemonic project. In
sum, the whole initiative consisted of 'criticisms of
marginal matters together with a large black hole of
intellectual nothingness at the centre'.[16] Unsurprisingly,
the predetermined policy outcomes of Kinnock's modernisation of Labour also owed little to the formulations of
the New Times theorists, although, the initiative was
plagiarised in the review process.

The British Left in Free Fall

One doesn't have to look far to realise that the accelerated
pace of change since 1988 has swept away so many pillars
of socialist thinking that much of the traditional left is now
in free fall.

Stalinism has ended in the East, and an enfeebled free
market has overreached itself in the rush for the
opportunities that have resulted. While war in the Gulf
and in Europe has dismayed a peace movement
habituated to earlier Cold War structures and issues,
closer to home, the process of European integration has
dismayed the left, most of which is neither willing nor
ready for Europeanisation. However, Charter 88
appeared within a few weeks of the launch of the New
Times initiative and has been able to sustain its

modernising, constitutional project. On the other hand, the green political bubble has swelled and burst, showering the established parties with fragments of policy and phraseology. There has been continued economic decline, despite the occasional blip or sighting of recovery. The election of President Clinton has shown that the centre-left can win elections but as Democrat trade policies were in the main directed against his political buddies in Europe, the honeymoon was brief. While the belated rise of the centre-left think tank has resulted in the Institute for Public Policy Research (IPPR), the Commission on Social Justice, and Demos, all the major political parties have lost support and membership, and the Communist Party has disappeared altogether. In fact television has become the predominant vehicle for politics and campaigns, as Band Aid, Comic Relief and similar enterprises have proven many times over. And, of course, Labour has lost yet another election.

Important policy changes on Europe, constitutional reform, democracy and the party's own internal structures have followed, but Labour's prospects of office via an overall Parliamentary majority remain remote. Labour's official position on European integration has been transformed. It no longer has a statist, nationalising view of alternatives to the free market. The party has reluctantly accepted much of the case for constitutional reform, but won't bring itself to take the most important step, electoral reform for the Commons. Labour has finally decided to redefine its relationship to unions, but even the partial changes adopted in 1993 – in the selection of the leader and parliamentary candidates – led to a tremendous and bitter polarisation. And at that point the role of trade unions at conference, on the National Executive Committee and on local general committees was not even up for discussion. And whereas during the Kinnock years it was the hard left which was expelled or marginalised, the new targets of a loyalty-demanding leadership are those who dare to talk of inter party co-operation or, even worse, coalition.

The far left is now living through its swansong,

deceiving itself and others, by pointing to minor and temporary membership increases as sufficient grounds for retaining its canonical texts and anachronistic perspectives. Purged by a determined leadership, Militant, once the largest Trotskyist organisation in British politics, has split. It is now in open competition with Labour, most effectively in Scotland, despite having lost its MPs, most of its members and its influence in the unions. The Socialist Workers party (SWP) scrapes a political living from the little that persists of an activist, student culture. The deadlocked residue of Bennism, the Socialist Movement, is tongue tied by divisions on today's key issues of Europe and electoral reform. Clearly, there is no longer a singular left with a common culture and language, but rather a series of incommensurate fragments that make the splits of the past look like tiffs in a political teacup. The in-house, soft left strategy of unfailing support to the party leadership, with all criticisms heavily coded, which has been pursued by the Labour Co-ordinating Committee, has failed to influence events; the original Bennite project has disintegrated, and the Leninists have still not built their mass party. As with the parties, so too with the publications. The loss of readerships and forums for debate compound the involution of the left and its isolation from wider civil currents. The best don't know what to think or do, and the worst still have no doubts.

The far left is intransigently oppositionalist and orthodox. It prefers familiar causes and ritual forms of action, fund raising and solidarity to hard thought. It displays, in equal measure, hostility towards Europeanisation, effective communications strategies and any explanation of its difficulties in terms other than leadership betrayal. The Leninist left is now a minor and myopic force, rallying to the defence of the very structures that many cut their political teeth confronting, the nation state; the block vote; the first-past-the-post electoral system. Can the darkness they inhabit be so very deep that they have still not recognised the faces of their erstwhile opponents right beside them? As for the soft left, it is still, inexcusably, shadowing the shadow Cabinet, even though

the leadership to which it was building bridges was washed
away long ago. Its journal *Renewal* showcases and gives
polemical edge to emergent leadership themes. A
'Modernisation Manifesto' issued in mid-1993 identified
the vested interests of the City and an antiquated state
structure as the source of Britain's problems and went on
to advocate regulation of the City, strong supply side
measures, a restricted notion of pluralism in which a
collaborative state would empower independent institutions, and the introduction of one-member, one-vote into
Labour Party selection procedures.[17]

Little remains of the left of the 1960s and 1970s that
first challenged the corporatist politics that Labour is now
so keen to ditch. Its temporary residence in London's
County Hall, where it tried to develop popular
participation and an accessible, empowering local state as
an alternative to the modernisation of the city by the
market, was ended by state decree. After many false starts
– *Beyond the Fragments*, the Socialist Society, *News on
Sunday, Socialist*, to name a few – the little that remains
seems fatally attracted to a dialogue with the Trotskyist
tradition from which it emerged, or yesterday's traditional
left of whose organisational strengths and resources, albeit
diminishing, it remains envious.[18]

And what of the original New Times left? Most of the
readers of *Marxism Today* were in fact outside the
Communist Party. And so were most of the contributors.
It was therefore always a homeless, shifting vision, indirect
in its impact on British politics and, as a cause, however
contradictory, the concern of few. The analysis lives on, in
disparate forms, in seminar groups, the Open University,
the work of Democratic Left, and in cultural studies
departments. It is everywhere and nowhere, fondly
remembered and forgotten at the same time.[19]

A Slow Awakening

Slowly, irreversibly, and usually without acknowledgement, elements of the New Times analysis have begun to
permeate the thinking and public pronouncements of

much left of centre politics in Britain. This is not just because the British left is a slow learner, redeemable only over time, but also because the diverse theses have been more carefully researched and disseminated, and the disparate processes to which the analysis pointed have persisted, further revealing the inadequacy of existing political formations to deal with them.

The left has been greatly discomforted by the new economic dynamic of flexible specialisation. Immediately posed was the question of whether its traditional attempts at social control over the market – nationalisation, co-ops or subsidy – were adequate to the process. And whether the Keynesian strategies which had provided the left with its only historical economic success could have any purchase on the behaviour of a polycentric, homeless corporation or flexible transnational like Honda, which, based in Japan, Europe and North America, always is in its bulk, located elsewhere as far as any national government is concerned. Inevitably, the goal of full employment became problematic as national, political elites recognised their limitations in the new situation.

Bewildered by the enormity of the challenge and the Lilliputian scale of its human, structural and policy resources, Labour's economic policy has meandered between intervention and accommodation to the market. Only mildly redistributionist in outlook, in the early 1990s Labour increasingly offered a supply-side aspiration to a high skill, high wage economy which would deliver competitive advantage as its main rejoinder to the government's development of a low skill, low wage and low tax economy, intended to be seductive to globally mobile capital. It rarely disassociated itself from the tight monetary management both parties thought necessary to avoid inflation. Front bench speeches on economic issues also went out of their way to suggest that improvements in welfare would be paid for by growth rather than increases in taxation. This was perceived as electorally crucial, as the only way to reassure the C2s and simultaneously win the votes of the poor. Qualitative issues about growth rarely troubled front bench economists, a large number of whom still hoped against the evidence – damning in the case of Mitterand's France – that Keynesianism could be exhumed and made to work in one small, and increasingly unimportant, corner of the globalised economy, notwithstanding the likelihood of capital flight and balance of payments crises. But there has also been a gradual realisation of the need for international co-operation if growth of any kind is to be generated, and increasing recognition of the fact that a reformed EC is the only agency immediately available.[20]

In addition, the momentum of flexible specialisation has enforced some rethinking in the political mainstream. Patricia Hewitt and Harriet Harman have spoken out in favour of flexible employment patterns and welcomed new approaches to working time;[21] trade union practice has changed, most famously in the Transport and General Workers Union's Link Up initiative, a recruitment campaign specifically oriented towards female part-time workers; and local authority economic policy has been significantly influenced by the London Industrial Strategy developed by Robin Murray, when he worked at the Greater London Council (GLC), the basic premises of which are still disseminated by the Centre for Local Economic Strategies (CLES) in its journal *Local Economy*. More widely, the realisation that jobless growth is the most likely consequence of any recovery has fuelled interest in Basic Income Schemes[22] and versions of Workfare.

Saying Goodbye to the Working Class

The working class, as traditionally represented in the folklore and the fantasies of the left, really is disappearing, numerically and politically. Given the institutional structures of the British left, the erosion of trade unionism and its decoupling from the political has been particularly significant. Neither the New Realist nor the Scargillite response to monetarism in government had any impact on the forced evanescence of organised labour. Four million members simply vanished from the public sphere into a twilight zone of unemployment, casualisation, non-unionised workplaces and the informal economy. Like the party they have sponsored for the best part of the century, the unions now suffer from falling membership, diminishing income and reduced political influence, a situation they are sensibly attempting to redress through mergers and more attention to Brussels. A phased reduction in their leverage over Labour is also underway, causing a great deal of bitterness and division and leaving their future role far from clear.

Nevertheless, the trade unions possess a role, membership and residual public popularity that should neither be overlooked nor ejected from the socialist project. We shouldn't underestimate their ability or willingness to keep up with a political project that acknowledges consumers and quality of service as well as producer interests, or the possibility that they might spend their political funds more wisely. But how well will they cope with post-Fordist forms, particularly as the economic sectors in which they are weakest grow at the expense of those in which they were once strong? Or with the fact that 90 per cent of the jobs created since 1979 have been taken by women? What provision have they made for the fact that almost half of the women now working (i.e. nearly half of the workforce) are in part time jobs and low paid? How will they deal with the highly mobile employers they confront at the transnational negotiating table? The New Times theses were generated just as a divergence between trade unionism and politics was being initiated. This is important unfinished business for any new left.

Becoming European

The Delors vision of a united and integrated Europe at first made great political headway in Labour circles, offering the prospect of additional countervailing powers and new allies in the confrontation with transnational economic forces. At the same time the regional programmes of the EC weakened the authority of national state elites by encouraging the potential recipients of funds to bypass their governments and bid direct to

Brussels. Something that was much bigger, but that was also more responsive than Westminster beckoned, and nationalist movements in Scotland and Wales responded. The new Jerusalem of the 1990s was a Europe of the regions which seemed to promise both increased purchase on the globalised economy and a simultaneous increase in local, democratic decision-making. But then the parliamentary left made common cause with the shameless Little Englandism of the Tory right in an attempt to prevent ratification of the Maastricht Treaty, citing the democratic deficit, an unaccountable bank and the loss of House of Commons sovereignty as their justification. This left had invented its own variation of a *Europe des Patries* and the process of political Europeanisation consequently stalled, just as the process of economic and monetary union faltered once the costs of German reunification were calculated. British exit from the ERM then lowered the economic and political tension and the uninspiring, extended drama of the ratification of a treaty from which Britain was largely exempt replaced a brief dawn of expanding horizons and possibilities.

Citizen Who

Fourteen years of untrammelled Conservative rule has ensured that the need to change the way in which Britain is governed, not merely the party in charge, is widely and popularly perceived. This revulsion against the British one-party state fuels a new politics of citizenship and empowerment. Labour has begun to reposition itself as a force for democratic reform. At long last it is committed to a Freedom of Information Act, A Bill of Rights incorporating the European Convention on Human Rights and electoral reform for European and Second Chamber elections. However the crude translation of the need to reform the Commons into the promise of a referendum makes the Plant Commission's two years of deliberation something of a fool's errand, despite its assistance in delegitimating the first-past-the-post system. Labour still has no firm commitment to electoral reform for the Commons nor has it taken the opportunity to initiate a process that will result in a modern, written constitution. The party is also unclear how to handle the enduring fiscal crisis of the welfare state in a way that won't jeopardise its chances of election by alienating the recipients of benefits, tax payers, or both. It clearly regards citizens as constitutional ciphers rather than as active participants and partners in its social and economic policy making or future practice as a government.

Fortunately, and belatedly, Labour has acknowledged its intellectual limits by sub-contracting out a number of these ideological and policy dilemmas to people who understand the issues far better. Important debates on new forms of social citizenship have taken place at the IPPR and the principles that underlay the Beveridge reforms are being refurbished by the Commission on Social Justice.[23] However, the exploration of citizenship still hasn't caught up with the original New Times agenda, in particular, the vexing and unresolved question of how to reconcile universal rights with an emerging diversity of secular and religious identities.[24]

War: Just War?

The end of the Cold War and the division of Europe has not resulted in a demilitarisation of the west, and neither has the widely expected 'peace dividend' been paid. Instead, military conflicts have proliferated. The Gulf War, conflict in the former Yugoslavia and the obstacles faced by the provision of aid to countries like Somalia have forced a transformation in the left's perception of conflict between states. Increasingly, military intervention by western powers has been endorsed. This has been accompanied, and in great part enabled, by the application of a highly reductive language of fascism, anti-fascism and appeasement to international relations. Post-Cold War battles are now frequently interpreted by reference to the 1930s and the Second World War.[25] While the language of anti-imperialism is treated as obsolescent, that of the United Nations and benevolent intervention is ascendant.

There have been few coherent objections from a peace movement which was largely demobilised by the ending of the Cold War, and which has found no consensus to replace the opposition to nuclear weaponry which unified it. Consequently there is no agreement on the centre left as to what constitutes the legitimate use of force, or what defines a just war.[26]

Fred Halliday argued that to interpret the Gulf War as imperialist was a blunder which allied the left with Iraqi fascism. Socialists had forgotten that there were occasions when the use of force was legitimate. He was both polemical and blunt, stating that 'If I have to make a choice between imperialism and fascism, I choose imperialism.'[27] Neal Ascherson, who charged that a socialism which judges all conflicts exclusively by the class interest of ruling groups is primitive, went on to declare himself a middle of the road warmonger.[28]

Their interventionist arguments have been taken much further by Martin Shaw, who argues that there has been a pacification of the core of the World system, and the development of global institutions whose purpose is to limit military conflicts. Consequently, ambitious state elites on the margins are wholly misunderstood if they are seen solely in the conceptual framework of anti-imperialism. The new settlement has its contradictions. Nationalist and ethnic polarisations have appeared in the core, and a self-interested, isolationist stance also tempts a number of key nation states. Shaw argues that frequent intercessions will be required of these core states and that their actions must involve a strengthened United Nations and regional institutions and be based on an aspiration towards a global community based on human rights. There are just and effective forms of economic, political and military intervention which can be undertaken without accommodating the military and economic priorities of the United States.[29]

Green Honeymoon Over

Equally global in its implication is the environmental crisis. In 1989, the British green vote hit an all time high in the

European elections. But the years since have witnessed the return of the Green Party's electoral support to insignificant levels, the departure of key figures from its leadership, a collapse in its membership and a decline in public donations to campaigning organisations like Greenpeace. Yet the ecological crisis to which these initiatives were a political response has deepened. Despite the political false start, the thinning and perforation of the ozone layer, defoliation by acid rain, pollution-induced poor health, the waste and exhaustion of scarce resources and other ecological issues remain a major civil concern and this is acknowledged by all parliamentary parties. Some important policy work has emerged from the left,[30] the concept of sustainability is more widely understood and featured heavily in the *Manifesto for New Times*, and Labour has set up an enquiry into ecological issues. But the diminished electoral challenge appears to have engendered complacency. Unlike the Commission on Social Justice and the Plant Commission, Labour's environmental rethink was set up as an entirely in-house review body.

Glitz and Spin

The increased mobility of capital, central to the developments summarised in New Times, had itself been enabled by developments in communications technology: the satellite, the silicon chip and fibre optics. Some on the left had viewed these developments with alarm, denigrating the new communications media and information retrieval systems as the carceral computer and the electronic panopticon.[31]. But of course the question is how to turn these new systems, with their contradictory potential for surveillance and interaction, into real forms of communication and mechanisms for creativity and decision-making. Instead of trying to answer that question, Labour's communicational preferences remain in the past. The party's ambition is limited to the introduction of neo-Morrisonian principles of public ownership, arguing that the governors of the BBC should be replaced with a more representative board of trustees supplemented by a viewers and listeners council.[32]

Beyond Left and Right

Baudrillard has argued that the intensified circulation of information by proliferating media systems has neutralised the difference between left and right, ended the social and silenced the masses. Although there was a brief flirtation with Baudrillard's work in *Marxism Today*, the transcendence of left/right distinctions celebrated by the magazine – and by David Marquand, the Green Party and the think tank Demos – is less apocalyptic. It simply suggested that the most significant of the counterposed responses to the issues raised by the New Times analysis would polarise around an axis radically different from that of the existing left/right division in British politics. The implication was that surprising political realignments and new forms of politics were on the agenda. But when the overcoming of left and right was articulated with psephology, electoral tactics and a commitment to pluralism, it actually engendered something much more commonplace; the endorsment of a left-of-centre electoral pact and/or tactical voting. The New Times analysis was the principal means by which the British, neo-Gramscian commitment to the formation of a national popular will effected this extraordinary, yet unstable, reconciliation between electoral pragmatism, and postmodern philosophy.

However, there is every reason to suppose that our real choice lies between a form of modernisation based on a commitment to democracy, equality, sustainability and compassion, and a form driven by the imperatives of the market. If that is so, the rhetoric of the transcendence, disappearance or deconstruction of the opposition between left and right, however well-intentioned, may obstruct the political learning necessary for renewal.

Finding a Prince

Some of the New Times theses were contradictory, and

many opened out onto political vistas that dazzled and frightened even those who initiated the analysis. Subsequent events have added to this body of unfinished business. The new nationalism did not lead to an enhancement of democratic rights and citizenship in the former Yugoslavia, for example. Some of the contrasts to which its contributors pointed were overdrawn, and much more of the old persisted alongside the new than its advocates were prepared to acknowledge.

Now that time has confirmed that the analysis had identified some real trends, the left is slowly, often reluctantly, and frequently without acknowledgement, beginning to draw on its insights and sources. But a major political problem remains. 'The very proliferation of new sites of social antagonism makes the prospect of constructing a unified counter-hegemonic force as the agency of progressive change harder rather than easier. Moreover, because the spread and pace of change is so uneven, the problems of the mind of political strategy required to unify old and new constituencies of change ... are profoundly complex'.[33]

Samson-like, the New Times analysis reduced its organisational base to rubble. The Communist Party in which it originated has been replaced with Democratic Left, a 1200 strong organisation which no longer regards itself as a party. As a political discourse it is a much weakened current. And somewhat ironically, the analysis has also become a victim of the processes it foresaw: the contraction and fragmentation of parties, the decline of grand explanatory theories, the implosion and depolarisation of politics. The connections have not been sustained, in theory or in practice. Gramsci wrote for a party; but British neo-Gramscianism, tired of kissing frogs, has failed to find a Prince of its own. The main beneficiaries have been the Trotskyist left, in particular the SWP, whose conferences and activism, by default, appear iconoclastic; and the modernising right in the Labour Party, whose complacency about the scale of change required goes unchallenged.

As parties across Europe contract in size; as old class

identities fragment and their cultures decline; as the
deliberations of nation states become less influential on the
economic, legal or cultural conditions of their populations;
and as new ways of organising proliferate outside the
established parties, it looks as if the era of the mass
national party has finally passed, however desperate the
measures taken to get members back. Impatiently waiting
in the wings, Green Realignment and the Socialist Society
assert that this condition is temporary or that it can be
overcome. It may be that some people realise the game is
up. During the 1992 Labour Party leadership election,
almost unnoticed, Bryan Gould confessed to a suspicion
that the era of the mass party had passed. The moment
was exceptional. Generally speaking, the centre-left and
radical left would both prefer the political clock to stop,
giving them the opportunity to conserve or replicate
failing and probably anachronistic organisational forms.[34]

Abandoned by key groups in the electorate, intellectually comatose, inhibited by a relationship with the trade
unions that both find joyless, Labour is certainly in need of
attention, as its modernisers half perceive. A routinised,
hierarchical coalition of diminishing or threatened
interests, the average age of its members, two thirds of
whom work in the public sector, is approaching 50 years
old. Its sclerosis has not gone unnoticed. Party research
repeatedly confirms that in the eyes of the public Labour is
associated with the past, the downwardly mobile, with
minorities and the unions. Consequently its vote in the
South remains sensitive to the advances of the right.
Double figure poll advantages have proved to be
ephemeral while the collapse in membership, finances and
ideas remains tangible and enduring. In public the party
has appeared confused about the economy, Europe,
electoral reform, taxation and the welfare state. The
desperately modernising, nonagenarian Labour Party has
become a tattered coat upon a stick, no longer knowing
what it stands for.

It has taken the Labour Party fourteen years in
opposition to make the tiniest of overtures towards other
forces left-of-centre. It will go further, although it is

unlikely to complement the process of shared thinking with common electoral action. But if this were more than a death-bed conversion Labour would also be acknowledging what the independent left, through the ghostly but still audible voices of the GLC, workers' alternative plans and women's committees could teach it about responsive forms of policy making and organisation, and exploring what the New Times theorists tried to tell it about the changing social and economic dynamic and its implication for contemporary political action. Sadly its growing self doubt doesn't run that deep.

Notes

[1] Stuart Hall and Martin Jacques (eds) *New Times: The Changing Face of Politics in the 1990s* Lawrence & Wishart, London 1989.

[2] Signs of the Times, c/o 28 Wargrave Avenue, London N15 6UD (see Founding statement on p 279 of this book).

[3] The work began with Ernesto Laclau and Chantal Mouffe, *Hegemony and Socialist Strategy*, Verso, London 1985: the debate commenced with Norman Geras' 'Post Marxism?' *New Left Review* 163, May-June 1987; Laclau and Mouffe 'Post Marxism without Apologies' *New Left Review* 166, Nov-Dec, 1987; and Norman Geras' 'Ex-Marxism without Substance in *New Left Review* 169, May-June, 1988.

[4] Scott Lash and John Urry, *The End of Organised Capitalism*, Polity Press, Cambridge 1987; Fredric Jameson *Postmodernism, or the Cultural Logic of Late Capitalism*, Verso, London 1991; David Harvey *The Condition of Postmodernity*, Basil Blackwell, Oxford 1989.

[5] Stuart Hall, *The Hard Road to Renewal: Thatcherism and the Crisis of the Left* Verso, London 1988.

[6] The main Marxist critique was offered by Bob Jessop, Kevin Bonnett, Simon Bromley and Tom Ling in *Thatcherism*, Polity Press, Cambridge 1980.

[7] There is evidence for this in Stuart Hall's contribution to the original anthology where he argues that there isn't a unified power game and that all politics may be positional. See *New Times op cit*, p 130 and the Foucauldian emphases of his most recent work, for example 'The West and the Rest: Discourse and Power' in Stuart Hall and Bram Gieben (eds), *Formations of Modernity*, Polity Press, Cambridge 1992.

[8] Colin Hughes and Patrick Wintour, *Labour Rebuilt: The New Model Labour Party*, Fourth Estate, London 1990, pp 92-3.

[9] The Socialist Policy Review, *Interlink* 13, 1989, p 6.

[10] A useful account of the life and death of the party can be found in William Thompson, *The Good Old Cause: British Communism 1920-1921*, Pluto Press, London 1992.

[11]*Interlink op cit*; Trevor Fisher (ed), *New Maps for the Nineties*, Chartist 1990.

[12] 'Modern Capitalism and Revolution' can be found in Cornelius Castoriadis *Political and Social Writings* Vol 2, University of Minnesota Press, Minnesota 1988, pp 226-325; The Port Huron Statement appears as an appendix to J. Miller *Democracy is in the Streets*, Simon and Schuster, New York 1978; *The May Day Manifesto* was published by Penguin, Harmondsworth 1968.

[13] 'Renovation', Democratic Left, January 1993.

[14] Alain Lipietz, *Towards a New Economic Order*, Polity Press, Cambridge 1992.

[15] For example, The Socialist Society, *Negotiating the Rapids: Socialist Politics for the Nineties*, 1989 which argued that the analysis was 'monolithic' with an 'obsessional emphasis on novelty'.

[16] John Saville, 'Marxism Today: An Anatomy' in *Socialist Register 1990*, The Merlin Press, London 1990, p 53.

[17] Labour Co-ordinating Committee, *Manifesto for Modernisation*, London June 1993.

[18] See Hilary Wainwright, *Labour: A Tale of Two Parties*, Hogarth Press, London, 1987, pp 252-286 and her article in *Socialist*, May 1992, p 7.

[19] A detailed history of the relationship between Gramscian analysis and the development of cultural studies in Britain can be found in David Harris *From Class Struggle to the Politics of Pleasure*, Routledge, London 1992.

[20] See Ken Coates and Michael Barratt Brown (eds), *A European Recovery Programme*, Spokesman Press, Nottingham 1993; The Tribune Group of MEPs, *Building on Maastricht: A Left Agenda for Europe 1993*, available from the South Wales European Office, 199 Newport Road, Cardiff CF2 1AJ; and the journal *European Labour Forum*.

[21]Patricia Hewitt, *About Time*, Rivers Oram Press, London 1993; Harriet Harman, *The Century Gap*, Vermillion Books, London 1993.

[22] Van Parijs, (ed) *Arguing for Basic Income*, Verso, London 1992.

[23] See Anna Coote (ed), *The Welfare of Citizens*, Rivers Oram Press, London 1992 and *Social Justice in a Changing World*, IPPR, London 1993.

[24]Stuart Hall and David Held in *New Times op cit*, pp 173-188. An introduction to the issues raised by identity politics can be found in Jonathan Rutherford (ed), *Identity*, Lawrence & Wishart, London 1990 and in Stuart Hall's 'The Question of Cultural Identity' in Stuart Hall, David Held and Tony McGrew (eds), *Modernity and its Futures*, Polity Press, Cambridge, 1992, p 273-316.

[25]For example, Neal Ascherson's claim that the position taken by the Communist JR Campbell in 1939 was also the appropriate response to the Gulf War in his 'Confessions of a Reluctant Middle of the Road Warmonger', *Independent on Sunday*, 10 February 1991.

[26] Although Mike Rustin did make an important start in his 'Justice and the Gulf War' in *Radical Philosophy* 61, Summer 1992, pp 3-9.

[27] Fred Halliday, *New Statesman and Society*, 8 March 1991, pp 15-16.

[28] Ascherson, *op cit*.

[29] Martin Shaw *Post Military Society: Militarism, Demilitarism and War at the end of the Twentieth Century*, Polity Press, Cambridge, 1992; Martin Shaw 'Grasping the Nettle' *'New Statesman and Society*, 15 January 1993, pp 16-17; Martin Shaw, 'War and Peace Politics' *Signs of the Times*, Discussion Paper, August 1993.

[30] Most notably Mike Jacobs *The Green Economy*, Pluto Press, London 1991 and Victor Anderson *Energy Efficient Policies*, Routledge, London 1993.

[31] D. Lyon, *The Information Society* Polity Press, Cambridge 1988; K. Robbins and F. Webster *The Technical Fix*, Macmillan, London 1989.

[32] Labour Party Discussion Document, 'Putting the Citizen at the Centre of British Broadcasting', London May 1993.

[33] Hall and Jacques, 1989 *op cit* p 18.

[34] On the expiry of the party as a political form see Sarah Benton in *Marxism Today*, March 1989; for Green Realignment see Sara Parkin in the *Guardian*, 3 June 1993; on the Socialist Society's aspirations see Richard Kuper 'We Need a New Left Party' *Tribune*, 20 March 1992; Bryan Gould made his comment during a leadership hustings speech at the LCC-Tribune conference 'New Directions', 26 June 1992.

Radical Democracy: Arguments and Principles

ADAM LENT

While many of the grand political doctrines of the nineteenth and twentieth centuries have seen their credibility wither in the last thirty years, democracy has remained constant. Its importance has actually grown with the changes in eastern Europe, even if these changes are proving somewhat ambiguous. Partly as a result of this situation, there has been increasing interest in the radical potential of democratic ideals and principles. Ernesto Laclau and Chantal Mouffe have developed a 'post-Marxist' theoretical analysis which, they assert, amounts to an argument for a radical conception of democracy.[1] Similarly, Roberto Unger and John Keane attempted to apply the fundamental principles of democracy to a radical political project.[2] These approaches have gained added inspiration from the growth of 'social movements', an apparently growing fragmentation of post-industrial society, and the declining faith in absolute values most clearly characterised by the increasing interest in postmodern thought.

Arguing for Radical Democracy

There are three main arguments in favour of a radical democratic perspective: two theoretical and one socio-political.

Explaining the Social Moment

The first theoretical argument seeks to explain the social moment. (By social moment, is meant an event, an idea and a particular, or a set of, human relationships analysed within their social context.) Throughout history, analysts have attempted to explain the social moment as the appearance, result of, or symptom of a higher order of things. This approach has been most significantly represented by religion through the belief that a social moment, such as a military victory or a certain political regime, is due to the designs of a mystical force or supernatural being. Alternatively, religious doctrine has also regarded the social moment as the result of the unfolding battle between good and evil, God and the Devil, or the sinful and the virtuous.

This approach, which can broadly be labelled epiphenomenal, was not, however, limited to the religious. Following the Enlightenment, there was a growth in the development and influence of epiphenomenal analysis that either rejected divine power and conflict absolutely or consigned it to a very limited or ambiguous role. The best known of these approaches are the Hegelian and the Marxist. The former explaining the social moment as the concrete form of the unfolding of human rationality or 'spirit'; the latter explaining the social moment as either resulting from class conflict or from the contradictions between productive forces and productive relations. It is important to state that not every social moment was seen as determined by the epiphenomena in Hegelian and Marxist approaches, but it is clear that the most important or cataclysmic social moments were seen as epiphenomena ie. as secondary events caused by other more fundamental or primary phenomena. It should also be made clear that in the Marxist, and more sophisticated Hegelian, analyses, the approach is somewhat more subtle, in that the primary phenomena, such as class conflict or 'spirit' is a social moment itself. Marxists, in particular, have emphasised this point, however this does not negate the fundamental critique of the epiphenomenal approach.

The influence of epiphenomenal explanations goes beyond the classic historicist approaches of Marxists and Hegelians. The writings of less explicitly ideological analysts, the pronouncements of politicians, our daily conversations, the assumptions of policy-makers; all are shot through with an understanding that explains social moments as the result of a higher order. Notions such as progress, 'history moving forward', civilisation, and the growing accuracy of scientific understanding all appeal to phenomena that are somehow guiding or designing various social moments. These phenomena might include the search for beauty or truth, the struggle for civilised values, or the inevitable march of industry and its goal of a technologically perfect world.

Any epiphenomenal analysis raises an awkward question that damages the credibility of the analysis at the most basic level. How is the analyst privileged in such a way as to observe or understand the influence or existence of the primary phenomena?

It is simply not convincing for an analyst to explain his or her own understanding as a result of the primary phenomena itself, because to accept this we have to accept the epiphenomenal explanation in the first place without yet being convinced of the correctness of the analyst's views. For example, if a Marxist was to say 'I am correct because I am for the working-class, the historically final and universal class' this assumes we accept the correctness of the class analysis already. It amounts to saying little more than 'I am correct because I am correct'.

Alternatively, epiphenomenal explanations can resort to explaining the analyst's privileged position in terms that immediately contradict the apparent influence of the primary phenomena. Marxism is the best example of this. Marxists have explained their superior understanding as a result of the power of scientific analysis. But it is never convincingly explained how this scientific analysis escapes the influence of class conflict or the contradictions of productive forces and productive relations. Why religious understanding is an 'ideological' or 'falsely conscious' result of the primary phenomena but scientific method is not is never clear. Such a basic flaw must seriously question the legitimacy of Marxism's whole approach to the analysis of history and society, as well as Marxist claims to political leadership.

To reject epiphenomenal explanation is not only a rejection of the belief that the social moment is the result of a higher order of things but also constitutes an acceptance of the more prosaic recognition that a social moment is only understandable, or is only imbued with meaning, through its articulation ie. 'any practice establishing a relation among elements such that their identity is modified'.[3] Essentially, social moments are constructed in the immediate world, through the conflict and articulation of already existing social moments.

If social moments are constructed through relations with each other, then that construction must be contingent. By contingent what is meant is that the social moment is constructed as an expedient, and at times highly complex, response to human purposes or needs that have themselves been constructed previously. This expedient construction, is not guided or determined by some ultimate purpose or transcendent force.

It is vital to recognise that the acceptance of the contingently constructed social moment has implications for the notion of objectivity. As objectivity can no longer be regarded as the result of a privileged analyst observing the primary phenomena and their creation of epiphe-nomena, then objectivity must itself be seen as a social moment that is just as contingent and constructed as any other.[4]

This is not an argument against coming to conclusions about one's world or environment. Quite clearly, conclusion is vital. Even if one managed to avoid making any pronouncements or value-judgements, one would still be making a conclusion by the very process of acting. In fact, this is the way in which most of humanity asserts the correctness of a particular conclusion.

We appear, therefore, to be at an impasse: no one, particular conclusion can be asserted as possessing greater value over another by appealing to objectivity or a higher understanding. Yet for a human to act is to assert, often silently, the correctness of a particular conclusion. This is more than a purely abstract issue as the results of our acts are often profound and the conflict between actors and their values or conclusions is obviously an important feature of human life.

This impasse can only be dealt with, rather than solved, by recognising and applying what might be called the 'democratic imperative'. This democratic imperative may be formulated as follows: to act is to conclude and to conclude is to assert the unsustainable, i.e. the superiority of a conclusion – one must thus ensure that any alternative conclusion is free to exist and to exercise challenges to one's own and other conclusions.

Such an imperative forms the basis for a radical democratic perspective. It is democratic because it demands behaviour that ensures plurality and allows for conflict between those elements making up that plurality. It is radical in the sense that it recognises, first, the absolutism contained within the concrete act not just within expressed viewpoints and beliefs (as in liberalism); and second, because it sees the absolutism that potentially exists in all social moments not just in those limited to the 'public sphere' (again, this stands in contrast to liberalism). As such the democratic imperative demands freedom of acts in all spheres not just freedom of expression and beliefs in the political sphere.

The Divided Subject

The second theoretical argument concerns the nature of the subject. By 'subject' I mean the individual human as a general category. In recent years there have been many analytical assaults on the notion of a 'unitary subject'.[5] The 'unitary subject' is a creature of the post-Enlightenment era: it is a notion of the human as a unified whole with one set of cultural, political and social values; a subject who can have one correct goal and come to one correct decision based on the power of reason; and a subject with one sexuality.

The notion of the 'unitary subject' took greatest hold in the so-called 'human sciences', where subjects are classified into grand categories with a set of distinct and indivisible characteristics. The technocratic obsessions of the nineteenth and twentieth centuries probably saw the high point in the use of the 'human science' notion of the 'unitary subject'. Not only were individuals categorised according to their rationally observed status but certain courses of action were deemed most appropriate for dealing with various 'types'. Incarceration in prison for the 'criminal type'; incarceration in a clinic for the 'insane'; incarceration in the workhouse for the 'undeserving poor'; labour camp for the 'Kulak'; concentration camp for the 'inferior race'.

Jacques Lacan has provided probably the most influential critique of notions of the 'unitary subject' by drawing on his own psychoanalytical ideas and methodology.[6] While Michel Foucault has provided the most influential historical studies on the way in which the various types of 'unitary subject' have been constructed through discourse.[7]

One can recognise the multiple identities and meanings that make up each subject simply by reflecting on an apparently singular and particular identity. If we take class identity, we can see that its elements go way beyond the traditional elements of job, wage relation or income. To take just one instance, the development of a male worker's class identity is quite clearly bound up with that of his family. A change in the wage relation, for example a cut in pay, is not necessarily a cause for a growth in class consciousness unless it has a knock-on effect in other identities – in this example, the failure of the male worker as father or as husband to provide for family and wife. Alternatively, the concern for family welfare may play a central role in actually preventing the growth of traditional class consciousness by weakening a tendency to militant industrial action. And this family identity is, of course, itself bound up with other identities based on gender and age. Quite clearly, these multiple identities exist in a complex dynamic that are constantly 'furrowing across individuals themselves, cutting them up and remoulding them, marking off irreducible regions in them, in their bodies and minds ...'.[8]

We should appreciate that the identities and values held by a subject are reproduced over time and in changing circumstances. We can call this feature of the divided subject, diachronic.

Consider the socio-political value of patriotism and its relation to the subject. Prior to and during war, there is nearly always a major upsurge in the potency of patriotism. Many individuals suddenly become ardent patriots whereas before they may have given little conscious thought to their national identity. Especially during wartime, this patriotism is deeply bound up with the associated values of xenophobia, racism and hatred of the enemy. We can easily appreciate the ways in which this patriotism draws much of its ability to reproduce itself from its antagonistic relationship to a particular characterisation of the enemy.

However, this process of reproduction is only that which occurs at the most general, social level; at the level of one particular individual subject the process of reproduction may be very different. For example, it is not hard to imagine a subject who, at the beginning of the First World War in Britain, had a belief in 'common decency' to all humans no matter what their nationality but, equally, felt enormous pressures to join in the patriotic fervour sweeping the nation and to fight for 'King and country'. This subject may very well feel the intense contradiction between these two identities and may apparently resolve the contradiction by explaining the war, itself, as a fight to enforce 'common decency for all humans' as a fundamental, international principle. The process of reproduction of the value of patriotism at the level of this particular human subject is different to that of many other, human subjects. For this subject, a blind hatred of the very character of 'Germanness' has no meaning, her or his patriotism is constructed through articulation with other previously held feelings or identities that may be common to some other human subjects but not to all.

Quite clearly, this means that a change in circumstances may affect the reproduction of patriotism in this subject in a fundamentally different way to that of other subjects. Direct experience of the brutality of war, and the ruthlessness of all armies involved in the conflagration, might mean that the articulation with the belief that the British are fighting for 'common decency' will be broken, leading to disillusion, desertion or even mutiny. Another subject, who might be motivated solely by a basic hatred for all things German, would not face the same change in the nature of his or her patriotism.

What is highlighted by this idea of the 'diachronic' and divided subject is the fact that any socio-political value or identity that claims to appeal to a large group of subjects will not be consistently reproducible, for all those subjects, over any decent period of time. There is a high probability for variation resulting from the fact that any socio-political value must attempt self-reproduction in a world already populated by subjects possessing a selection of diverse and conflicting identities. The nature of reproduction, therefore, will also be diverse and will have a high probability of being liable to diverging processes of development.

One response to this reproductive failure is the attempt by powerful or privileged groups to reimpose a socio-political value or identity through authoritarian means. This amounts to an attempt to counter the power of conflicting values and identities by forcing repro-duction through the use of violence, the threat of violence, or through the manipulation of other social identities and values, such as removal or provision of status and material reward. Such a method is inherently weak and unstable because it is always involved in conflict or tension with emerging identities and values. But it is also weak because it does not acknowledge that the methods it uses to reproduce its own values, are themselves just as vulnerable to probable reproductive failure as the values they try to reproduce. It is often assumed, especially by dictatorships, that a threat to the body or life (or equally a threat to status or material standing) somehow escapes the vagaries of socio-political values, that it has a reproductive capacity specific to itself of great, almost indestructible, power. This fails to recognise that just as the reproduction of a socio-political value over time will also have a high probability of collapse, so the constant reproduction of violence, or other authoritarian means, will have a high probability of collapse. New identities and values, such as martyrdom or simply a willingness to die for a cause, will ultimately break the articulation between fear of pain or death and authoritarian violence.

An alternative response is to opt for the radical democratic development of identities and values. This, in part, means not attempting to impose a universal value on a large group of people. But it also means developing a system of interaction that not only allows for the free development of identities and values but also allows for their peaceful conflict and collapse. Such a system would be inherently more stable, peaceful and stronger than that which opts for authoritarian imposition.

Social Dislocation

The failure of a socio-political value or structure to reproduce itself effectively often occurs on a much greater scale than at the level of the subject. A part of this process, is 'social dislocation'. 'Social dislocation' is the situation in which a set of meanings or a particular identity lose their explanatory power or their ability to provide moral or political guidance.[9] It is a notion that is central to the third – socio-political – argument in favour of radical democracy.

Recent years have seen an increasing sense of social dislocation throughout western Europe. This dislocation stretches across the whole political spectrum (with the possible exceptions of fascism and ultra-nationalism) but is nowhere more visible than in the decline of support and faith in the most influential progressive ideology of the post-war era – parliamentary socialism. Parliamentary socialist parties have either seen vital parts of their traditional social base switch allegiance, or simply fragment and decline. Where parliamentary socialism remained in power, such as in France and Spain, the ruling socialist parties clearly lost faith in their traditional principles and pursued a directionless revisionism.

The reasons for this state of social dislocation are undoubtedly manifold but, with regards to parliamentary socialism, we can point to two factors that have played a central role in the ideological discrediting of these two doctrines.

First, despite the efforts of social democratic and socialist ideals and structures, both these creeds have shown themselves consistently unable to deal with an abiding inequality in the possession of power resources. In Britain, in the 1990s, after fifty years of a campaigning and influential parliamentary socialism – power over the political, economic, social and cultural aspects of life still remains massively imbalanced. Second, the institutions of the labour movement have not been able to adapt their ideology, programmes or structures to an increasing, popular concern with identity and difference. Identities that differ from that of the able-bodied, white, male, heterosexual continue to face discrimination and disenfranchisement.

It has often been noted how Margaret Thatcher responded to some aspects of this social dislocation by building her rhetorical and ideological appeal around the introduction of greater choice and individual liberty and by portraying herself as a warrior against the inequalities brought about by excessive bureaucratic and political power. She picked up vital parts of the electorate by appealing to a spirit of individual freedom that grew partly out of an exasperation with the conformity and bureaucracy created by the structures and ethos of post-war, social democracy.

Nevertheless, parliamentary socialism has not been able to capitalise on the discrediting of the Thatcherite project. The concentration on large-scale, state provision of financial resources funded by continuous economic growth, has proved not only unrealistic, in the post-imperial economy of Britain, but also fails to respond to demands for changes in unequal possession of resources in areas outside the economy. Furthermore, an ever-closer betrothal to the values of the market has restricted its ability to seriously address unequal possession of power resources.

Parliamentary socialism has also failed to reflect difference by limiting the resolution of conflict to a severely narrow political, parliamentary arena. Parliamentary socialism has done little to reconstruct the nature of democracy in Britain or to build a new, more active and participatory notion of citizenship. A strong strand of elitism, technocracy and awe for parliament in the labour movement has ensured that its ability to involve large sections of the population in the day-to-day building of a social democratic state is extremely limited. For many, the welfare state, the trade unions, and Labour local authorities have become symbols, not of liberation and change through active participation, but of drab bureaucracy, elitism, careerism, and white, male domination.

Most fundamentally, the traditional movements of the left have centred their activities, reforms and revolutions on the economic sphere. This has been the result of three trends: a belief in economic determinism, ie. that egalitarian changes in the economy will automatically bring egalitarian change in other spheres; a belief that changes in economic relations are the most important for the 'working class' and that other changes in politics, culture or social relations can be postponed indefinitely; and the trend of elitism, technocracy, and parliamentarianism that has already been indicated. This approach has proved overly shallow: not only have spheres of human interaction other than the economy grown in political importance in the last thirty years, but also the whole gamut of political, social, cultural, and economic relations all play a role in reproducing and deconstructing each other. Thus the attempt to introduce economic egalitarianism, whilst reinforcing centralised state power or traditional gender relations, is a flawed project. Either the other forms of inequality will assert themselves with a new ideological and structural power as they are used by a new hierarchical class (usually, in the case of parliamentary socialism, a class made up of bureaucrats and politicians) to legitimise their power, or the whole, economic, egalitarian project will be undermined by the inequalities existing elsewhere.

The old progressive movements and ideologies are proving unable to explain or provide satisfactory guidance for those people most directly affected by unaddressed problems and new issues. This situation suggests the need for a political approach based upon a radical reassessment of the methods by which power resources are allocated within every sphere of life, as well as a need for a radical shift towards pluralism in lifestyle and behaviour. It is in these areas that the political principles and strategies of radical democracy, which I will outline, go beyond those of parliamentary socialism.

PRINCIPLES OF RADICAL DEMOCRACY

Extending Democratic Processes

The 'democratic imperative' asserts: 'one must ensure that any alternative conclusion is free to exist and free to exercise challenges to one's own and other conclusions'. Such an imperative demands that the processes that are part of human interaction be as democratic as possible. The 'democratic imperative' is based on a recognition, distinct from liberalism, that all social moments contain within them an element of absolutism.

It is important that structures are established that allow for the peaceful conflict and collapse of differing socio-political values and identities. This suggests that a radical democracy that is responding to the 'democratic imperative' and to the 'diachronic', divided subject should hold as a central principle the introduction of democratic processes into spheres of human relations beyond that of a narrowly defined state. There are undoubtedly areas where the introduction of some of the traditional, liberal democratic processes of election of officials, accountability, checks and balances, and majority rule would be beneficial. The great organs of state power such as welfare agencies, the police, the military, education institutions, the judiciary, the civil service and local authorities have all become centres of absolute control and therefore require the introduction of democratic processes for those who work and use their services. Similarly large and small economic ventures would require the introduction of democratic processes.

Any introduction of democratic processes must also involve a decentralisation and a diffusion of power. By diffusion of power what is meant is the provision of certain public services by a variety of agencies. For example, there is no reason why health-care should be provided solely by various institutions under the strict control of the Department of Health or even of some decentralised body. The same applies to other welfare agencies. Imagination should be employed to discover ways in which communities can be facilitated and resourced to ensure some of their own health, education and wealth needs. With the wilful decline in the provision of state-sponsored welfare, there are already small-scale attempts by some communities to 'fill the gap' in this provision.

However, it is clear that not all aspects of human interaction are structured in such a way that an extension of the processes used by the democratic state are appropriate or practical. For example, consenting personal relations and artistic expression thrive in an environment where individuals are free from any interference, whether that be by the state or a democratically constituted majority. The often cumbersome processes of democracy which are based on compromise and political conflict would only force dilution of artistic expression and deny free-choice in personal relations. Therefore, an application of democratic ideals in a form that goes beyond formal decision-making is important for these areas in particular. A central feature of such an application should be the notion of access. Providing individuals and groups, especially those who do not usually possess such opportunities with the resources and the time to produce television and radio programmes, theatrical productions, and all forms of publications. Clearly, personal relations, must be free from any form of state interference and must not be subject to attack by those possessing power elsewhere in society. Means by which diversity in personal relations can be encouraged might also be considered through such things as free and easy access to counselling and through the creation of a social ethos of acceptance of different types of personal relations.

It is important to recognise the indispensible nature of promoting a rich political culture to support formal democratic processes and other applications of democracy. Radical democratic processes without a rich political culture built on understanding of the system, lively, diverse debate and the desire to get involved, ensures not democracy but clientism, corruption, apathy and abuse of the processes. Part of creating this richer political culture will be the result of individuals actually combatting inequality and absolutism but an emphasis must also be placed on the role of a democratic media and a democratic education.

The media must be subject to more diversity in control and output. The setting of priorities for news and entertainment by a tiny elite based upon personal or group prejudices and codes is unacceptable. The need to ensure diversity, access and greater accountability in the mass media is vital. Similarly in education there is an urgent requirement to diversify types of teaching and options offered, to enforce childrens' rights and give them the prime say in the running of their educational institutions, and (most importantly for the sake of a rich political culture) to establish organic links between the intellectual resources education can provide to people and the organisational and social needs of communities.[10]

Therefore with regard to democratic processes inspired by the 'democratic imperative', we have three central tenets: the introduction of democratic processes into all spheres of public life where appropriate or just; the need to go beyond simple majority processes of decision-making and introduce decentralisation, diffusion, access, and

defence of freedom from interference in personal
relations; and the need to ensure democratic processes are
not abused or wasted by creating the conditions for a rich,
political culture.

Pluralism

Beyond the extension and adaptation of democratic
processes, a radical democracy must also encourage
diversity. The instability and suffering caused by the
authoritarian imposition of absolute and singular principles on divided subjects, and the consequent failure to
respond to and reflect difference, suggest that a radical
democracy should defend and encourage pluralism not
only in views and beliefs, but also in identities and modes
of behaviour.

It is through socio-political interaction that individuals
and groups construct a diversity of identities, values and
rights but those can only be fought for if others – who
have an interest in denying certain rights, do not possess
an unequal share of power resources. Therefore,
pluralism can be partly encouraged and facilitated
through the extension of democratic processes and the
maintenance of a rich, political culture, but creating new
notions of citizenship, and combatting inequalities in
power resources elsewhere, are also central.

Differentiated Citizenship

The reflection of difference by public authorities has been
exceptionally poor in Britain. The sovereign body of the
state is notoriously exclusive. It is hardly surprising that an
apathy and hostility towards parliament has grown in
recent years alongside a growth in the sense of difference.

As Iris Marion Young has pointed out in her essay
'Polity and Group Difference',[11] this difficulty is partly
due to the ideology of 'universal citizenship' that
dominates public life.

Young sees 'universal citizenship' as having three central
features: the belief that citizenship should be extended to

everyone; building public life around what citizens have in common as opposed to how they differ; establishing laws and rules 'that are blind to individual and group differences'.[12] However, as Young points out, social movements have been asking recently why this long-standing notion of a universal citizenship has favoured very specific groups and excluded many others.[13]

Young asserts that the notion of 'universal citizenship' is self-contradictory while there remain disfavoured groups in society. Ignoring differences, by consigning all particularity to the private realm and allowing the public realm only to deal with commonness, only perpetuates an exclusionary citizenship. A 'universal citizenship' fails to recognise, first, that different outlooks in the public sphere are the result not just of conflicts of interest, but are about very different identities and life experiences; and, second, that the presiding notion of what is 'universal' or 'common' in public life is that which is particular to the dominant groups and individuals.[14]

Young argues for a notion of 'differentiated citizen-ship'[15] that recognises difference and the way in which public life, as presently conceived and structured, excludes large sections of the population. For Young, 'differentiated citizenship', would ensure group representation in the processes of state and public authorities. This would require institutional and public resources supporting three activities: self-organization of group members; decision-makers being required to consult groups on policy and prove that they have taken their perspectives into consideration; groups having veto power over specific policies that affect them directly eg. women and reproductive rights, black people and race relations legislation.[16]

To this one might add the right for certain communities to maintain a semi-autonomous relationship to the state and the rest of society. This would allow certain communities to establish their own infrastructure of welfare, education and even their own mini-state. Their involvement with broader society might be largely through exchange of goods and a regular negotiation with the authorities of broader society regarding use of various services in return for a levy, the size of which could be open to negotiation.

Equality

Inequality in power resources may be gradually and partially dealt with by the introduction of democratic processes into spheres of life beyond the purely political. Such a change would provide the forum within which the disfavoured could legitimately and legally alter the way in which social goods are distributed in a community, an association, or a firm. However, it is important to encourage clarity about what form a radical democratic equality might take.

In his book *Spheres of Justice*, Michael Walzer, reassesses ideas of equality.[17] He asserts that 'complex equality' is preferable to 'simple equality'.[18] The latter is essentially the form of equality adopted by social democracy and parliamentary socialism. In 'simple equality', a dominant social good (in social democracy and socialism's view, wealth), is redistributed to end or limit inequality.

Walzer attacks this approach because, he argues, the redistributive process requires too much interference by the state. Furthermore, it ignores the fact that other social goods apart from wealth, that cause inequality, such as political or bureaucratic power, become more potent ways of gaining privilege if wealth is redistributed. 'Complex equality' on the other hand does not involve the redistribution of a particular social good, but involves rather the attempt to prevent any one social good gaining dominance over all spheres of life. So, for Walzer, rather than money being able to buy the wealthy material goods, political power, health care, good education, and better leisure time etc; money might only be useful for the buying of material goods while political power would be distributed according to more relevant criteria such as health care according to need and education for all. As such, Walzer is willing to accept inequalities but not inequalities for the same people across all spheres of life.

As he puts it, 'complex equality' would 'narrow the range within which particular goods are convertible and ... vindicate the autonomy of distributive spheres'.[19]

While, at a philosophical level, Walzer's notion of 'complex equality,' does present a sophisticated advance on 'simple equality', it is never clear how 'complex equality' is to be achieved. Enforcing 'complex equality' might well require state intervention. To create and maintain the autonomy of distributive spheres, to just as high a degree as 'simple equality', might demand state intervention to administer and police the redistributive process.

If a move towards greater equality was to come from grassroots activity, as it should if such a move is to remain democratic, what might be created is not 'complex equality' but a complex form of 'complex equality'. In this scenario, there would not only be different criteria for different spheres of distribution, but there may be more than one criterion active within each sphere of distribution. For example, in 'complex equality' political power might be distributed according to the ability to win votes through persuasion, whereas major commodities such as washing machines or televisions are distributed according to free exchange or wealth. However, if a grassroots approach is taken based on the establishment of alternative lifestyles from the bottom-up, we may find that in the political sphere some communities choose their local representatives or authorities through election, or on a rotating basis, or on a voluntary basis, or even according to the drawing of lots; while major commodities might be distributed according to free exchange by some members of a community while others might distribute according to immediate need, or through communal sharing.

This 'complex form of complex equality' raises serious problems of integration amongst different parts of the community. It may be dealt with partially by a notion of differentiated citizenship, but it does not need to involve interference by the state and it should prevent any one particular social good being able to dominate all spheres, or rather large sections of each sphere. Furthermore, this is a logical vision of equality if one hopes to combine a drive against inequality with a drive to pluralism and democracy.

Notes on Strategy

The fundamental factor in determining a strategy for a radicalisation of democracy must be to 'decentre' the state. For the vast majority of socio-political campaigns the state has come to possess a central role as a target of their activities and as an agency for change. Parliamentary socialism, despite its origin in broad social movements, has become transfixed by the power of the state and its apparent ability to bring justice and equality to society. However, for any campaign that hopes to democratise major aspects of our lives, I have argued that the state cannot play a role as the main agent of change.

Democracy is as much a cultural state of mind as it is the existence of democratic processes. The state cannot create such a culture as it cannot impose pluralism or a spirit of democratic interaction. The state might be able to help defend pluralism and democracy, it might even be able to help facilitate pluralism and democracy but it cannot impose these values and practices. A radical democracy, which sees its strategic goal as the seizing of the power of the state with which to building a more equal, democratic, pluralistic society, is a movement bound up in self-contradiction.

The consciousness of one's rights that is associated with citizenship, the diversity that is associated with pluralism, and the political culture that is associated with democratic processes can only be created through political campaigning and struggle. It has long been a liberal belief that rights are extended to various groups or that rights are won from the state. In fact rights are often created by disfavoured groups and individuals recognising their subordinate position and building a set of demands; creating a conception of the rights they require through the struggle to escape that subordination; by building on and adapting older values, and by existing in conflict with other groups.[20]

So, while a radical democratic campaign may aim to democratise the state, may aim to defend itself against the state and may force the state to help facilitate democratic change, the state cannot be a central agent of change itself.

Interestingly, some of the most effective campaigns of recent years have not been those which aim primarily at the state as the target of their activity. Social movements like anti-racist groups, the women's movement, gay and lesbian liberation, and green campaigns have attempted to place pressure for change only partly on the state. They have looked to other sources of authority which play a central role in maintaining absolute power. Trans-national corporations, the electronic media, the press, advertising, employers, trade unions, educational institutions, political parties, the family, the medical establishment have all faced campaigns specifically directed against them. This phenomenon, should indicate a strategic approach that goes beyond simply campaigning against, or for, a change in state authority.

Recent years have also seen a growth in what might be called 'here-and-now' politics; groups and communites coming together to organise concrete, alternative ways of distributing power, usually in the economic sphere. While to date this has been far more widespread outside Britain, there is now a growing interest in credit unions, local economic and trading systems, consumers' co-operatives and producers' co-operatives. It is vital that radicals and democrats begin to recognise the important of such activities. They are methods, not only of introducing pluralism into communities and into the economy at a grassroots level, but they also work for communities in the here-and-now. It is an approach that goes beyond the 'wait until the next election' approach of the Labour Party and the millenarianism of revolutionary socialism.

Therefore we can identify a three-fold strategy for a process of radical democratisation: democratisation of the state and legislation to facilitate and defend democratic change; undermining non-state sources of authority which reproduce absolute power; and activities to establish alternative modes of distributing resources 'here-and-now'. Like the labour movement in its pioneering heyday, these initiatives and principles have the power to combine achievable political goals, with the long-term vision of a society where equality and pluralism are the fundamental principles of human association.

Notes

Thanks to Anne Coddington, Mark Perryman and Martin Smith for their comments on earlier drafts of this chapter.

[1] E. Laclau & C. Mouffe, *Hegemony and Socialist Strategy*, Verso, London 1985. E. Laclau, *New Reflections on the Revolution of Our Time*, Verso, London 1990. C. Mouffe (ed), *Dimensions of Radical Democracy*, Verso, London 1992.

[2] J. Keane, *Democracy and Civil Society*, Verso, London 1988; R. Unger, *False Necessity*, CUP, Cambridge 1987.

[3] E. Laclau & C. Mouffe, *op cit*, p 105.

[4] For a more detailed analysis of how articulation and contingency affect notions of objectivity, see: E. Laclau, *op cit*, pp 17-27.

[5] For an excellent overview and development of the critique of the notion of the 'unitary subject', see: J. Henriques et al, *Changing the Subject*, Methuen, London 1984.

[6] Lacan is a notoriously inaccessible writer. For a clear introduction to all his work including notions of the 'divided subject', see: B. Benvenuto & R. Kennedy, *The Works of Jacques Lacan*, Free Association Books, London 1986.

[7] The construction of subjects runs through nearly all of Foucault's work. The following is a small and arbitrary selection: M. Foucault, *The Order of Things*, Tavistock, London 1970. M. Foucault, *Birth of the Clinic*, Tavistock, London 1973. M. Foucault, *The History of Sexuality, Vol 1. An Introduction*, Penguin, Harmondsworth 1978. M. Foucault, *Discipline and Punish*, Penguin, Harmondsworth 1979.

[8] M. Foucault, *op cit*, 1978, p 96.

[9] For a more detailed exploration of social dislocation, see: E. Laclau, *op cit*, pp 39-61.

[10] For a fascinating theoretical and practical insight into how democratic education can play a constructive role in communities, see: G. Kirkwood & C. Kirkwood, *Living Adult Education*, Open University Press in assoc. with the Scottish Institute of Adult and Continuing Education, Milton Keynes 1989.

[11] I.M. Young, 'Polity and Group Difference: A Critique of the Ideal of Universal Citizenship', *Ethics*, No 99 (Jan, '89) pp 250-274.

[12] *Ibid.*, p 250.

[13] *Ibid.*, pp 250-251.

[14] *Ibid.*, p 257.

[15] *Ibid.*, p 258.

[16] *Ibid.*, p 261.
[17] M. Walzer, *Spheres of Justice: A Defence of Pluralism and Equality*, Basil Blackwell, Oxford 1983.
[18] *Ibid.*, p 17.
[19] *Ibid.*, p 17.
[20] E. Laclau & C. Mouffe, *op cit.*, p 105.

Towards a Postmodern Conservatism

MARC-HENRI GLENDENING

Since the mid-1980s a torrent of books, articles and academic seminars has posited the belief that western society is on the verge of, or has already partly entered, a qualitatively new epoch. A variety of terms have been used to evoke and describe this distinctive period of history: 'new times'; 'post-Fordism'; 'disorganised-capitalism'; 'the third wave' and 'postmodernity'.

The postmodernity idea has been portrayed in a wide variety of ways by the various articulators of the concept. Hudson, for example, has listed fourteen different accounts of postmodernity, some of which are contradictory.[1] However, whether postmodernity is characterised as a radically different economic condition; a new ideological climate; a distinctive type of intellectual discourse; new modes of artistic representation, or whatever, common dominant themes emerges. The modern era's alleged hallmarks – standardisation, centralisation, homogeneity, conformity and totalisation – are said to be giving way to an 'altered state' which is typified by a movement towards diversity, fragmentation, decentralisation and ever more rapid changes in the way human beings order their lives.

The postmodernity assertion is potent, in part, because the idea that we are experiencing a dramatic and distinctive historical transition is adhered to by analysts and activists from a wide variety of political positions. The postmodernity thesis was adopted in Britain and promoted with the greatest vigour by the Communist Party of Great Britain, principally through its celebrated journal *Marxism Today*[2] and its *Manifesto for New Times*.[3] This publication provoked an intense debate on the left and has been the subject of a vitriolic and sustained attack by orthodox Marxists (Stalinists and Trotskyites alike). Among the non-socialist 'futurologists' who have reached a similar social prognosis to the writers associated with *Marxism Today* are Professors Robert Skidelsky and David Marquand, respectively of the (late) SDP and Liberal Democrats, and the two American techno-analysts Daniel Bell and Alvin Toffler. The Conservative MP David Howell and the journalist Norman Macrae have been the principal articulators and analysers of a postmodernist economic order on the British right.

Postmodern Conservatism[4] is motivated by the belief that in order for Conservatives to change the world in a progressive direction they must first understand it. Postmodern Conservatism is thus premised on an awareness that there needs to be an intimate relationship between theory and action. There is a need to reject the voluntarist approach which states that political principles are timeless and universal. Voluntarists argue that the moral objectives individuals adhere to are not determined by the particular historical periods they live through; the ideas inside our minds are independent of material reality. According to this view social reality is a reflection of the dominant ideologies and perceptions of self-interest that are hegemonic during any one period of time. Mind determines matter in a linear, causal manner. Political success is therefore gained by the political force which can communicate its message most effectively, it is believed.

At the other extreme is the old Marxist view which sees ideas as a passive reflection of material reality, and the evolution of the productive, economic base in particular. The minds of men are ciphers through which the winds of historical materialism blow their impersonal tunes. Matter determines mind. Our ideas and perceptions of self-interest are shaped by our objective 'class' position which, in turn, is a function of our relationship to the means of production.

A third position needs to be considered which proposes, instead, that the relationship between human consciousness and material reality is a dialectical one. While our minds are indeed autonomous (in that no environmental factor, supernatural deity or inherited gene can make us believe or do that which we do not will freely ourselves); changes in the 'outer space' of the objective world do precipitate changes of attitude in the 'inner space' of the subjective mind; consciousness does not exist in a vacuum. As the material conditions people are confronted by alter so their perceptions and evaluations of the world, and what constitutes their own self-interest also change, though not in any fixed, pre-determined way. The hierarchy of needs, according to which each of us operates, undergoes revision with the result that certain objectives we previously desired become downplayed or even rejected outright, and lower order goals then get moved up the scale of personal priorities. Equally the strategies we hope will realise our self-chosen ends are also subjected to constant re-evaluation in the light of new insights derived from empirical experience.

The distinction that is commonly drawn between 'pragmatists' and 'dogmatists' is therefore a false one. Individuals are differentiated from one another not by virtue of being more or less dogmatic but, rather, with regard to the differing goals they seek to advance. Equally, if pragmatism is defined as being the view that the correctness of a theory, and the actions it gives rise to, is directly proportionate to its practical efficacy in terms of aiding the achievement of the particular goal desired, then all human beings are also pragmatists.

So it is that in political, as well as personal life, the commitment we assign to numerous competing goals changes over time in response to developments taking place both outwith and within ourselves. What we value in our minds may not be causally determined by factors external to consciousness, but is nevertheless highly influenced by material changes beyond our immediate control. It is entirely appropriate and necessary therefore for Conservatives to try and analyse the times we are living through and, in addition, to extrapolate from current trends the texture of the political and social period we are embarking upon. Only then will we be able to carry out an audit of our current ideological profile with a view to developing a coherent response to the new political agenda we may have to confront.

Instead of describing each individual account of postmodernity separately, certain claims, considered to be of key importance, have been selected here and grouped under one of the three following headings: economy; civil society; and politics.

Economy

At the heart of most descriptions of the New Times we are said to be experiencing is the restructuring of private capital. Two economic systems and epochs are contrasted; the first is sometimes described as Fordism and the second as post-Fordism. There is little indication from those who believe in new economic times as to how complete this revolution is. For Stuart Hall, the extent of post-Fordism's progress is not the main issue. He believes that we have to make assessments 'not from the completed edge, but from the "leading edge" of change ... The question should always be ... where is the ... "leading edge" and in what direction is it pointing?'.[5]

Fordism (the term is derived from the system of mass-production pioneered by Henry Ford and imitated by other manufacturers in the early twentieth century) is associated with a number of key features: the standard-ised, mass-production of consumer durables by large companies employing vast armies of semi-skilled or unskilled manual workers concentrated in huge factories; a hierarchical and authoritarian structure of business organisation based on rigid, vertical lines of command; ownership of capital restricted to a very small percentage of the population; high rates of trade union membership; and largely autonomous, national economies with little foreign investment.

The postmodern school see advances in technology, and in marketing analysis and strategy as catalysts for change in the way people both produce and consume. This, in turn, is thought to have significant repercussions for the way in which they conduct their lives in general. In particular, a heavy emphasis is placed on the advent of the information technology revolution in explaining the demise of Fordist economy. This revolution has enhanced methods of transmitting, storing and retrieving information quickly, minimising the amount of space necessary for productive activity and cutting down on the deployment of labour. In addition, there have been great advances in the theory of production – the development of evermore sophisticated theories about the most efficient ways of combining energy and resources in order to transform natural resources into products.

Significant, also, are new modes of marketing products and analysing demand. Market research no longer only takes into consideration peoples' objective details, such as income, occupation, age and sex. Now, subjective factors including values, lifestyles and personal motivations are the criteria according to which marketing campaigns are planned and waged.

There are several physical manifestations of the 'new times'. One of the major differences between the Fordist and post-Fordist eras is the introduction of small batch production targeted at a particular audience of consumers. There is now an attempt to ensure that the supply of commodities and services on offer takes into account the personal priorities of individual purchasers. The ability of manufacturers to ensure that their clothing, furniture, cars and so on reflect the cultural signals that consumers want to identify themselves with, is what gives them a competitive edge. The fragmentation of society into ever greater numbers of sub-cultures and 'style tribes' necessitates, in turn, a wide diversity of goods and services.

This new productive sensitivity to consumer wishes is

achieved in a number of ways. With the advent of the micro-processor, equipment can be easily reprogrammed to ensure a far greater degree of productive flexibility. Programmable machines can be switched from product to product with a minimimum of manual resetting. Robin Murray writes that: 'instead of using purpose-built machines to build standard products, flexible automation uses general purposes machines to produce a variety of products'.[6] This means that more attention is given to design and the packaging of commodities. This is all the more important because product life is becoming shorter for consumer durables – the periods between changes in fashion are getting shorter and shorter. And computers, in enabling vast quantities of information to be relayed extremely fast, aid the matching of supply to demand at extremely short notice. Sainsbury's, for example, record the quantities they have sold for each particular line every day. In this way they are able to adjust their order correspondingly for the following day, so as to minimise shortages and excess, and to cater for minority tastes. Large retailers like Marks & Spencer are moving from in-house production and are sub-contracting work to small, independent companies who specialise in particular areas of production. Contracts are for short periods and can be cancelled or extended in accordance with the selling success of the output. In the television world Channel 4 is an exemplar of a post-Fordist economy. Its programmes are made by small outside film companies and the aim is to target specific groups of viewers rather than attract huge mass audiences for each screening. Narrow (rather than broad) casting is now the name of the game in television. The introduction of the new technology to printing has similarly resulted in a proliferation of new magazine titles and newspapers which can now afford to pitch for relatively small groups of readers because of the declining real costs of production.

It is claimed that the work environment of the late twentieth century is also undergoing far-reaching change. New theories of business organisation stress that decision-making should be decentralised; communication

within enterprises should be horizontal rather than
vertical; and the distinction between mental and manual
labour should be eroded. Workers are perceived as human
capital to be invested in, rather than as substitute robots.
Geoff Mulgan explains: 'the authoritarian, vertical
corporation is beginning to outlive its usefulness;
dictatorial organisation may still work in assembly plants
and supermarkets, but this is inefficient in research and
development ... If people are treated like things, they will
behave like things, unwilling to care about what they
produce, or to use their intelligence to solve the problems
that inevitably arise'.[7]

New management theories advocate the creation of
quality circles; the establishment of semi-autonomous
units within companies, which are driven by internal and
external rates of return; and the introduction of flexi-time
and individually-specific contracts.

Production has become increasingly internationalised.
Multi-national corporations are spreading their nets even
wider. This has been facilitated by the new technology as
business strategists are quickly alerted to new profit-
making opportunities abroad. Enhanced transport facilities make it relatively cheap to have different components
manufactured in different countries before they are finally
assembled. There has been a spatial reorganisation of
capital. Most traditional centres of economic and industrial
activity have suffered losses in jobs and people in the latter
part of the century. Liverpool, for example, now has half
the number of people it did in 1900. Firms are less dependent than before upon particular raw materials, sources of
energy, railways, ports and large supplies of labour. The
new technology has resulted in the net transfer of jobs and
capital to what were previously small provincial towns such
as Swindon, Basingstoke and Bedford.

The decline of the smokestack industries and the
changing nature of labour, and the environment within
which it takes place, have transformed industrial relations.
The miners strike of the mid-1980s and the print workers'
dispute with Murdoch at Wapping were probably the last
of the old style, Fordist, industrial conflicts. No strike

agreements; employee share ownership; individually specific contracts and semi-autonomous units are the wave of the future. The tensions between those workers remaining in industries and unions tied to the past and those, on the other hand, who have accommodated themselves to the future has brought about a number of intra-union disputes which are likely to grow, rather than to diminish, in the future.

Civil Society

The theoretical approach of the writers associated with *Marxism Today* was, as Mike Rustin points out, Marxist in its basic frame of analysis, in that the sphere of production is attributed with the power to set the general tone of all other aspects of human existence. For Rustin, the post-Fordist idea 'has the great merit of being an attempt to theorise structures and their effects. It thus become possible, in principle, to derive explanation, prediction and strategic choices based on assessments of possibility. By contrast, liberal and social democratic models tend to confine us to ahistorical and normative choices ...'[8]

Therefore, for many of the theorists of postmodernity, the new, high-tech based economy is thought to be responsible for changes in civil society (that set of relationships that reside outside the productive base and the state) and popular culture. Strong, class-based identities are said to have been eroded by the rising affluence a majority of the population have experienced. The declining real costs of a wide variety of consumer items has meant that the hard divisions that once existed in the way the middle and working classes used to live outside the workplace have now become blurred. Similar types of clothing, music, entertainment and recreation are available to a much larger percentage of the population across the management/shop-floor divide than was the case thirty years ago. The collapse of many collectivities of human beings centered on certain smokestack industries, such as coal, steel and docking, and the simultaneous rise of the service sector has signalled a new cultural pluralism in previously homogeneous communities. Residential areas in the big cities are more socially confused than they once were. Another important factor in the fracturing of once dominant patterns of living and social mores has been the infusion into the inner cities of immigrants with very different cultural backgrounds. While the advent of multi-racial areas has sometimes resulted in culture clash it has also led, gradually, to a dilution of established ways of living and thinking in both the host and immigrant communities.

Access to different ways of seeking cultural self-fulfillment has been facilitated by post-Fordist production, mass communications, improved travel facilities and the collapse of residential 'zoning'. These factors have helped to produce a proliferation of 'style tribes' which evolve, dissolve and fuse with other cultural segments. Individuals now enjoy the means to change cultural identity far more easily than their parents. The 'organic' communities of pre-industrial and Fordist Britain, which were largely the result of circumstance (where you were born, where you worked), are being replaced in the big cities by a multiplicity of 'designer' communities composed of individuals who share similar attitudes and lifestyles, and seek each other out on that basis.

This fragmentation of once monolithic social blocs into small sub cultures finds an analogy in other areas. Postmodern architecture is characterised by the refusal to design buildings according to any one architectural tradition. Instead, the type of buildings being erected today combine an array of different approaches. The functionalism of the modernist period is fused with the classical emphasis on decoration. This incorporation of diversity and confusion of styles can also be found in the modern novel down to the typography employed in a Gap catalogue.

It is possible to hypothesise, a vision of a not too distant future culture.[9] A growing number of people, particularly those involved with the processing, interpretation and dissemination of information, will work from home. An accountant from Humberside will just as easily to be able to work for a firm based in, say, Birmingham, or Madrid, as Hull. The advent of fax machines and two-way television computers (TCs) will make the office superfluous. Commuting to and from work will become a thing of the past. This holds the contradictory prospect both of increasing individual anomie and the transformation of dormitory suburbs and satellite towns into more vibrant communities as local people will have less incentive and need to socialise and seek entertainment in the city centres. Luton might even develop its own version of Las Vegas in time, Bromley its own Covent Garden. As people increasingly define themselves in terms of subjective aspirations and cultural values, rather than their relationship to the means of production, they may well choose to live in communities that reflect their lifestyle preferences. Thus, if bohemians and carnally orientated individuals wish to exist together as a community they may well turn Milton Keynes into a new Soho.

Likewise, schools may become an irrelevance as pupils communicate directly with their teachers on a one to one basis through TCs. The educational day will be cut to no more than two or three hours as children will no longer have to waste time travelling to and from school and spend time playing games and taking lunch breaks. However, new modes of social interaction may need to be developed in the additional time that will be liberated by the making of school redundant. The new mechanisms and practices that come into place, to fill the vacuum, will be geared more to the individual preferences of children and their parents, than the present situation in which a standardised educational and recreational programme is imposed on all children in a given school. TCs might likewise transform positively the lives of pensioners and disabled people living alone by enabling them to keep in visual contact with people without having to leave their own homes.

The gradual erosion of traditional belief systems, that were the product of settled and more culturally homogeneous communities, will probably accelerate certain trends in the way human beings organise their domestic lives. Fewer people will choose to get married; those who do will divorce with increasing rapidity; couples will have fewer children and a declining percentage of women will be prepared to carry out the traditional home-making and child-raising roles they previously assumed. A multiplicity of domestic living arrangements will become more prevalent, ranging from individuals who live alone to extended families.

The hard home/work distinction may break down as the new technology and the trend towards sub-contracting and self-employment gathers momentum. This raises the prospect of a return to child labour: children may come to be viewed as economic assets who, instead of continuing to remain the passive beneficiaries of their parents largesse, will be expected to make an active contribution to the success of the family 'enterprise', much as many children of Asian shopkeepers do at present. Increasing computer literacy among the young will greatly facilitate the commercialisation of those families that remain in existence.

Politics

According to the *Marxism Today* set, the political development of the 'altered states' epoch renders much of traditional Marxist theory redundant. Stuart Hall writes:

'The wider changes remind us that "new times" are both "out there", changing our conditions of life, and "in here", working on us. In part it is us who are being "remade".' He quotes Marshall Berman: 'Modern environments and experiences cut across all boundaries of geography and ethnicity, of class and nationality, of religion and ideology – not destroying them entirely, but weakening and subverting them, eroding lines of continuity.'[10]

Hall believes that we can no longer perceive human beings in terms of having a single, coherent and unchanging identity. Individuals exist simultaneously in a variety of different spheres of existence and their lives and consciousness cannot be reduced to a single area of personal activity or experience. At different times people adopt different political personalities, according to what is of paramount significance to them at that particular time. Postmodernist politics is thus an evolving patchwork made up of fragmentary minority interests, whose size and composition is constantly changing as individuals undergo the never-ending process of defining and redefining themselves. From what Hall writes we can deduce something that Marxists fail to understand: that a dialectical process is at work within each and every human being. The way in which we define ourselves politically at any one time can give rise to an 'opposition', that is to say, a new and contrary mode of self-understanding and identification provoked by new, external circumstances. For old school socialist revolutionaries, human beings live in a single dimension. To return to Hall:

> The conventional culture of the left, with its stress on "objective contradictions", impersonal structures and processes that work "behind men's backs", have disabled us from confronting the subjective in politics in any very coherent way … classical Marxism depended on an assumed correspondence between the "economic" and the "political": one could read off our political attitudes, interests and motivations from our economic class interests and position. This correspondence between "the political" and "the economic" is exactly what has now disintegrated – practically and theoretically.[11]

Two crucial hypotheses emerge from the postmodernity commentators. The first is that the working class, as Marx originally defined the concept, can no longer be seen as the agency for a revolutionary transition to socialism. The second is that new sources of political division have emerged which do not relate to the productive base. These new forms of collective identity owe more to civil society. Postmodernist political conflict centres on issues relating to gender, race, sexuality, ecology and civil liberties, unlike the predominantly economic production/ownership conflicts of the Fordist period.

It must be pointed out that even in the heyday of Fordist economics, when the labour movement was numerically, organisationally and electorally at the peak of its powers, manual workers in the developed western economies showed little enthusiasm for mass nationalisation of the means of production, and for central planning of the economy. Labour tended to support political parties whose principal point of appeal was a commitment to welfarism. Thus, most workers tended to attach significance to their lives as consumers rather than their lives as producers. They demanded redistribution of wealth and state-financed services, but they never supported a massive redrawing of the boundary between the private and the public sectors, with the public sector being favoured with regard to ownership. Commitment to nationalisation tended to manifest itself only among those trade unionists already employed in state-owned enterprises and bureaucracies, because of the perceived advantages of protection from market forces and competition.

A number of factors can be identified that help to explain the decline in support for collectivist policies and the demise of a working class sense of political identity:

1) With the advent of the joint stock company and the spread of share ownership that has grown over the past ten years, an increasing number of individuals occupy what is, from a Marxist perspective, an ambiguous class position. They are simultaneously owners of capital and producers of surplus value. The extension of share ownership has further undermined the appeal of nationalisation.

2) The new post-Fordist modes of small batch, consumer-sensitive production combined with the diminishing real costs of consumer items – once the preserve of the privileged few – have added to the popular appeal of a competitive market economy. It is through consumer choices that most individuals express themselves. The idea that people might gain self-fulfillment and meaning while living in an economy in which all productive assets are subject to centralised, bureaucratic direction now appears bizarre.

3) Rising standards of living have resulted in a changing structure of demand; affluence has resulted in a decreasing dependence on state provided services such as transport, housing and health care. This, in turn, has created a new point of political division: workers in the public sector have a vested interest in rising state expenditure, whereas affluent, private sector employees have exhibited a tendency to support cuts in taxation.

4) The trend towards subcontracting production to small firms, to semi-autonomous units within large companies, and to self-employed individuals who were once directly employed workers, has caused the working class to be subverted. And the same effect has been achieved with the dramatic rise in the number of workers engaged in providing services, and the corresponding decrease in unskilled and semiskilled manual employees. Changing work environments, and new management practices and structures, have done much to provoke a new psychological attitude to the labour process on the part of employees.

Conclusion

Certain challenges present themselves to Conservatives if the postmodernity thesis is accepted as having validity. The first task is to develop an understanding of the new left, and respond to it. The anti-socialist revolutions in eastern Europe in 1989; the disintegration of the Soviet Union and its various satellite regimes and the marginalisation of the hard left within the Labour Party, has resulted in a smug triumphalism in some quarters of the right. Now only a hardcore of committed hard leftists still believe the goal of a society in which all productive assets have been expropriated, and are then made to comply with a centrally conceived plan, is desirable.

If the old left are a declining irrelevance this should not blind us to the possibility that a new left is in the process of emerging which is a much more potent adversary for those who adhere to liberal values. The new left is characterised in the economic sphere by an abandonment of mass nationalisation of the means of production and its replacement, instead, by a commitment to extensive regulation of enterprise and a limited redistribution of wealth. It is thus both corporatist and social democratic in nature. However, this is corporatism of a special type since the impetus behind it is no longer solely to do with seeking to subordinate private capital to the economic imperatives of the state. Instead, the driving force of the new left's interventionism are the new social movements that have their origins in civil society rather than the productive base. While the demands of these groups spring from the senses of identity that have gained increasing currency over the past twenty years, they are nevertheless designed to encourage government to impose new, bureaucratic regulations and restrictions on free enterprise. There is a feminist lobby who want *Penthouse* and *Playboy* 'off the shelf'; a green lobby who want further curbs on the activities of business; animal rights lobbyists seek to stop the pharmaceutical industry from carrying out the research needed to develop new medicines, to name but a few.

The new left's potential danger for the right is partly a consequence of the fact that its political project lacks the dramatic and sinister quality of the Marxist grand narrative. Instead, the new left represents the bringing together under a single umbrella of a variety of different group demands. Furthermore, whereas the demands of the supporters of old style collectivist politics were essentially contingent upon their own material status at any one time (thus rising affluence resulted in many changing political allegiances), the aspirations of the new lobbies are, by their very nature, less negotiable and less transitory. These demands can only be satisfied by direct state intervention. Many of the policies that the new lobbies pressure for also contain a populist appeal which can enlist the support of individuals outside the traditional confines of the left, on an issue by issue basis.

The second key area of concern for the right relates to the Conservative Party's lack of interest in, and understanding of, civil society and the postmodernity agenda that is emerging. Unless it is able to formulate a strategy for the next terrain of ideological conflict, the new left will enjoy the kind of hegemony the old left once possessed with regard to the economy. The Tories had to ape many of the Keynesian, welfarist, and mixed economy policies of the Labour Party in order to stay in electoral business in the 1940 s, 50 s and 60 s. The danger today is that the right will simply be forced to echo the policies of the revamped corporatism, mentioned above. To some extent this has already occurred. Despite over fourteen years of Conservative government the Equal Opportunities and Race Relations Acts have not been repealed. Some senior Tory politicians have given support to the idea that the tabloid press should be regulated. Draconian laws against so called 'video nasties' have also been introduced. Further restrictions on tobacco advertising have been implemented.

How such a strategy to counter the dominance of the new corporatists of the left can be formulated is not immediately apparent. A starting point might be to reconsider which particular sites of political conflict Conservatives should direct their energies towards; and then look again at the content of the ideological message being communicated by the right. With regard to the first point, a criticism that can be made of the Conservative Party is its unimaginative and slavish devotion to parliamentary politics. Virtually all its organisational and intellectual capacities are directed to the electoral process. Little effort has been devoted to those other, intermediate social processes and institutions which are of growing significance. This, despite the fact that voters' consciousness as developed in civil society, will obviously influence the electoral choices they make.

In a period when narrow calculations of immediate economic self-interest, in terms of both ownership and consumption, were the chief determinants of political success, the fact that the Conservative Party restricted itself to electoral politics was not a great disadvantage to the right. The propaganda war was of virtually no significance in dictating the outcomes of elections since voters made up their minds in accordance with direct, empirical experience and usually self-evident calculations of gain and loss from the various competing policy proposals. The manner in which people come to align themselves when such materialistic concerns are no longer paramount is altogether more problematic and complex.

One hypothesis worth considering is that in an era when other, more amorphous, 'quality of life', desires/values are becoming prioritised by a growing number of people, dominance of the institutions of civil society will itself be a key factor in determining political success. The craving for a sense of 'belonging', 'community' or 'moral righteousness', in an age when the organic collectivities of the past (and the traditional value systems that went with them) are in the process of disintegration, provides a window of opportunity for the ideology that is most widely adhered to within the cultural sphere. If the way in which society is represented artistically – through drama, literature, comedy, and popular music – is characterised by the hegemony of a particular world-view, then a precondition of gaining that sense of belonging and ethical superiority will be adherence to it.

To feel part of a community, be it an artificial, fictitious one that manifests itself electronically through the television or film screen, demands conformity to a particular set of beliefs. The absence of right-wing alternative comedians of the stature of Jo Brand or Ben Elton; dramatists like Alan Bleasdale; writers such as Hanif Kureishi; popular musicians like Carter USM; or film makers such as Derek Jarman, gives the new left a considerable advantage over the right. At a time when Hollywood and the British film industry are so dominated by the ethos of the bourgeois new left, conservatives should be acutely aware of how fortunate the right is that 'dissident' American film makers such as David Lynch and John Millius have been prepared to puncture some of the sacred cows of collectivism. Lynch's films, in particular *Blue Velvet* and *Wild at Heart*, juxtapose a virile existentialist individualism against the sentimental, 'caring and sharing' values of much modern politically correct cinema. Of course, the satellite TV revolution and the continued success of the *Sun* should not be underestimated politically. Rupert Murdoch's various cultural interventions have been crucial to the conservative fight back in civil society.

Prime illustrations of the Conservative Party's failure to recognise the importance of, and the opportunities that exist in, civil society have been the government backed campaigns against Acid House and for the introduction of soccer ID cards. Imaginative Conservatives, with any degree of understanding of the deep political importance of popular culture, would attempt to incorporate ravers and football fans into a pro-freedom coalition since many within these two sub-cultures share progressive, anti-statist impulses. If Conservatism is to prosper in the coming decades the activists of the right will need to enter and contest the various spheres of popular culture, the churches, broadcasting, education and sport.

The third challenge that Conservatives must face and develop an attitude towards regards Britain's constitutional make-up and the future of the nation-state. The British state is being undermined from 'below' and 'above' by a variety of forces. The technological revolution will seriously compromise the ability of any government to control the flow of visual and aural messages in society. Video recorders and camcorders; TCs; fax machines; the increasing number of pirate radio stations; portable phones and satellite TV will make censorship more problematic. Likewise, the state's capacity to exercise control over the national economy may decrease as the inter-continental movement of capital becomes more difficult to trace because of the proliferation of computers.

As well as the welcome challenge to the power of the state arising from the empowerment of individuals through technology, there are also a number of negative threats to the British nation-state from projects which aim radically to transform the character of the state. Such attacks tend to originate from those who perceive the British constitution and political system as an obstruction to their ideological ends.

Tom Nairn, in his anti-monarchist polemic *The*

Enchanted Glass,[12] has characterised the British state as 'early modern', pointing out that although Britain was at one time the most liberal and enlightened state in Europe, there has been no fundamental overhaul of the constitution since before the industrial revolution. He views the now 'archaic' system, with its lack of written rights and emphasis on custom, practice and continuity as a major obstacle to the implementation of socialist policies. Nairn's theory finds an echo in Charter 88 which demands a written constitution for the UK. Supporters of Charter 88 are clearly frustrated by the seeming inability of the British state to be user-friendly to socialism.

Prior to the advent of Thatcherism, the principal left critique of the British state centred around its alleged antipathy to progress and its almost mystical capacity to uphold the essence of the status quo in the face of 'popular' demands for change. Since 1979, however, many on the left have shifted their emphasis. Their priority is no longer the creation of a unicameral 'enabling' state which can bypass vested interests in order to transform society. Instead new leftists, including Charter 88, wish to enshrine institutions and introduce safeguards against radical changes (especially those relating to the welfare state) in order to frustrate the incipient changes posited by Thatcherism.

The British state, unlike other constitutional models, provides no *a priori* rationale for intervention. It is therefore easier to implement reforms that are based upon a concrete property/rights perspective than it is to impose abstract rights favoured by socialists – such as the right to a job. The British tradition has no theoretical limitation on the power of Parliament to interfere in the affairs of individuals, yet has substantially failed to go down the road of enforcing theoretical 'rights' which entail curbing the real property rights of others.

As we approach the new millennium there is a substantial and growing threat to the integrity, even the survival, of the British state. This comes from the European Community to which the United Kingdom, despite rhetorical reservations, is fully committed. The EC is determined to usurp many of the constitutional prerogatives of its member states. In the name of 'harmonization' the European Commission is attempting to impose a mechanistic, artificial state structure on the United Kingdom. It inevitably draws upon the continental tradition of written, second generation, rights based on a series of subjective abstractions. There is an overpowering flavour of social/christian democratic consensus, hence the clear corporatist aspirations of the Delors Social Charter.

The projected European superstate is a linear descendant of the absolute monarchies of pre-revolutionary Europe – governance from above. It has also incorporated the formularised traditions of the Napoleonic Code. There are few in Britain who view the prospect of a united Europe with any real degree of enthusiasm, but some see it as a panacea to the alleged excesses of Thatcherism. It is a measure of the alienation among many socialists, social democrats and Tory corporatists that they would prefer to jettison the British state as it is presently understood rather than attempt to persuade the British people to accept their values and policies. In other words there is a substantial body of political opinion in Britain that is working towards the effective winding up of the British state, constitution and legal systems, not because of a principled objection but rather because of a belief that another formula may better help them facilitate their ideological aspirations.

The relentless drive towards a federal Europe advocated by the main political currents of all the EC countries will prove to be a key issue in future British elections. This will almost certainly have permanently divisive implications for the Conservative Party. Liberalism and the cause of national autonomy may once again become bedfellows as Tory free marketeers oppose full European integration in order to defend the ideological gains of Thatcherism. Conversely, the left of the Conservative Party, which has a history of fidelity to the European ideal, will move ever closer to the federalist position as a means of facilitating its preferred brand of continental-style corporatism. 'One nation' will be eclipsed by 'One Europe'.

Notes

1 W. Hudson, 'Postmodernity and Contemporary Social Thought', in P. Lassman, (ed.), *Politics and Social Theory*, Routledge, London 1989.

2 See Robin Murray, 'Fordism and Post-Fordism'; Geoff Mulgan, 'The Power of the Weak'; and Stuart Hall, 'The Meaning of New Times', in Stuart Hall and Martin Jaques, (eds), *New Times, The Changing Face of Politics in the 1990s*, Lawrence and Wishart, London 1989.

3 The 'Manifesto for New Times' was initially published as a discussion document by The Communist Party in June 1989 as part of the process of redrafting the party's official programme. It was finally adopted, in a slightly modified form, at the party's Congress in December 1989.

4 This chapter was first published as 'Altered States: Towards a Post-Modernist Conservatism'. It served as an introductory paper to a series of monthly forums organised under the auspices of The National Association of Conservative Graduates. The paper and forums were an attempt to replicate within Conservative and libertarian circles the debate concerning the implications of New Times that *Marxism Today* had initiated within the left.

5 Stuart Hall, 'Brave New World', in *Marxism Today*, October 1988.

6 Robin Murray, 'Life after Henry (Ford)', in *Marxism Today*, October 1988.

7 Mulgan, G., 'The Power of the Weak', in Hall, S., and Jacques, M., (eds), *op cit.*, Lawrence and Wishart, 1989.

8 Rustin, M., 'The Politics of Post-Fordism: Or the Trouble with "New Times" ', *New Left Review*, no 175, May/June 1989.

9 See Toffler A., *The Third Wave*, Chapter 11-17, Pan, London 1980.

10 Hall, S., *op cit.* 1988.

11 Hall, S., *ibid.*

12 Tom Nairn, *The Enchanted Glass*, Radius, London 1988.

Rethinking Socialism: New Processes, New Insights

ANNE SHOWSTACK SASSOON

The more challenging the period, the more urgent it is to find the space to reflect. Those who earn their living as intellectuals need to cast arrogance aside. Any polished end product may be the result of individual intellectual effort, but it inevitably reflects a collective process. However 'expert' someone is, however much someone has read, ideas with any claim to validity must be tested and based on *listening* and most importantly on *hearing* as they take account of the responses they elicit. Academic seminars and specialist conferences provide one kind of terrain for this, party commissions and independent think tanks still others. Small discussion groups are perhaps one of the most 'thinker-friendly' because of the opportunity they provide to share some thoughts and to get feedback. Above all, they help, along with private conversations, which can provide such rich 'food for thought', to overcome some of the isolation which intellectual work forces on those who engage in it.

Having a practical object, or a political commitment, or even belonging to a group, or working with others is useful but not sufficient if debates continue to reproduce old ideas as answers to questions which are rendered outmoded by historical transformations. That new thinking, which somehow manages to leap out of the traps of old dichotomies, while taking insights from the past which are still useful in the present, and which aims to innovate in ways corresponding to the needs of a new epoch, must be grounded in the messy, often confusing tangle of developments, while constantly allowing for uncertainty and ambiguity.

Unsettled and Upended

We are without any doubt living through extraordinary times and any attempt to rethink socialism is little short of daunting. The central and eastern European socialist regimes have collapsed. We read in the newspapers, hear on the radio, and see on television reports about what is being destroyed, and what is left behind. Without personal contact it is difficult to get a sense of what is being created in the spaces opening up. In the West many of us have the sensation of being buffeted about from one financial crisis to another, as people lose jobs and homes, as we walk past people sleeping on the streets, as even once steadfast regimes, like the Swedish welfare state, cease to be a beacon of light. Yet while socialism has collapsed, capitalism certainly doesn't seem to work all that well. In Britain it cannot house a significant section of the population adequately. In the United States it has not been able to provide good health care. Those starving in Sudan, or being bombarded in the former Yugoslavia, have little to thank capitalism for. But what, we ask, is the alternative?

As we think about an answer, we can, and must, each examine our own feelings about this situation. For it is a period which requires reflection, the deeper the better, as much as reading, or listening or talking. The process of self-reflection must not be short-circuited precisely *because* of the *necessity* of trying to go beyond our individual limitations, the narrow confines of the groups and places we each inhabit, in order to try to connect with society more widely. We must be in touch with our own feelings, and relate our thinking to them, if we are to have any chance to be in touch with others. That is, a rethinking which shares concerns with others must come from the inside as well as the outside. We need to listen to our hearts as well as our heads and to reflect on *our* daily experiences to begin to check whether our ideas and our policies are valid. How else can we have empathy with others, however much we recognize the distance between different experiences? And if we do not listen to ourselves, let alone others, how can our activities, our ideas, our policies have a ring of authenticity on the one hand and of necessity on the other? How can they attract, and reflect, more than a handful of intellectuals unless they *feel* right?

Putting *feelings* on the agenda is hardly the usual mode of proceeding for rethinking politics, or indeed, for engaging in intellectual activities. The usual mode, in its most dogmatic form, is to lay down the line, to give the definitive version. We are supposed to subjugate our feelings and to conquer our anxiety and our ambivalence as we search for the certainty of generalities outside of ourselves. The dichotomy which has been set up historically between thinking and feeling has been much criticized, not least in important work by feminist writers. But can we overcome the seeming contradiction between a naive belief in the obviousness of reading our feelings and a sophisticated, detached intellectual analysis? Can we understand how subjectivity can itself be a *resource* in expanding our comprehension of the social order?

If we can recognize the parallels between politics and the kinds of creative intervention undertaken by novelists and artists, then an illustration of what I am getting at is provided by an interview of some years ago with the German writer Christa Wolf in the context of a fight to justify a particular creative space in the GDR. Talking about her work she says,

> This mode of writing is not 'subjectivist', but 'interven-
> tionist'. It does require subjectivity, and a subject who is
> prepared to undergo unrelenting exposure ... to the
> material at hand, to accept the tensions that inexorably
> arise, and to be curious about the changes that both the
> material and the author undergo. The new reality is
> different from the one you saw before. Suddenly,
> everything is interconnected and fluid. Things formerly

taken as 'given' start to dissolve revealing the reified social relations they contain and no longer that hierarchically arranged social cosmos in which the human particle travels along the paths pre-ordained by sociology or ideology, or deviates from them. It becomes more and more difficult to say 'I', and yet at the same time often imperative to do so. I would like to give the provisional name 'subjective authenticity' to the search for a new method of writing which does justice to this reality. I can only hope that I have made it clear that the method not only does not dispute the existence of objective reality, but is precisely an attempt to engage with 'objective reality' in a productive manner.[1]

Reflection, of course, goes hand in hand with other ways of learning. We all try to read those things which can give us insight into our current situation. We listen to those who can teach us something. We seek knowledge from a variety of sources. But at the same time many of us are all too aware of the difficulty we have in really understanding what is going on. First of all, the rapidity of events is breathtaking. Sometimes it feels like a film which has speeded up and gone haywire. But secondly, and this is an example of an old question reappearing, we all face the problem of how to get in contact with what is going on in society. Although one would never know it from the bad press political parties receive, this is actually a question which in part has to do with the need for a new kind of party.[2] As political parties of the left lose elections, or try to redefine themselves but find it difficult to regenerate, people search for alternatives and talk about social movements or civic groups or whatever else seems to provide an unsullied, organizational form.[3] Yet, if history has irrevocably undermined the parties of old, our problem is how to move from a party which sees itself as the be all and end all (a vice of social democratic parties no less than communist ones) to one, or better, ones, which see themselves as *part* of an overall process in relation to and alongside other organizations which represent a diversity of peoples, ideas, other interests and serve a variety of political functions. Parties are needed to formulate political programmes, based on a vision of society, which reflect and influence pressures for change. They are needed for an effective democratic process answerable to the electorate and responsible for the actions of governments and policy makers. They are needed as an important mediator, if by no means the only one, of knowledge about society as it connects with some sense of a collective project which millions of people are willing to lend (and I mean lend, not grant once and for all) their allegiance to.

It should be obvious that this is not just any old party. Nor is it an organization which already exists although some of its *attributes* have existed. Much of this concerns a new way of the political being reflected in an organization which is deeply rooted in society, which functions as a conduit for ideas and feelings, which listens and tries to understand, and which connects that understanding to knowledge at a higher, societal and indeed international level, that is, to policies and political programmes. This is what mass, social democratic and communist parties used to set as their task. Admittedly, it was in a manner which is today increasingly inadequate, since the complexity of society, and consequently of governing, requires manifold channels of knowledge and sources of creative policy making. Moreover, the imperatives arising from this situation have enormous implications, not only for rethinking the party, but also, for restructuring the state.

On the Ground and Down to Earth

Yet if the current situation requires, parties plus a myriad of other organizations, institutions, and processes, we *still* have to have our ears to the ground, to learn from people's daily lives and aspirations, from people's needs, however they are being defined, not because of some populist vocation, but because the name of the political game is the need for popular support. This is not just essential for winning elections, but because any policy worth its salt has inevitably to be translated on the ground by millions of people as they simply get on with life within the confines of the possible and with the dreams of the desirable. Of course the form and content of these needs are contested and constantly evolving, and are the product of many influences, structures, and agencies. But *whatever* we encounter, and *however far* from the political vision we may have strayed, popular aspirations are the context and the mediator of any politics and policy.[4] Given that the experience of any of us or of our families, friends, workmates, acquaintances is inevitably circumscribed, we can only come into contact with a minute part of this society directly. We therefore depend on what others know and communicate, and overall we require some kind of evolving, never fully defined, always contestable synthesis as the basis for constructing what Gramsci called a 'collective will', that is, one which does not lose the complex texture of contemporary society, the depth of individual experience, or the quality of openness and process. We need to hold together the subjective and the analytical. However finely honed the intellectual argument, however convincingly argued a political position, however complex a policy analysis, if it is to be translated *on the ground*, it is of necessity situated in this reality, it will be constantly tested as society changes.

However, the question of knowledge and understanding is not an abstract, theoretical matter. It is very down to earth and concrete. As Marx wrote, 'The educators must be educated.' To change his language somewhat, we who have come some way down the road to articulating political ideas, who organize or manage in the work we do, who aim to intervene to change society for the better, need the confidence that our politics are valid, confidence in ourselves, but eventually and much more importantly, we need to gain the confidence of wider sectors of the society. And we cannot achieve that confidence simply by being in an organization with a particular name, or because our hearts are in the right place. Our politics can only be validated if they are rooted in the profound needs of our society.

The greatest danger in such a rapidly evolving situation is to assume that we already know all the *questions*, let alone the *answers*. Yet that does not mean that none of the old questions are useful, or that we have to throw away all the old categories. Quite the opposite. What is happening is that some very traditional questions are reappearing in new, and sometimes rather old forms. At the level of intellectual debates, for example, there are attempts to reformulate very traditional questions; about the nature of citizenship, the problems involved in arriving at the common good in conditions of plurality and difference, and the tensions and contradictions within liberal democracy which can serve as the motor of a process aimed at expanding conditions of democracy. What is too often missing, however, is an understanding that social and historical changes require the development of new and adequate conceptual apparatus.

The inadequacies of left thinking, and the disastrous aspects of socialist regimes, do not mean that other traditions of political thought, such as liberalism, however relevant it may still appear, however it may be dressed up in inspiring, radical language, is sufficient to analyse the dramatic changes we are living through. At the same time, being 'post' something else, identifying with a 'post-ism', be it post-Marxism or postmodernism, runs the risk of simply repeating the insights of Locke, or Rousseau, or Nietzsche, or Freud, in a language much more convoluted than they ever employed. Recent debates in philosophy and social theory, carrying the name of postmodernism, have been essential in liberating us from the dead weight of those ideas which prevent us from seeing and seeking to understand the multifarious and complex nature of social reality. But, to put it crudely, the baby has all too often been thrown out with the bath water.

Back to Reality

Because debate is posed at such an abstract level with little, if any, recognition that we need to move between theoretical abstractions and reality and back again, we tend to lose sight of some inescapable, if very old-fashioned, features of society. Let's jump to the specific and the concrete: the recent league tables of secondary schools, highly flawed that they are, highlight how *class* differences are crucial in educational achievement in this country. The same could be said of health statistics or other indices. Yet we are all aware how class is but one of a configuration of factors and how any automatic, knee jerk response to these facts which assumes an obvious protagonism of some mythical working class (mythical in the sense that it tends to be conjured up in its superficial generality) is completely inadequate politically. Again, this is not a question of abstract theory, but of something very concrete. As I sat recently in a sparkling, new, international style shopping mall in Kingston upon Thames, I thought to myself how very distant, metaphorically, the society it represented was from what, in spatial terms, was just up the road, Brixton. *Both* realities must be taken into account, and the similarities, as well as the differences, entered into our frame. After all, unemployment and house repossessions have risen rapidly in Kingston, just as material gratification is alive and well in Brixton. But, for all sorts of reasons, we must not underestimate the challenge such a mixed reality presents to us both analytically, and politically, as it forces us both to arrive at new understandings and to build on those from the past which are still useful.

To consider another question, when we speak about developing civil society, we need to realize two things. First, that we must study what is *already going on* in civil society, in both organized and unorganized ways. Second, civil society cannot be conceptualized in limbo. It always exists in some kind of relation to the state. We cannot avoid the traditional concern with the state, yet this concern has taken on a new meaning in a context where the state/society relationship is being reorganized so dramatically. With regard to both civil society and to the state, if we fail to begin with studying what is already going on, and instead assert a politics which we weave out of our heads, we risk at best being irrelevant and at worst failing to connect with precisely those elements which could constitute the basis for socialist advance. The development of policy which is worth fighting for, because it is appropriate for what is *really* going on and is not just proceeding in well worn channels, or reflecting the untested ideas of a few experts, must derive from a reflection on the actual processes of society, the ones we like and also the ones we do not.[5]

Reinventing the State: Theory Learning from Practice

Any attempt at what has been called 'reinventing the state',[6] must learn from an examination of those practices which are developing in public institutions, as the people who work in them try to 'push back the walls' of the constraints they face and take advantage of the new spaces which are opening up. This could include everything from local authority service contracts to new teaching practices, to equal opportunities policies and attempts to get what is good out of community care legislation. We have to study those intermediate levels and to listen to those people, the practitioners, who are trying to do good jobs, to develop more democratic practices, and at the same time to maintain some kind of job satisfaction within the most difficult constraints. To learn about the concrete dimensions of citizenship in Britain today, we would do well to study, for example, the local service contracts which a number of local councils have introduced between specific services and their users. These have required detailed and practical thinking, service by service, about how to give people some effective control to make the contract meaningful,[7] or the attempts at more democratic and empowering practices in social work,[8] or examples of good community care practices furnished by voluntary sector services run by users, practitioners and managers together,[9] or the development of effective multi-cultural and anti-racist policies.[10]

If our politics and our rethinking does not build on the good practices being developed (which, incidentally, cannot be claimed to be the achievement of any political party) by creating the conditions needed to fulfil their potential, not least by funding them properly, then our very vision of what is possible and desirable will not be grounded in concrete reality. Theoretical debate, however stimulating and inspiring, would then remain floating in the air, unrelated to ongoing processes, real problems and structures. We would be reproducing the worst aspects of traditional, intellectual practice without effectively feeding into a process of political regeneration. We would remain out of touch and out of date. As we aim at a strategic dimension, not only nationally but internationally, we would be trying to re-invent the wheel without the benefit of the knowledge and experience of those who constitute the link between citizen and state.

What is actually being suggested is something which was hinted at, if not spelt out, by Marx, on the one hand, and by Gramsci on the other. Marx provided what remains an incisive critique of attempts to develop philosophical and social thinking as if it could be generated without reference to the historical, socio-economic context. He and Engels based their own prognosis of socialism on what they understood was the potential of capitalism, that is, from an engagement with the cutting edge of contemporary developments. Going well beyond them, but developing many of their ideas, in a period of enormous political and theoretical crisis, Gramsci was sharply critical of political parties or intellectuals who acted as if they had nothing to learn from the ongoing, complex historical process. He analysed the latest historical developments, while criticizing the limitations of existing theory which was available to give us some of the most creative and original insights into twentieth century society, insights which managed to escape the sterile dichotomies of contemporary debates. The point is not to have any illusions about the possibility of basing the analysis which we need today on thinkers whose own works are full of limitations. Moreover, there are many different sources of wisdom. But at the same time, we should be open to learning from the way they worked, and from the criticisms they made of abstract, detached intellectualistic pretence.[11]

The Resources for a New Understanding

Learning and thinking about social change must be tackled by *all* reforming political organizations, whatever their position in the political spectrum, but no political party in today's conditions can hope to accomplish this task on its own. There is a *functional* need for non-sectarian openness and democratic change. We must go beyond even the most open communist tradition informed by Gramsci, and we need more political and intellectual resources than even a reforming Labour Party or a host of think tanks can provide, useful though they may prove to be. Society is simply too complex, and the amount of knowledge too great. One consequence of the complexity of social needs is the inevitability of diversity and flexibility if social provision is to be adequate. And if we begin to reformulate our ideas about social provision to include fundamentally the state, but as a facilitator (and funder) as much as direct provider, with much of policy being invented in a creative way 'on the ground' and probably 'on the move' as well, then we have also to rethink the party which can no longer be conceived of as an all-knowing, all-providing organization. Further, if a different kind of party is a necessary but not a sufficient condition, it will require a regeneration of a whole range of organizations, of everything from trade unions, to women's groups, to voluntary organizations, to professional associations, and, crucially, educational institutions.

This implies embarking on that kind of intellectual and moral reform described by Gramsci when he discussed what he called the 'political' question of the intellectuals. By this he meant not just the academic élite, but all those in society whose jobs and training mean that they organize institutions or ideas, who connect people in civil society; the experts, the managers, the professionals, the technicians, the practitioners, in short, anyone with some kind of advanced education or training. Gramsci chose the word 'reform' with care. It indicated the kind of sea change in the way people view themselves and their socio-economic roles, from top to toe of the social ladder,

associated with the Protestant reformation or the creation
of a modern secular society. Elements of a transformation
of this order are already under way within the difficult
conditions of the present. And since these processes *are*
already under way, we can be comforted that we are not
simply idealistic utopians, cut off from the needs of our
neighbours or indeed out of touch with our own.

Out of the anger with the failure of what is no more and
the vast distance between on the one hand, what is needed
and, on the other, what seems to be within our grasp, it is
so easy to reject all of what went before or, on the other
hand, to hold on for dear life. There is the tendency to
come up with a formula which seems to be original but
which is created in a very old-fashioned, outdated way,
that is, by intellectuals who are detached from the ongoing
processes.

Rethinking socialism inevitably implies rethinking how
we go about things, individually and collectively. The ends
will never be achieved if the means are not the right ones.
And if the means are faulty we will not, in any case, know
what those ends are or could be. This rethinking, then, is a
task on the agenda for everyone who is trying to make
some kind of sense of the present situation. It may be
easier to come up with a slogan or mobilizing call or neat
theoretical formulation than to contemplate the brutal
reality that what is needed has to be painstakingly created.
It is not created in conditions of our choosing, to
paraphrase Marx, but what *we are able to create*, for politics
is a creative process, will depend on how far it harnesses
the potential of people and sectors of society who would
never turn out on a dark winter's night to a meeting.

A good starting point is to add to our usual sources
conversations, films, novels, television programmes, plays,
whatever – and our own deepest feelings. Let me give you
a few examples of how I have been given a much greater
understanding of some major issues and profound
questions by batting them around in my own mind and
gaining insights from unexpected sources. They all
concern women. I think that both changes in women's
lives, the contradictions they and the households in which

they live encounter, and the theoretical and political advances made by feminism, give us the basis for a real advance in understanding.

The first story has to do with a woman who was my daughter's childminder some years ago. She was a single mother, with two primary-school-age children, who had applied several times to return part-time to a job which she had held before as a lab technician in a large London teaching hospital. However, she never even got an interview. By sheer coincidence her mother used to work in the personnel department of this same hospital, and she explained that they simply would never consider anyone who had small children. Hearing this story made something click inside me. First, what might seem obvious, the necessity of a law on equal opportunities was brought home along with the fact that we have to make sure that it is enforced. The rules of entry to jobs and the practices of personnel departments should resemble justice blind-folded, disregarding irrelevant differences and, in partic-ular, keeping childcare responsibilities out of court. This single, concrete example drove home to me that the traditional, liberal democratic guarantee of the rule of law still needs to be fought for and applied equitably.

Yet there was also something else. This specific, concrete woman *did* have responsibility for the care of two small children. While entry to a job should not be blocked because of this, once she was in a job (and she finally did get one), she did not in fact leave this responsibility on the side, and no one anywhere in the world, however good the childcare provision, has come up with any possibility of doing that. What we (and I include myself) need is a transformation of the logic of work itself to be able to develop adequate flexibility to address the different caring responsibilities, of both men and women, in different points of their life cycles. This is difficult to imagine, but while it would be revolutionary, it is not utopian, because it adheres to the actual needs of millions of people, even if it goes beyond the logic of much, if not all, of contemporary working life. Of course, this everyday example was deciphered by me through lenses which I had because of some reading and knowledge of theoretical debates, but I understood the theory so much better from thinking about the real dimensions of this woman's life, and my own life and the lives of other women I knew. This kind of engagement helped me to understand how we both need to fight to make liberal ideas of equality real, and to construct a new terrain in which we give full credence to difference. Taking this one step further and relating it to discussions about women and different welfare states, I arrived at a much better understanding of the highly differentiated relationship we each have with the state, not only through the system of laws but mediated by the institutions of the welfare state and how our citizenship is much more complex than it once was.[12]

The second example has to do with something I have been puzzling over for a long time. Why is it that in Britain, unlike say Italy or Finland, women experience such guilt and anxiety over combining paid work and childcare responsibilities? Yes, there was the influence in the post-war period of oversimplified, psychoanalytic theory as mediated by social policy and inadequate social provision.[13] But, why did it seem to stick to women's guts in Britain in such an uncomfortable way? Why do so many women in Britain see childcare as their *individual* responsibility? (And I stress the word responsibility – the place of joy and desire has all too small a place in these discussions). What gave me a greater insight into this came from an account of a friend's emotional experience having been evacuated as a six year old child to the United States. It was at the beginning of the Second World War and she was shipped off with her sisters, changing from one set of relatives to another, before finally being reunited with her parents at the war's end. Could it be that the trauma of a *policy* of evacuation, mediated through parental choice, as opposed to unforeseen and unchosen separations which involved so many millions in Europe in the last war,[14] scarred the national psyche so deeply that discussions of childcare are overdetermined by it? And weren't the fresh memories of millions of women of the difficult conditions of combining work and childcare in wartime, which were only partially mitigated by the existence of nurseries and the benefits of an independent wage, an element in influencing the desire for 'normality', sex stereotyped that it might be, with women having only *one* job, in the home, and men having, *at least one*, in paid work? Could a further contributing factor be the emotional experiences of early separation of a small, but influential minority of people, whose parents have sent them to boarding school, who form part of the nation's elite? When it comes to developing a policy of good quality, socially provided childcare, could these in part explain some of the resistances? When they are reinforced by the lack of experience of good quality provision, which, for example, as a Danish friend told me, makes it as automatic in Denmark for a parent to decide to place a young child in a nursery as it would for British parents to send their children to school, we are talking about long-term historical and cultural factors which shape the context for policy making in which no political party in Britain places adequate childcare provision at the fore. Of course anecdote does not provide systematic knowledge, but combined with reading and research, it can provide leads and ground for more abstract discussion.

And finally, a very different example. At a recent London Film Festival I had the good fortune to see the Istvan Szabò film, *Sweet Emma, Dear Böbe* about the experiences of two young women teachers in the Budapest of today, and to hear his comments afterward. *Sweet Emma, Dear Böbe* is about coping and survival. It is a tremendously moving, at times funny, and incredibly sad story about how tough it is to survive a change of regime, a low income, the need to take a second job, the loss of ties with family and rural culture, the experience of living in a dormitory with no privacy and the upheaval of an institution where colleagues constantly accuse each other, pupils could not care less about learning, and where one's previous training, to teach Russian, is worth nothing. Added to these immense problems were the torments of loving a man who cannot respond to your needs, the institutionalized sexism of the police, and some, little, humanity and joy.

What was striking in the film was the sympathy and

understanding with which the characters were portrayed. When Szabò responded to questions about the bleakness of it all, the role of religion, the conditions of making films in Hungary today, and so on, he told some stories from his own life, explaining that since he was born in 1938 there have been eight changes of regime in Hungary. He described how he learned about the situation of these teachers from the inside through long discussions, showing them the film before it was released. And he said some things that I will never forget: 'It is really hard to live through these changes. Some people make it and some don't. People need to believe in something. Our future lies with the education of our children. I had already made several films about opportunistic men. Now I wanted to show the story of a strong woman.'

It is this kind of authenticity, sensitivity, and dedication of our talents and skills to a politics which is rooted in the depths of our society, and in a reflection on our role as intellectuals in the wider Gramscian sense, which must be the basis of our rethinking socialism. There are no easy prescriptions for accomplishing this, but at the centre of our agenda there must be an expansion of our ways of seeing, hearing and understanding, and a critique of the inadequacies of all those prognoses and programmes, which seem to have little if anything to do with daily life. We have to get in touch with the positive things which are being created as well as provide a critique of the negative features of society. We need to wed policy making, the reconstruction of organizations, and theorizing to the lived experience of millions of people. Only then can we hope to regenerate ourselves and our politics.

Notes

[1] Christa Wolf, *The Fourth Dimension: Interviews with Christa Wolf*, Verso, London 1987, p 22.
[2] Although most of the context and many of the terms of Gramsci's discussion have been superseded, his writings on the party still have much to offer and influence in part what follows here. See Anne Showstack Sassoon, *Gramsci's Politics*, second edition, Unwin Hyman, London 1987.

[3] See Anne Phillips, *Engendering Democracy*, Polity, Oxford 1991 for a thoughtful critique from a feminist perspective of the difficulties of political practice in small groups.

[4] The extensive debate about how to define needs often fails to grasp the political nettle in an attempt to provide a baseline which can be defended. See Kate Soper's review article, 'A Theory of Human Needs,' in *New Left Review*, 197, January/February, 1993. Nancy Fraser has a good sense of the contested and constructed nature of needs. See 'Talking About Needs: Interpretive Contests and Political Conflicts in Welfare-State Societies,' in *Ethics*, vol 99, no 2, January, 1989.

[5] Analyses of the changes being forced on the public sector, and a critical re-evaluation of the assumptions of much modern management and organizational theory, are rich sources for anyone trying to think through the theoretical implications of current developments. See, for example, 'New Forms of Public Administration,' *IDS Bulletin*, vol 23, no 4, October, 1992.

[6] The terminology is slightly different, but this notion has been very influential in Clinton's project. See for example, Dave Osborne and Ted Gaebler, *Reinventing Government*, Addison-Wesley Publishing Co., Inc., Reading, Massachusetts 1992.

[7] See Wendy Thomson, 'Realising Rights Through Local Service Contracts' in Anna Coote, ed., *The Welfare of Citizens*, Rivers Oram Press, London 1992 and Wendy Thomson, 'Local Experience of Managing Quality,' in Ian Sanderson, ed., *The Management of Quality in Local Government*, Longman, London 1992.

[8] See, for example, Nina Biehal, Mike Fisher, Peter Marsh, Eric Sainsbury, 'Rights and Social Work,' in Anna Coote, ed. *op cit*.

[9] One example of such a 'user lead' service, and one which is consistently threatened by under funding, is the community mental health support service organized by a voluntary agency, the Family Welfare Association, in North London, but there are many others.

[10] Again within a context of inadequate funding, the London Borough of Lambeth, for example, has made great strides in changing its staffing policy through positive action programmes to ensure that services are run by people who reflect the ethnic and racial mix of the local community and respond to specific needs in ways easily and comfortably accessible to different groups. In addition, although there is a long way to go, a number of voluntary agencies are beginning to take on board the lack of fit between how they work and what they offer, on the one hand, and the needs of ethnic minorities on the other.

[11] I have developed some of these ideas in 'Postscript. The People, Intellectuals and Specialised Knowledge,' in *Gramsci's Politics, op cit* and in 'Gramsci, the Left and the 1990s: an Agenda for Research,' in Chronis Polychroniou, ed., *Socialism: Crisis and Renewal*, Praeger, New York, 1993. For a beautiful essay about Gramsci's creative way of working see Joseph A. Buttigieg, 'Introduction to Antonio Gramsci', *Prison Notebooks*, Vol I, Columbia University Press, New York, 1992.

[12] These arguments are developed at greater length in 'Equality and

Difference: The Emergence of a New Concept of Citizenship', in David McLellan and Sean Sayers, *Socialism and Democracy*, Macmillan, London 1991.

[13] See Denise Riley's rich and complex discussion, *War in the Nursery*, Virago, London 1983.

[14] Of course many parents in other circumstances made even more horrendous choices, for example, in sending Jewish children to Britain from Nazi Germany and Austria. The psychological effects have often extended across several generations.

About Signs
of the Times

Signs of the Times was founded in early 1992 as an independent and open discussion group. Its founding statement sets out the following perspective and aims –

We are living through New Times. Our world is being remade. A fundamental political, economic and cultural restructuring is taking place – the outcome of which remains uncertain. Through these changes, our identities, our sense of self, our subjectivities are being transformed.

Signs of the Times *is a project committed to exploring the new times analysis pioneered by* Marxism Today *in the late eighties and developing an understanding of the profound changes which are redrawing the political and cultural map. We aim to chart this new landscape and shape new agendas for the nineties.*

Signs of the Times *is independent and open. We are creating a free-thinking and participative culture sadly lacking in party politics. By this process we seek the remaking of the political.*

To date Signs of the Times *has published four discussion papers –*

Loves Labour Lost, by Andrew Gamble
Preparing the Ground – Life after the Party, by Mark Perryman
War and Peace Politics, by Martin Shaw
In These Times – New Times Revisited, by Suzanne Moore, Geoff Mulgan, Robin Murray and Judith Squires.

All of these discussion papers are available **free**, please enclose a large SAE, from Signs of the Times, c/o 28 Wargrave Avenue, London N15 6UD.

Signs of the Times organises regular seminars, workshops, an annual summer school and conferences. If you would like details of our forthcoming programme, including correspondence courses, please write to the above address.

Index